Exceptionally Blessed
Understanding the Real Cause of American Exceptionalism

KENNETH L. BRADSTREET

Copyright © 2019 Kenneth L. Bradstreet.

All rights reserved. No part of this book may be used or reproduced by any means, graphic, electronic, or mechanical, including photocopying, recording, taping or by any information storage retrieval system without the written permission of the author except in the case of brief quotations embodied in critical articles and reviews.

This book is a work of non-fiction. Unless otherwise noted, the author and the publisher make no explicit guarantees as to the accuracy of the information contained in this book and in some cases, names of people and places have been altered to protect their privacy.

WestBow Press books may be ordered through booksellers or by contacting:

WestBow Press
A Division of Thomas Nelson & Zondervan
1663 Liberty Drive
Bloomington, IN 47403
www.westbowpress.com
1 (866) 928-1240

Because of the dynamic nature of the Internet, any web addresses or links contained in this book may have changed since publication and may no longer be valid. The views expressed in this work are solely those of the author and do not necessarily reflect the views of the publisher, and the publisher hereby disclaims any responsibility for them.

Any people depicted in stock imagery provided by Getty Images are models, and such images are being used for illustrative purposes only.
Certain stock imagery © Getty Images.

Cover Portrait: First Prayer in Congress, 1774 by Tompkins Harrison Matteson (1813-1884)
Graphics from Granger Historical Picture Archive, Used by Permission.

Scripture taken from the King James Version of the Bible.

ISBN: 978-1-9736-7524-2 (sc)
ISBN: 978-1-9736-7525-9 (hc)
ISBN: 978-1-9736-7523-5 (e)

Library of Congress Control Number: 2019914331

Print information available on the last page.

WestBow Press rev. date: 10/29/2019

Dedication

To my children and my grandchildren, and to the children of your generation who have been robbed of a knowledge of the true history of America: I want you to know how America really came about, and I want you to know what any country can be when God and His Word are honored above all, and what will inevitably happen to a country where God is not honored.

Special thanks to Rev. Rusty Chatfield, my pastor, my radio partner, and my friend. Without his encouragement and assistance this book would never have been written.

Also, a special "Thank You" to my daughter, Melissa Croll, who helped me with editing this book.

Contents

Preface ix
Introduction - They Are Lying to Us xi

Part I - The Way We Were

Chapter 1 - Vidal v. Girard's Executors 1
Chapter 2 - By Order of the Court 15
Chapter 3 - America's Early School System 27
Chapter 4 - America's Early Colleges 47

Part II - The Way We Thought

Chapter 5 - Our Charter of Freedom 65
Chapter 6 - Natural Law, The Created Order 79
Chapter 7 - On the Shoulders of Giants 97
Chapter 8 - More Giants 117
Chapter 9 - Federalism, Safeguard of our Liberties 127

Part III - The Corruption of the Original Ideal

Chapter 10 - Judicial Tyranny 155
Chapter 11 - The Great Swamp – A Comfortable Aristocracy 189

Part IV - True Exceptionalism

Chapter 12 - Opposing Views of American Exceptionalism 205
Chapter 13 - Divine Providence, The Missing Ingredient 217

Part V - America on the Brink

Chapter 14 - Understanding Where We Are Headed 243
Chapter 15 - Can the Blessing Be Restored? 261

Appendix A - Early Education Laws of New England 273
Appendix B - Blue-Backed-Speller, Moral Catechism 277
Appendix C - McGuffey's Third Reader Excerpts 287
Appendix D - Essex Convention 291

Index 295

Preface

American exceptionalism – what does it mean to invoke that phrase? The idea of American exceptionalism has been the topic of numerous books and limitless political debates, speeches and disputes.

The idea that there has always been something unique about America has been with us since our founding. The economic progress of the 1800s led to America's emergence at the dawn of the twentieth century as the greatest nation on earth in terms of wealth and freedom. Economically, the United States was the richest country in terms of per capita gross domestic product for most of the twentieth century. As we all are aware, America from the early 1800s through the present, has been the dreamed for destination of millions of immigrants from all over the world, looking for opportunity, a chance at the American dream, when the doors to opportunity had been closed back home. And here they have thrived.

Any knowledge of American history will lead to the conclusion that there is a uniqueness in the American experience compared with other countries. Over the past two hundred years when we combine the ingredients of wealth, opportunity, and freedom, America stands out as exceptional. Most historians will agree with the premise that the American experience has been exceptional among nations. That part is obvious, and that is where the agreement ends.

It is the cause of this greatness which provokes a wide range of opinions. These theories cover the entire scope of good and evil, from the idea that our righteous founders and system of government has fertilized this unprecedented growth, to the idea that the evils of capitalism and exploitation of our own people, of slaves, of indigenous peoples, and of poor colonial countries all over the world has made us unjustly prosperous. A modern European view of American exceptionalism is that America copied all of its great ideas from Europe, and prone to exploit the powerless, combined with limitless land and resources that Europe did not have, what else might we expect?

There is one thing certain about the topic of American exceptionalism. Assuming we can agree that American exceptionalism is, or at least can be, a force for good, and if so, that American exceptionalism is something worth being preserved, we have the best chance of preserving it only if we understand how it came about in the first place. Our only chance of keeping it is to understand it. Are freedom and prosperity values to be embraced and defended? Then we need to understand what got us here.

The key to understanding American exceptionalism is understanding the American historical experience, particularly its founding. American history is one of the key battlegrounds of today's academics. If we wish to have an exceptional future we must get the history right, and most of all, we must understand why that history is important.

Introduction
They Are Lying to Us

One of the clear memories from my childhood is my mother answering a question I had asked her about communists. This was back in the 50s at the start of the cold war, and I had heard my mother discussing with someone how communists lie to their people in order to advance their cause. In my childhood innocence I asked my mother, "But isn't it wrong for them to lie?" "Yes, it is wrong for them to lie," my mother responded, "but communists don't really believe it is wrong. They believe it is ok to lie if the lie helps them."

That answer really confused me. I had been taught that lying is wrong – always. I just assumed that everyone knew that. My mother was trying to explain relative morality to a child that was not old enough to understand abstract reasoning or situational ethics. I didn't really understand her answer until I was much older, but I always remembered it.

There is, and always has been, a conflict between those who believe in God and in absolute morals and those who believe there are absolutely no absolutes. George Washington in his farewell address spoke of the importance of a society which embraces a world view that believes in God and in absolute right and wrong:

> *Of all the dispositions and habits which lead to political prosperity, religion and morality are indispensable supports. In vain would that man claim the tribute of patriotism, who should labor to subvert these great pillars of human happiness, these firmest props of the duties of men and citizens. The mere politician, equally with the pious man, ought to respect and to*

cherish them. A volume could not trace all their connections with private and public felicity. Let it simply be asked: **Where is the security for property, for reputation, for life, if the sense of religious obligation desert the oaths which are the instruments of investigation in courts of justice?** [emphasis added] *And let us with caution indulge the supposition that morality can be maintained without religion. Whatever may be conceded to the influence of refined education on minds of peculiar structure, reason and experience both forbid us to expect that national morality can prevail in exclusion of religious principle.*

A quick historical note here: in the writings of our founders the word "religion" was often used synonymously with Christianity, and certainly that is the context here. Notice the reason Washington used to emphasize the importance of religion and the absolute honesty that springs from it. Whether in a court of law or whether standing before a judge to assume an office of trust, oaths of truth, conformity or purpose are worthless if they are not based in honesty and in the fear of a just, powerful God who enforces absolute morals.

Everything hinges on honesty, ultimately even our very lives, and as Washington put it, honesty hinges on religion. When an elected official takes the oath of his or her office, our entire lives and well-being rest on that person's integrity. Swearing an oath before man and God is a sobering experience – if you believe in the justice and power of that God. If you believe that you are accountable to God, that He corrects his erring children, sometimes painfully, and that you must stand before Him in the future as your judge, that will affect the solemn promise you make. If not, the oath is simply a ceremony, and it is unlikely to affect future actions.

Nothing is more certain from American history than that the formation of our American colonies, our States, even our federal government was based on Christianity and the Bible. That unassailable fact is under constant attack today, and its attackers are relentless in their attempt to reshape American history to conform to secularist beliefs. Simply put, they attack our history by lying about it.

Through the first 175 years of our existence, our country embraced a common world view. We believed in the Creator, the author of our liberty. We believed that all citizens are accountable to Him and His law. In the wake of the Civil War we enthusiastically embraced the phrase "In God We Trust" which was first stamped on our coins in 1864. We embraced the notion that religion matters and that there are moral absolutes, honesty being one of the more important absolutes, which spring from religion.

Alexis de Tocqueville in his great work *Democracy In America* tells a story that demonstrates how a judge applied Washington's parting advice in an 1831 New York court of law.

> *Whilst I was in America, a witness, who happened to be called at the assizes of the county of Chester (State of New York), declared that he did not believe in the existence of God, or in the immortality of the soul. The judge refused to admit his evidence, on the ground that the witness had destroyed beforehand all the confidence of the Court in what he was about to say. The newspapers related the fact without any further comment.*
>
> *The Americans combine the notions of Christianity and of liberty so intimately in their minds, that it is impossible to make them conceive the one without the other . . . .*

What de Tocqueville observed was a simple test of veracity. The judge understood that people of faith who believe that they are ultimately accountable to God for their actions are credible witnesses in a court of law. People who do not believe they are accountable to any absolute lawgiver follow no absolute standard of honesty. Therefore, the witness's testimony could not be assumed to be credible.

Relativism is the philosophy that nothing is actually right or wrong in absolute terms. There being no real Creator/Lawgiver, an action is only right or wrong depending on the particular situation and how it affects outcomes. Today most liberals and secularists are relativists. In their world telling the truth can be wrong if it leads to a bad outcome. They defend their relative honesty with such trick questions as, "If your wife asked you, 'Does this dress make me look fat?' is it wrong to say no when the truth is clearly yes?"

In that event it would be wrong to tell the truth, they would argue, and it would be right to lie.

In March 2013, Director of National Intelligence James Clapper was asked under oath before a Congressional committee whether the National Security Agency was collecting "any type of data at all" on millions of American citizens. He answered, "No sir...not wittingly." A few months later we all learned that the NSA routinely collects all types of data on American citizens across the country, and that James Clapper was intentionally lying to Congress and to the American people while under oath. Clapper was told in advance he would be asked this question, so he knew it was coming, and presumably his answer was premeditated. He perjured himself.

Evidently Clapper is a relativist. He believed that it was better for the American people not to know to what degree their government was spying on them. I will assume that he believed in the value of government spying to the degree that he thought telling the truth about it could endanger this important work, and it would therefore be wrong.

We could add numerous other examples other than Clapper. For instance, the case against Supreme Court appointee Brett Kavanaugh was based on disputable recollections mixed with outright, outrageous lies, some so transparently false as to be embarrassing to the teller if embarrassment were possible. However, taking Kavanaugh down was the highest good in the minds of most of the Democrats on the Judiciary Committee, and truth was not part of the equation. The objective was to destroy the man by any means necessary. If outright lies were part of that process, so be it.

Today we are in a war – a war for our culture and ultimately for our liberty. This culture war, generally speaking, pits people of faith who believe in honesty against relativists who do not believe in absolute right or wrong. We battle using different rules. Those who believe in honesty tell the truth, embrace the truth, and even admit the truth when the truth places us at a disadvantage. The other side tells whatever "truth" might advance their cause in reshaping America.

Secularist historians, generally speaking, are relativists. They have a mission, a mission to manipulate the minds of Americans, particularly young Americans, to believe that the Christian founding of America never happened. It is more than anything else a giant public relations venture. It is manned by media and academia and the tools are textbooks, TV channels, periodicals, and best sellers – all aimed at convincing us that our founders were secularists, deists, skeptics, and yes, let's not forget Thomas Paine the atheist.

To the Christian who believes in absolute truth our objective is to prove a point using actual history. To prove a point requires investigation and application of facts. The objective of the other side is merely to win the war, and along the way to win arguments. Winning arguments does not require truth. Winning an argument can consist of anything from complete truth to complete falsehood or anything in between. All that is important to win an argument is that you have to convince someone of something. It need not be true at all – just believable.

Through the years, from our founding until the mid-1900s, the vast majority of Americans knew from their own educational experience that America was a Christian nation – Christian in a general sense, not Baptist Christian, Lutheran Christian, or Catholic Christian, but Christian in the sense that we believed in God as Creator. We believed in the truth of "the Good Book" and we embraced the basic morality of the Bible which is summarized by the Ten Commandments and the Golden Rule.

Before the mid-1900s American children were taught about our religious heritage, and we grew up thinking of our country as a Christian nation. Those early generations were taught how the Pilgrims and other early inhabitants of America were persecuted, often jailed, even executed, for their religious beliefs back in England, so they came here seeking refuge from religious persecution. American children before the mid-1900s were taught that the religion clauses of the First Amendment are about "freedom of religion" so that persecution of this nature does not happen in the future.

Contrast that with students from the 60s and beyond who are taught today almost nothing about the religious persecution which brought us here, but rather are taught that the religion clauses in the First Amendment are all about "separation of Church and State." Religion is no longer something to be protected, but rather is something to be protected against.

The arguments of the secular historians of academia concerning the Christian founding of America are mostly not true, and most of these historians are smart enough and studied enough to know that. In spite of commonly known historical truth concerning the Christian nature of our founding, they seek to hide that history by putting a purely secular spin on it. They know that most people in our society are not studied enough to know any better.

Their objective is not to advance truth, which for educators should be the ultimate goal. Rather it is to put down Christianity and absolute morality by any means at their disposal. The means they have chosen is to ignore real American history, or to intentionally revise our history to fit their argument, and ultimately to win the argument.

A good case in point is the story of noted historian and secular author Joseph Ellis. Ellis is a champion of secularists and has authored a number of best-selling books on American history. Among these are *Founding Brothers*, *His Excellency: George Washington*, *American Creation*, and *American Sphinx: the Character of Thomas Jefferson*. *Founding Brothers* won Ellis a Pulitzer Prize. Ellis is a talented writer, and he is an evangelist for secularism. He is embraced by the media and academia alike.

I have read one, and perused several others of Ellis's books, and in each one I found him to be on a mission to convince his readers that America's founding was a completely secular undertaking. In *American Creation* he writes of the founders,

> ... *they created the first wholly secular state. Before the American Revolution it was broadly assumed that shared religious convictions were the primary basis for the common values that linked together the people of any political community, indeed the ideological glue that made any sense of community possible. By insisting on the complete separation of Church and State, the founders successfully overturned this long-standing presumption.*

In *His Excellency*, Ellis quotes W. W. Abbot, another secular historian, in describing Washington as something less than a true Christian,

> *Never a deeply religious man, at least in the traditional Christian sense of the term, Washington thought of God as a distant, impersonal force, the presumed wellspring for what he called destiny or providence. Whether or not there was a hereafter, or a heaven where one's soul lived on, struck him as*

> one of those unfathomable mysteries that Christian theologians wasted much ink and energy trying to resolve. The only certain form of persistence was in the memory of succeeding generations, a secular rather than sacred version of immortality..."

In one of his early works, *After the Revolution*, writing about Noah Webster's famous school textbooks, including the famous *Blue Backed Speller*, Ellis wrote that Webster's *Blue Backed Speller* books taught five generations of American children how to spell and read, and made their education more secular and less religious. According to Ellis he gave Americans "a secular catechism to the nation-state."

Ellis claimed that it was Webster's intent to get religion out of the school books, and that he wanted to provide an alternative to the overtly religious *New England Primer*.

> *The speller concluded with two pages of important dates in American history, beginning with Columbus's discovery and ending with the battle of Yorktown. This litany of national names and dates replaced any mention of God, the Bible, or sacred events. "Let sacred things be appropriated for sacred purposes," wrote Webster. In place of* **Christian myths** *[emphasis added], Webster began to construct a secular catechism to the nation-state. Here was the first appearance of "civics" in American schoolbooks. In this sense, Webster's speller was the secular successor to* The New England Primer *with its explicitly biblical injunctions.*

Anyone who has looked at Webster's *Blue Backed Speller* knows that such a claim is ludicrous. Where it deals with complete sentences rather than just spelling words, Webster's *Blue Backed Speller* is overtly religious, filled with Christian principles and numerous references to the Bible and Biblical truths. Later in this book we will look in more detail at these American school books including Webster's speller, but suffice it to say that Ellis' description of Webster's speller is inaccurate at best, and it is hard to imagine a historian of his esteem not knowing any better.

Well, perhaps he did know better. You see, in a not-so-glamorous episode in his life, in 2001 Ellis was relieved of his classroom duties at Mt. Holyoke College and suspended for a year without pay for lying to his students. He claimed to have been a combat officer, a paratrooper in Vietnam, not to mention a football hero. When it was discovered that he was never in Vietnam during the war years, and that he never played football exceptionally well, he was called to account, losing his teaching position and the coveted Ford Foundation Chair in History. The college was forced to act, not because they wanted to, but because Ellis's "stolen valor" had become so generally known by the public from media reports.

In announcing his reinstatement to that same position four years later, the college, in a May 20, 2005, release on their website, described his history with the college as follows:

> ... Ellis served Mount Holyoke as dean of faculty from 1980 to 1990. At the end of his term the trustees named him to the then-new Ford Foundation Chair, noting Ellis's uncommon achievement and excellence in his field, his commitment to excellence in the teaching of history, and his encouragement of students to stretch their intellectual and analytical abilities to the fullest measure of their potential. Ellis <u>stepped down</u> [emphasis mine] from the Ford Chair in 2001. After four years of teaching, scholarship, and service of the highest standards and integrity, he has earned the chair anew.

The above deception is typical of the "truth-seekers" in academia in their various responses to Ellis's lies. They just treated the incident as though nothing important really happened. The American media was strangely silent as well.

Nancy Pearl was the executive director of the Seattle-based *Washington Center for the Book*, a subsidiary of the national Library of Congress. Just as Ellis was being relieved of his duties as a professor, the Center for the Book was planning a lecture from Ellis featuring his new book, *Founding Brothers*. This scandal brought many questions to the center as to whether they still wanted Ellis to speak.

As the Seattle based *Post Intelligencer* reported, Ellis was not disinvited, and Nancy Pearl defended the decision by saying, "It seemed to us that Ellis's personal life -- what he did or didn't do as a teacher -- really has nothing to do with the scholarship that went into his books about Jefferson and the 'founding brothers.' He is coming here as an American historian with valuable things to share about American history. To me, that is entirely separate from his personal life."

Really?! Do we really believe that a dishonest person is only dishonest in one compartment of his life? Honesty is a general character trait. Do we really believe that Ellis can lie profusely in his classroom but be honest in his treatment of American history? The secularists would like us to believe this.

A New York Times editorial opined that Ellis's lies should not be used to raise larger questions about his honesty. "According to Arnita Jones, executive director of the American Historical Association, Mr. Ellis's case 'has provoked a conversation about the limits and the values of truth.' In a sense, that is exactly what this case should not do. . . It takes no great insight to realize the inner strain that teaching history at West Point might have caused Mr. Ellis at a time when its graduates were going off to fight in Vietnam."

Another academic, obviously a relativist, Ronald Hilton from Berkeley, even went so far as to suggest that the structure of our colleges gives incentive for professors to embellish their teaching, so what else are we to expect a professor to do? Of course they are going to lie in class just to make it more interesting. Hilton described the problem on the Stanford University website with this lengthy rationalization:

> The academic world has been shaken by the case of Joseph Ellis, Professor of History at Mount Holyoke College. A specialist in US colonial and early republican history, he had won great acclaim by his book Founding Brothers, which describes the founding fathers, not as secular saints deserving the awed respect which used to be accorded to the kings of England, but as typical politicians, ambitious and squabbling. His reputation has been shattered by reports that in his classes on the Vietnam war he lied about serving in it, as well as about other matters, such as his prowess as a football player. The case was broken by brilliant Boston Globe investigative reporter Walter Robinson and has since become a subject of national debate . . . Every

aspect of the case has been covered except one: a serious flaw in the American university system.

Berkeley was the scene of many noisy and stupid protests, but one was justified. With encouragement from a junior professor of German, who was looked upon as a traitor, indeed an academic sinner, by older colleagues, students started publishing assessments of the professors, often unfavorable. Now this procedure has become routine. Students began demanding more attention, and university administrators began listening to these customers. Teaching became a key component in decisions about tenure and salary.

Professors had to attract students in order to ensure a good enrolment, and then to keep them happy, thus ensuring the approval of the administration. History professors began putting on acts. One was famous for his reenactment of the death of Lincoln. It was hard to jazz up teaching foreign languages that way, and this is one of the reasons enrolment in those courses began to decline. Professor Ellis was jazzing up his course on the Vietnam with "I was there" accounts. It was indeed a pathetic breach of ethics, both professional and general. However, **he was really a victim of the system.** [emphasis mine] . . . *It's the system, stupid. It's the stupid system.*

So the system made Ellis lie. What a poor, pathetic victim! Faced with all the pressure of his esteemed professorial position, he had to perform, and perform he did. The question I have is obvious, assuming for the sake of argument that pressure to perform did really cause Ellis to lie. Does that end justify the means? Is it ok to lie to add to your performance in the classroom – to be rated more highly by the students – to give them a more rewarding college experience?

Asked another way, isn't it ok to lie to advance a more noble philosophy? If you are of the view, as most secularists are, that there is no absolute morality, and you believe that America is better off today as an entirely secular society, what would be wrong with "shaping" American history to conform to that view? What would be wrong with labeling George Washington non-religious or Noah Webster a secularist that today's academics could more readily relate to?

In the political world, most leftists are relativists and nearly all leftists operate from the premise that the end justifies the means. This is true of liberals in both major parties. In my own political experience and observation, when it comes to planting misinformation in a campaign or dirty tricks, it is far more common for the non-religious to engage in that sort of thing than for principled statesmen who embrace honesty as a prerequisite for their personal and political lives.

That explains why feminists gave President Bill Clinton a complete pass in the Monica Lewinsky affair. Though Clinton was their worst nightmare when it came to the treatment of women, he was useful to their side in the abortion battle. Liberal reporters and pundits likewise gave him a pass while all singing from the same chorus sheet, "Everyone lies about sex – no big deal." Never mind that the life of an intern in her early twenties had been ruined by a powerful man in his fifties.

To liberal secularists honesty is only important when it advances the secularist narrative, and with respect to American history, almost nothing from actual history advances the narrative of a secular founding. In the foreword to *George Washington's Sacred Fire*, their exhaustive work on the Christian faith of George Washington, Jerry Newcombe and Peter Lillback wrote of this revising of American history:

> *In many of America's secondary schools and schools of higher education, history is considered irrelevant to the post-modern and multi-cultural world. Entire curricula on American history have been written with only passing reference to our founding fathers, including George Washington.*
>
> *But this is not a sudden event. The roots of this historical revisionism go back to the early nineteen hundreds as many elite leaders and educators in America began, intentionally, to move in a direction away from America's Christian heritage.*
>
> *George Washington, the preeminent figure at the beginning of America as a new, independent nation, has been subjected to the reinterpretation of American history by numerous, secular scholars. Motivated by a world view that*

rejects the foundational doctrine of George Washington's world view—Divine Providence—these scholars have filtered out and misrepresented the extensive evidence of George Washington's faith. As a result, they have created a secular George Washington as a truncated figure from the heroic figure known by his contemporaries...

... Because some early American patriots, like Thomas Paine, were Deists, that is those who believed in a distant and remote Deity, many more recent historians have tried to label a number of the luminaries of the founding fathers of America as also being Deists. For example, it is often said today that Thomas Jefferson and Benjamin Franklin were Deists. Yet, each man in a variety of contexts spoke earnestly of their conviction as Theists—that God was both approachable by man and that God played an ever-active role in the affairs of man. Consider Thomas Jefferson's declaration: "God who gave us life gave us liberty. And can the liberties of a nation be thought secure when we have removed our only firm basis, a conviction in the minds of the people that these liberties are the gift of God?" It is not surprising, therefore, that Thomas Jefferson and his fellow founders would have referred four times in the Declaration of Independence to a Creator God of Providence. Likewise, consider the statement of Benjamin Franklin delivered at the Constitutional Convention in Philadelphia in 1787: "I have lived, Sir, a long time, and the longer I live, the more convincing proofs I see of this truth: that God governs in the affairs of man."

... Washington later in his public life said: "It is the duty of all nations to acknowledge the Providence of Almighty God, to obey his will, to be grateful for his benefits, and humbly implore his protection and favor." (Thanksgiving Proclamation, October 3, 1789)

It is sad to contemplate that many of our children's teachers finish their years in secular colleges with a completely false understanding of American history and the role played by Christianity. It is not entirely their fault that they pass on this misinformation to their students. Many of these teachers are good and honest people who would gladly teach the truth if they knew the truth.

Today truth comes to us far less frequently than we need. We are becoming accustomed to being told falsehoods by our politicians and especially our media. This has become increasingly clear since Donald Trump became President. As much of the media dishonesty is found in what they don't say as in what they do say – that is, what they refuse to report. It seems okay to secularists to not tell the whole truth. Several media outlets have even deleted portions of the quotes of newsmakers in such a way as to completely change context in order that you embrace the narrative they want you to hear rather than what was actually said within its context. Truth has become a relative virtue, useful at times, but just as often not useful, or even counterproductive.

The study for the truth surrounding our founding is an objective study of the words and deeds of those who were there and the books and documents that they left behind. It is no more complicated than that. It does not need to be filtered through a nuanced modern perspective. We need no "experts" to explain it to us. We must be willing to sort through the American attic for the real true story. With respect to our founding purpose, the evidences from history are plentiful and conclusive if we take the time to look. Otherwise we will be taken in by wannabe war heroes.

The real question remains, what are we to do with that information? I am hopeful that we can all learn the truth about America's founding. Once we understand the founding principles, we need to understand why it worked so well to make America the greatest nation in the history of mankind. And having worked so well, can it still work? It is my hope and prayer that I can prove my point, not just win an argument.

Part I
The Way We Were

"Industry and constant employment are great preservatives of the morals and virtue of a nation. Hence bad examples to youth are more rare in America; which must be a comfortable consideration to parents. To this may be truly added, that serious religion, under its various denominations, is not only tolerated, but respected and practiced. Atheism is unknown there, infidelity rare and secret; so that persons may live to a great age in that country without having their piety shocked by meeting with either an atheist or an infidel. And the Divine Being seems to have manifested his approbation of the mutual forbearance and kindness with which the different sects treat each other, by the remarkable prosperity with which He has been pleased to favour the whole country." Benjamin Franklin, 1784, *Information to Those Who Would Remove to America.* (Pamphlet printed in London: M. Gurney)

In 1776 America's population was approximately 2.5 million people. It was comprised almost entirely of English Protestants. While there were numerous sects of Protestant Christianity, these together accounted for about 98.4% of all of the American colonialists. There was a small number of Roman Catholics, mostly in Maryland and Pennsylvania, numbering about 35,000, which represented an estimated 1.4% of the population. The other estimated 5,000 (0.2 %) were either Jewish or were not affiliated with any religion. [From Benjamin Hart, *Faith & Freedom: The Christian Roots of American Liberty,* published by Christian Defense Fund, 1997]

Chapter 1
Vidal v. Girard's Executors

Article VIII Education; Sec. 1. Religion, morality and knowledge being necessary to good government and the happiness of mankind, schools and the means of education shall forever be encouraged. Michigan Constitution, 1963

Fortune magazine lists him as the fourth richest American who ever lived – just ahead of Bill Gates, the fifth richest American who ever lived. That calculation is based on his amassed fortune as compared to the nation's Gross Domestic Product (GDP) – allowing for the comparison of fortunes of tycoons from widely differing eras in American history. Only the fortunes of John D. Rockefeller, Cornelius Vanderbilt, and John Jacob Astor rate higher than the fortune amassed by Stephen Girard (1750-1831) which was $1/150^{th}$ of the GDP.

In his day, Stephen Girard of Philadelphia was the richest man in America, a banker who, it is said by some, single-handedly prevented the country from going bankrupt following the War of 1812. While many historians consider this an exaggeration, Girard helped the US Government raise millions of dollars to conduct the war, money that the US Government simply did not have and probably could not raise any other way. Of the millions of dollars in loans Girard raised, about half of that money was Girard's, and he underwrote most of the rest, the balance coming from other American investors and bankers.

Stephen Girard was born in Bordeaux, then the largest seaport in southwestern France. As a young man he followed in his father's footsteps as a sea captain. In 1776, being chased away from New York harbor by British ships blockading the city, he sailed his ship into the port of Philadelphia for refuge. He decided to settle in Philadelphia and to expand his shipping business as a resident – later naturalized citizen – of America. He earned his initial fortune in the merchant and shipping business. He later would expand his vast fortune in banking, and late in his life even profited from such varied enterprises as coal mining and railroads.

In late December of 1830, at the age of 80, Stephen Girard was run over by a horse and wagon in downtown Philadelphia, the wheel of the wagon running right over the left side of his face. Although he was able to get up and stagger home, he was never quite able to recover from the accident. He was unable to work for two months. A year after the accident, in his aged and weakened state, he would succumb to an influenza epidemic – the day after Christmas, 1831, with his faithful slave Hannah at his bedside. His body was interred in Holy Trinity Catholic Cemetery in Philadelphia. Eventually, it was transferred to its final resting place at Girard College, the college that would bear his name and would become the subject of one of the most interesting Supreme Court Decisions in American history.

As a young man Girard had married Mary Lum of Philadelphia. Soon after their marriage his wife became insane and had to be committed to an institution. He spent most of his life with two mistresses, first, Sally Bickham and then Polly Kenton. Polly left him about three years before the horse and wagon accident, and at his death he had no companion other than his slave Hannah. He died childless, and the world wondered what would become of the vast fortune of the most wealthy man in America who had no obvious heirs.

Stephen Girard had always kept his will secret. When the will was read, his slave, Hannah, who had served him for fifty years, discovered that she was now a free woman with an annual income that would assure her comfort for the rest of her days. Girard's will was very detailed about how his wealth would be divided, and it was generously beneficent toward a number of relatives in France as well as numerous charitable causes and institutions in Philadelphia and French-oriented New Orleans.

Philadelphia at that time was wracked with civil unrest over the issue of which religion was to be taught in the public schools, as were New York City and Boston. A large influx of Roman Catholic immigrants, predominately from Ireland in the early decades of the 1800s, resulted in an anti-Catholic backlash among the Protestant majority. This migration had created a large population of Irish Catholics in these cities, and the bishops and priests had raised a number of issues with the city governments concerning the education of Catholic youths. Specifically, they did not approve of the use of the King James Version of the Bible that was currently in use in the schools, and they did not want the Catholic youths indoctrinated in Protestant theology and hymnology.

In New York City the Catholic bishop even demanded from the city government the right to a pro rata share of the tax dollars with which to build their own schools in Catholic neighborhoods. This was refused, although New York had such a great number of Irish Catholics that by the middle of the nineteenth century, due to pressure from the Catholic Church, more than 30 New York City schools had abandoned Bible reading in the schools because the version used had been Protestant. The issue of Catholics having to attend these "Protestant schools" led eventually to the Catholic, parochial school movement.

In Philadelphia the issue grew so contentious that it would ultimately lead to armed riots between Protestants and Catholics. Both Protestants and Catholics resorted to small arms fire in the Kensington area of Philadelphia in the infamous Philadelphia Bible Riots of 1844. This was followed by actual cannon fire from both sides in follow-up riots in the Southwark district of Philadelphia following a fourth of July celebration. This was the culmination of several decades of growing religious unrest in Philadelphia, and it was in this context of religious strife, dating back to the early 1800s, that Stephen Girard wrote his will in the late 1820s.

Perhaps the most striking thing about Stephen Girard's will was a bequest to the City of Philadelphia of a large portion of his will for the founding and maintenance of a school for poor, white fatherless boys – "orphans" as he referred to them. That school exists to this day as Girard College, which is actually a K-12 school, not a college in the normal sense of the word.

Girard's religious convictions are not known – some say he was a deist while others claim he was an atheist. We do know that he was from France, a secularist but predominately Roman Catholic country at the time, and that he was initially laid to rest in a Catholic cemetery. We also know that this generous man had given thousands of dollars to various Protestant charitable causes throughout his life. And we do know that schools within the City of Philadelphia were almost entirely Protestant when he wrote his will, engaging in religious service, Bible reading and instruction, and Protestant hymns.

Whatever his motives, Girard directed that this school, to be built and maintained by the City of Philadelphia, was prohibited from having any clergy as teachers, or administrators – even as visitors. His will stated:

> ... I enjoin and require that no ecclesiastic, missionary, or minister of any sect whatsoever shall ever hold or exercise any station or duty whatever in the said college, nor shall any such person ever be admitted for any purpose, or as a visitor, within the premises appropriated to the purposes of the said college...
>
> In making this restriction, I do not mean to cast any reflection upon any sect or person whatsoever, but as there is such a multitude of sects and such a diversity of opinion amongst them, I desire to keep the tender minds of the orphans who are to derive advantage from this bequest free from the excitement which clashing doctrines and sectarian controversy are so apt to produce; my desire is that all the instructors and teachers in the college shall take pains to instill into the minds of the scholars the purest principles of morality, so that, on their entrance into active life, they may, from inclination and habit, evince benevolence towards their fellow creatures and a love of truth, sobriety, and industry, adopting at the same time such religious tenets as their matured reason may enable them to prefer.

The above two clauses of Girard's will would lead to a major contest between the City of Philadelphia, which wanted both the money and the school, and a few of Girard's surviving relatives from France who simply wanted the money. That contest eventually was settled in the United States Supreme Court, and it is known today as *Vidal v. Girard's Executors* (1844). It is this lawsuit, the manner in which it was argued in the courts, and the language contained in the decision, that tells us much about the United States in the mid-1800s, its practices and its values. What it teaches us clashes with the version of American history that is taught in most secular universities today.

The case was originally made before the Federal Circuit Court of the Eastern District of Pennsylvania. The plaintiffs argued that there were two major defects in the will which made the major bequests to the City of Philadelphia legally flawed. They raised the question whether the City of Philadelphia, as a corporation, could lawfully administer the bequests as a trust. Claiming that the city could not so administer this trust, they demanded that the monies thus bequeathed should instead go to themselves, the largest portion of which was the large bequest for the college for orphans.

The second flaw that the plaintiffs claimed against the will of Stephen Girard was that the terms set out concerning the orphans' college were incapable of being executed, that they were in violation of Pennsylvania common law, and that they were a practical absurdity and thus, null and void. The terms that they attacked in particular were the provisions that clergy were to be excluded completely from the school.

The Federal Circuit Court dismissed the case, ruling that the City of Philadelphia could administer the trust, and that it could apply the provisions of the will as instructed. The plaintiffs then appealed the decision to the U.S. Supreme Court, and they hired no less than the nation's premiere attorney, Daniel Webster, to plead their case. The City of Philadelphia retained the equally esteemed attorney Horace Binney. The plaintiffs made these two claims – that the city as a corporation could not legally administer the trust, and that the college could not possibly be operated legally as prescribed by Girard.

For the purpose of this discussion we will not get into the first question in any depth – that of the capacity of the City of Philadelphia to administer a trust as a corporation. That represented a technical legal question which was settled in the court opinion beyond any question. Suffice it to say, when the will of Stephen Girard was first made public, both the City of Philadelphia and the State of Pennsylvania passed a number of ordinances and statutes designed to enable both the State and city to legally accept and administer these bequests, and those ordinances and statutes were affirmed by the Supreme Court.

The second charge, however, was as much a philosophical question as a legal one. The question raised was whether a school as described in Stephen

Girard's will could be legally operated as ordered without severe damage to the orphans that it was trying to help. Supreme Court Justice Joseph Story, writing the unanimous opinion, described it thusly:

> This objection is that the foundation of the college upon the principles and exclusions prescribed by the testator, is derogatory and hostile to the Christian religion, and so is void, as being against the common law and public policy of Pennsylvania, and this for two reasons: first, because of the exclusion of all ecclesiastics, missionaries, and ministers of any sect from holding or exercising any station or duty in the college, or even visiting the same, and secondly because it limits the instruction to be given to the scholars to pure morality, and general benevolence, and a love of truth, sobriety, and industry, thereby excluding, by implication, all instruction in the Christian religion.

In other words, in the view of the plaintiff, the terms of the will seemed to be explicitly aimed at the Christian religion, and since the Christian religion was part of Pennsylvania common law, such a provision was on its face illegal. Prior to this time there were no purely secular schools in the United States, at least not as we understand the term today.

There were, at this time, non-sectarian colleges which operated independently of any specific church denomination such as the University of Virginia, but these non-sectarian colleges still promoted Christianity in general. They revered and used the Bible and had religious services which were exclusively at least Judeo/Christian. At the elementary and prep school levels, many schools were run by clergy, and all schools promoted Christianity as a necessary part of preparing moral, productive citizens. A school without Christianity was unthinkable, and that is exactly what *both sides* argued before the Supreme Court.

Both sides? Yes, both the lawyers for the plaintiffs and the lawyers for the City of Philadelphia argued that an education for these orphans *must* include Biblical instruction and Christianity, and that Christianity was indeed a part of the common law of Pennsylvania. The chief difference in their arguments was that the plaintiffs argued that it was Girard's wish not to teach Christianity in the school, and the defendants argued that this was not at all Girard's wish – that his will excluded clergy, but it didn't exclude the Bible or Christianity.

The plaintiffs' case began,

> ... A part of this devise would make it a curse to any civilized land; it is a cruel experiment upon poor orphan boys to shut them up and make them the victims of a philosophical speculation. By the laws of Pennsylvania it is blasphemy to attack the Christian religion, but in this case nothing is to be taught but the doctrines of a pure morality, and all the advantages of early impressions upon the youthful mind are entirely abrogated.

Attorneys for the City of Philadelphia countered,

> But it is said that the use is not good because the proposed college is unchristian. The bill filed in the cause makes no such objection.... The purest principles of morality are to be taught. Where are they found? Whoever searches for them must go to the source from which a Christian man derives his faith -- the Bible. It is therefore affirmatively recommended, and in such a way as to preserve the sacred rights of conscience.... Girard did not mean to reflect upon Christianity. It is true [clergy] cannot hold office.... Girard only says that laymen must be instructors, and why cannot they teach religion as well as science? ... All that is done by the will is to secure the college from controversy.

Attorney Daniel Webster responded,

> The plan of education is derogatory to the Christian religion, tending to weaken men's respect for it and their conviction of its importance. It subverts the only foundation of public morals, and therefore it is mischievous and not desirable. The clause is pointedly opprobrious to the whole clergy; it brands them all

> *without distinction of sect. Their very presence is supposed to be mischievous. If a preacher happens to have a sick relative in the college, he is forbidden to visit him. How have the great body of preachers deserved to be denied even the ordinary rites of hospitality?*
>
> *... There are two objectionable features in this restriction in the will. The first is, that all clergymen are excluded from the college; and the second, that a cruel experiment is to be made upon these orphans, to ascertain whether they cannot be brought up without religion.*

Justice Joseph Story wrote the opinion of the court, and that opinion was **unanimous.** Story reiterated the argument made by Horace Binney on behalf of the City of Philadelphia, that the will did not prohibit the teaching of Christianity, but rather could be interpreted to require it. The will provided that "... all the instructors and teachers in the college shall take pains to instill into the minds of the scholars the purest principles of morality..." Binney had argued that the purest principles of morality are only to be found in the Bible, thus the will requires Biblical instruction in the school.

Justice Story in the court's order stated,

> *It is also said, and truly, that the Christian religion is a part of the common law of Pennsylvania.... So that we are compelled to admit that although Christianity be a part of the common law of the state, yet it is so in this qualified sense, that its divine origin and truth are admitted, and therefore it is not to be maliciously and openly reviled and blasphemed against, to the annoyance of believers or the injury of the public. Such was the doctrine of the Supreme Court of Pennsylvania in Updegraff v. Commonwealth, 11 Serg. & R. 394.*
>
> *It is unnecessary for us, however, to consider what would be the legal effect of a devise in Pennsylvania for the establishment of a school or college, for the propagation of Judaism, or Deism, or any other form of infidelity.* **Such a case is not to be presumed to exist in a Christian country**

[emphasis added], *and therefore it must be made out by clear and indisputable proof. Remote inferences, or possible results, or speculative tendencies, are not to be drawn or adopted for such purposes. There must be plain, positive, and express provisions, demonstrating not only that Christianity is not to be taught, but that it is to be impugned or repudiated.*

But the objection itself assumes the proposition that Christianity is not to be taught, because ecclesiastics are not to be instructors or officers. But this is by no means a necessary or legitimate inference from the premises. Why may not laymen instruct in the general principles of Christianity as well as ecclesiastics?

. . . Why may not the Bible, and especially the New Testament, without note or comment, be read and taught as a divine revelation in the college -- its general precepts expounded, its evidences explained, and its glorious principles of morality inculcated? What is there to prevent a work, not sectarian, upon the general evidences of Christianity, from being read and taught in the college by lay teachers? Certainly there is nothing in the will that proscribes such studies. Above all, the testator positively enjoins, "that all the instructors and teachers in the college shall take pains to instill into the minds of the scholars the purest principles of morality, so that on their entrance into active life, they may from inclination and habit evince benevolence towards their fellow creatures, and a love of truth, sobriety, and industry, adopting at the same time such religious tenets as their matured reason may enable them to prefer."

Now it may well be asked what is there in all this which is positively enjoined, inconsistent with the spirit or truths of Christianity? Are not these truths all taught by Christianity, although it teaches much more? Where can the purest principles of morality be learned so clearly or so perfectly as from the New Testament? Where are benevolence, the love of truth, sobriety, and industry, so powerfully and irresistibly inculcated as in the sacred volume? The testator has not said how these great principles are to be taught or by whom, except it be by laymen, nor what books are to be used to explain or enforce them.

All that we can gather from his language is that he desired to exclude sectarians and sectarianism from the college, leaving the instructors and officers free to teach the purest morality, the love of truth, sobriety, and industry, by all appropriate means, and of course including the best, the surest, and the most impressive...

Story's opinion in a nutshell was this: One, yes, Christianity is part of the common law of Pennsylvania, but; two, the question in this case is whether the will demands teachings hostile to Christianity, and; three, such an interpretation is absurd on its face since a school hostile to Christianity could not be imagined in a Christian country such as this one, and that; four, Christianity will be taught in this school operated by the City of Philadelphia because that is what the will requires – that is, the "purest principles of morality."

Bear in mind, here we have the singular most esteemed authority on the U.S. Constitution writing the opinion. Joseph Story was appointed to the Supreme Court by President James Madison in 1812 and he served on the court for more than thirty-three years. During that time he authored a number of legal textbooks, but none was more revered and authoritative than his three volume *Commentaries on the Constitution of the United States* published in 1833. Through the remainder of the nineteenth century and much of the twentieth, Story's commentary on the U.S. Constitution was regarded as the most authoritative work on American jurisprudence since Blackstone's Commentaries.

This authoritative and brilliant legal mind had written a decision which went directly to the heart of the question of religion in the public schools. The school in question was to be established and maintained by a local unit of government, the City of Philadelphia. The question was not whether teaching Christianity in this government run school was permissible. The question was whether it should be regarded as necessary, and both sides plus the court agreed that it should be viewed in that way.

And no surprise that the people and the court would hold this opinion. Indeed, from the very founding of the country an ordinance was written in 1787 under the Articles of Confederation which provided for the development of lands "northwest of the Ohio River" which had become property of the United States after the treaty of Paris had settled the War for Independence. This ordinance was to become known as "The Northwest Ordinance," and included new territories now known as Ohio, Indiana, Illinois, Michigan, Wisconsin, and Minnesota.

After the government under the new U.S. Constitution was formed in 1789, the Northwest Ordinance was re-ratified so as to make it part of the new government statutory law. The Northwest Ordinance provided the template for the development of new States – not just those northwest of the Ohio River, but new territories added to the west following the Louisiana Purchase in 1803. Under the Northwest Ordinance, a U.S. territory could apply for statehood once it reached a population of at least 60,000 persons and had fulfilled several other provisions of the ordinance.

One of these additional provisions was that the territories, as they developed, were to establish a system of education for the children. The exact wording was as follows:

> Art. 3. Religion, morality, and knowledge, being necessary to good government and the happiness of mankind, schools and the means of education shall forever be encouraged...

In other words, before a territory could approach the U.S. Government and request admission into the Union as a State, it first needed to establish schools which taught the children these three indispensable pillars of a free society: "religion, morality, and knowledge." The new United States Congress ratified this ordinance in August, 1789. The next month the same U.S. Congress presented twelve proposed amendments to the U.S. Constitution to President Washington for dissemination to the States. Ten of these would be ratified by the States, and they became known as the "Bill of Rights."

So in August, 1789, Congress established the principle that if you are a U.S. territory that wants to become a State, you have to have a school system which, among other things, teaches religion. Are we to believe that the same men, the following month, September, 1789, proposed the First Amendment to the States for the purpose of prohibiting the teaching of religion in public schools? Clearly that was not their intent, and historically that never happened until the 1960s.

The framers' purpose in establishing the religion clauses of the First Amendment had nothing to do with prohibiting religion in public schools or in the public square. Back then there was no such thing, no such sentiment, as "separation of church and state." To the contrary, the purpose of the Amendment was to prohibit a national church from being established while at the same time encouraging personal freedom of conscience and encouraging Christianity in general.

In 1840 Justice Joseph Story, in his abbreviated *Familiar Exposition of the Constitution of the United States* wrote this concerning the First Amendment:

> *We are not to attribute this prohibition of a national religious establishment to an indifference to religion in general, and especially to Christianity (which none could hold in more reverence than the framers of the Constitution) ...*
>
> *Probably, at the time of the adoption of the Constitution, and of the Amendment to it now under consideration, the general, if not the universal sentiment in America was, that Christianity ought to receive encouragement from the State so far as was not incompatible with the private rights of conscience and the freedom of religious worship.*
>
> *Any attempt to level all religions, and to make it a matter of state policy to hold all in utter indifference, would have created universal disapprobation, if not universal indignation.*

In his more expansive work *Commentaries on the Constitution of the United States* Story added this:

> *The real object of the amendment was, not to countenance, much less to advance Mahometanism, or Judaism, or infidelity, by prostrating Christianity; but to exclude all rivalry among Christian sects, and to prevent any national ecclesiastical establishment, which should give to an hierarchy the exclusive patronage of the national government. It thus cut off the means of religious persecution, (the vice and pest of former ages,)*

and of the subversion of the rights of conscience in matters of religion, which had been trampled upon almost from the days of the Apostles to the present age.

Today Article VIII of the Constitution of the State of Michigan (1963) begins the section on education as follows: "Article VIII Education; Sec. 1. Religion, morality and knowledge being necessary to good government and the happiness of mankind, schools and the means of education shall forever be encouraged." Sound familiar? It should, of course. It is taken word-for-word from the Northwest Ordinance of the U.S. Congress. Just one problem - this version of Michigan's Constitution was ratified in 1963. At that same time the United States Supreme Court was ruling that religion in the schools is unconstitutional. The arrogant Court claimed to know better what Congress intended than Congress itself.

Wait a minute!! Hold everything!! I was always taught in school that the founders of the United States created a government which required "separation of Church and State," and that the First Amendment to the U.S. Constitution prohibited the teaching of religion in public schools. If that is your reaction, you are not alone. Most young people who have grown up in America since the 1950s have been taught that. However, as we shall see later in this book, "separation of Church and State" is a concept that started relatively recently as a result of a Supreme Court decision in 1947.

If you are an older American like me, you were taught that the First Amendment religion clauses were all about "freedom of religion." If you attended elementary school beginning in the 1960s and since then, you were likely taught that the religion clauses were about "separation of Church and State." If you are a younger American you will discover in this book that you have been misinformed about much of what you were taught growing up in public school.

What we learn from this particular Supreme Court case is that America's founding was never intended to be a secular undertaking, contrary to many historians in academia today. Many secularists claim that the First Amendment was added to prevent any religion from encroaching in schools or in the public arena. While it is easy to make claims of this nature, nothing carries historical weight quite like a unanimous decision of the United States

Supreme Court which provides written, on-the-record commentary on America's history.

The First Amendment was NOT about separation of Church and State, nor was it ever intended to be. America in 1844 was a Christian nation; Justice Joseph Story unmistakably states that in his decision. As we read the arguments from both sides, it was assumed by both sides that Christianity *must* be taught in the schools, or education would be incomplete and indeed even abusive to the students, just as the Northwest Ordinance of 1789 prescribed. Both sides *and the court* acknowledged that Christianity was part of the common law of Pennsylvania. Everyone in the country recognized that teaching children religion was a practical necessity, consistent with the Northwest Ordinance, and, most importantly, the First Amendment.

As we shall see in Chapter 9, the very design of the First Amendment was to preserve the Christian essence of the States and their people, and to prevent the Federal Government from interfering in any area of religious life. America was from the beginning a Christian nation, not a secular one. The people of the nation held exclusively to a Judeo/Christian world view. The nation was not just Christian in its founding documents, but it was as a practical matter completely Christian in every way – in all of its institutions, from its elementary schools all the way up to the Supreme Court of the United States. And as we shall see in the latter chapters of this book, the reason expressed by many of our founding fathers was rather simple: when the United States ceases to be a Christian nation, it ceases to be free.

(See *The Story Behind Vidal v. Girard's Executors: Joseph Story, The Philadelphia Bible Riots, and Religious Liberty* by Jay Sekulow and Jeremy Tedesco, Pepperdine Law Review, 2005, Volume 32, Issue 3)

Chapter 2
By Order of the Court

On February 29, 1892, the United States Supreme Court issued an order in the case of *Church of the Holy Trinity v. United States*, one of its most important decisions up to that time, and certainly with respect to religious issues, the most important in its history. It eclipsed even *Vidal v. Girard's Executors*. During the latter part of the 1800s, there were a number of attacks on orthodox Christianity, including modernism and Darwinism. Harvard University, which for over two hundred years had trained America's ministers, and had been a bastion of the Christian faith, had sunk into infidelity and unbelief. (Read all about the development of our early colleges in Chapter 4.)

The late 1800s – this was the modern age – one in which you could board a train in New York City on Monday morning, and be in San Francisco on Thursday night, a trip which a few decades earlier would have taken months. There were a lot of new "things" and a lot of new thoughts.

During the mid-1800s there was an effort on the part of entrepreneurs all over the country to link the nation together through a system of railroads. In 1862 Congress began to pass legislation to facilitate linking east with west, even providing financial backing for the investments in various railroads. The final product of that effort was the link-up of the eastern system with the western system. The last "golden" spike in that construction was driven on May 10, 1869, completing the connection between the eastern lines and Sacramento.

From that first connection numerous new rail lines branched out all over the continent, both in the east and in the west. Railroad tycoons sought ways to reduce construction costs and maximize profits. One of the ways these tycoons accomplished that was to go to other countries and recruit labor, offering impoverished men a ticket for passage to America in exchange for a certain amount of time in labor on the railroad at extremely low pay. In this way, many thousands of immigrants were brought in from around the world, particularly from China.

Other industrialists in the north, and the textile industry in the south, began to dip into this type of labor pool as well. By the 1880s, America was experiencing a flood of new immigrants who provided the cheap labor which, in turn, drove the rapid expansion of industrialization throughout the country.

This created two problems; one it artificially lowered the cost of labor for American workers, and two, it established an underclass of foreigners who did not speak English or understand the culture. This in turn produced an understandable backlash among the American public, and in 1885 Congress decided to remedy the problem, passing the *Alien Contract Labor Law*. The law was a sweeping, thorough reversal of immigration policy, written broadly.

> *Be it enacted by the Senate and House of Representatives of the United States of America in Congress assembled, that from and after the passage of this act it shall be unlawful for any person, company, partnership, or corporation, in any manner whatsoever, to prepay the transportation, or in any way assist or encourage the importation or migration, of any alien or aliens, any foreigner or foreigners, into the United States, its territories, or the District of Columbia under contract or agreement, parol or special, express or implied, made previous to the importation or migration of such alien or aliens, foreigner or foreigners, to perform labor or service of any kind in the United States, its territories, or the District of Columbia.*

In 1887, the Church of the Holy Trinity, a church belonging to the Anglican Communion in New York City, was in need of a pastor. It had heard of a reputable minister in England, the Reverend E. Walpole Warren, who they believed would be just what the church needed, and they contracted him to be their pastor and rector. They may not have been aware of the prohibition against imported labor, and if they were, certainly would have no reason to believe that such a law, with its obvious intent, would apply to hiring a minister of the gospel.

Once Rev. Warren arrived in New York City, the church was sued for violating this *Alien Contract Labor Law*. The case was brought to trial in the Circuit Court of the United States, Southern District of New York. The court ruled that this was indeed a violation of the law, and the court ordered the contract with the pastor voided. The church appealed to the U.S. Supreme Court.

The Supreme Court decision, like the *Vidal v. Girard's Executors* decision discussed in the first chapter, was a *unanimous* decision. It was written by Associate Justice David J. Brewer. The decision of the court was that the Circuit Court had erred in applying the *Alien Contract Labor Law* to a minister. The court gave two reasons for why they did not believe the *Alien Law* should apply to Rev. Warren in the landmark decision *Church of the Holy Trinity v. United States (1892)*.

The first reason was discussed in some detail, and has often been referred to in succeeding Supreme Court decisions as an important precedent. This reason is summed up by the Court as follows:

> *It is a familiar rule that a thing may be within the letter of the statute and yet not within the statute because not within its spirit nor within the intention of its makers. This has been often asserted, and the reports are full of cases illustrating its application. This is not the substitution of the will of the judge for that of the legislator, for frequently words of general meaning are used in a statute, words broad enough to include an act in question, and yet a consideration of the whole legislation, or of the circumstances surrounding its enactment, or of the absurd results which follow from giving such broad meaning to the words, makes it unreasonable to believe that the legislator intended to include the particular act.*

The Court decision pointed out the broad language of the statute, seemingly to include no exceptions whatever. The Court then discussed at some length the underlying reason for the legislature to create this law in the first place, that being to prevent industrialists from importing cheap, unskilled manual labor from abroad, with the consequences mentioned above.

The Court then cited a number of prior cases in which broad language in the letter of a law produced an absurd result never intended by the legislature. The Court decision concluded that the law's clear intent, both from the context of the law as well as the historical context, was to prevent the importation of cheap, unskilled, manual labor, not brain power, and that the law did not apply to any profession in which the main thing being contracted was a man's unique knowledge.

The Supreme Court could have ended the opinion right at that point, and it would have been understood and well-received by the country, that the broadly worded law produced an absurd result never intended by Congress. However, the Court did not end there. Instead the decision concluded with a lengthy explanation communicating in detail the second and main reason the court did not view the law applying to a Christian minister.

The Court began this section of the decision in this way, "... no purpose of action against religion can be imputed to any legislation, state or national, because this is a religious people. This is historically true. From the discovery of this continent to the present hour, there is a single voice making this affirmation." By implication, the Supreme Court was saying that such a law *could* not apply to a Christian minister because of the nature and purpose of this country, founded on the Christian religion.

In this section of the decision, the Supreme Court took the time to go back through American history to the very founding of the colonies, then to the founding of individual States, and ultimately the founding of the United States as a new and separate entity, its Declaration of Independence, and its Constitution. The decision included numerous quotes from the various founding documents throughout our history.

> *The commission to Christopher Columbus, prior to his sail westward, is from "Ferdinand and Isabella, by the grace of God, King and Queen of Castile," etc., and recites that "it is hoped that by God's assistance some of the continents and islands in the ocean will be discovered," etc. The first colonial grant, that made to Sir Walter Raleigh in 1584, was from "Elizabeth, by the grace of God, of England, Fraunce and Ireland, Queene, defender of the faith," etc., and the grant authorizing him to enact statutes of the government of the proposed colony provided that "they be not against the true Christian faith nowe professed in the Church of England." The first charter of Virginia, granted by King James I in 1606, after reciting the*

application of certain parties for a charter, commenced the grant in these words: "We, greatly commending, and graciously accepting of, their Desires for the Furtherance of so noble a Work, which may, by the Providence of Almighty God, hereafter tend to the Glory of his Divine Majesty, in propagating of Christian Religion to such People, as yet live in Darkness and miserable Ignorance of the true Knowledge and Worship of God, and may in time bring the Infidels and Savages, living in those parts, to human Civility, and to a settled and quiet government; DO, by these our Letters-Patents, graciously accept of, and agree to, their humble and well intended Desires."

The Court continues with a lengthy series of quotes from various founding documents. I have included several excerpts because I believe it is imperative that we understand not only where the nation was politically and spiritually at the close of the nineteenth century, but also the exclusively Christian nature of the founding of every one of the States.

Language of similar import may be found in the subsequent charters of that colony, from the same king, in 1609 and 1611, and the same is true of the various charters granted to the other colonies. In language more or less emphatic is the establishment of the Christian religion declared to be one of the purposes of the grant.

The celebrated compact made by the pilgrims in the Mayflower, 1620, recites:

"Having undertaken for the Glory of God, and Advancement of the Christian Faith, and the Honour of our King and Country, a Voyage to plant the first Colony in the northern Parts of Virginia; Do by these Presents, solemnly and mutually, in the Presence of God and one another, covenant and combine ourselves together into a civil Body Politick, for our better Ordering and Preservation, and Furtherance of the Ends aforesaid."

The fundamental orders of Connecticut, under which a provisional government was instituted in 1638-39, commence with this declaration:

"Forasmuch as it hath pleased the Allmighty God by the wise disposition of his divyne prvidence so to Order and dispose of things that we the Inhabitants and Residents of Windsor, Hartford, and Wethersfield are now cohabiting and dwelling in and uppon the River of Conectecotte and the Lands thereunto adioyneing; And well knowing where a people are gathered togather the word of God requires that to mayntayne the peace and union of such a people there should be an orderly and decent Goverment established according to God, to order and dispose of the affayres of the people at all seasons as occation shall require . . .

Coming nearer to the present time, the declaration of independence recognizes the presence of the Divine in human affairs in these words:

"We hold these truths to be self-evident, that all men are created equal, that they are endowed by their Creator with certain unalienable Rights, that among these are Life, Liberty, and the pursuit of Happiness. . . . We therefore the Representatives of the united states of America, in General Congress, Assembled, appealing to the Supreme Judge of the world for the rectitude of our intentions, do, in the Name and by Authority of the good these Colonies, solemnly publish and declare," etc.;

"And for the support of this Declaration, with a firm reliance on the Protection of Divine Providence, we mutually pledge to each other our Lives, our Fortunes, and our sacred Honor."

If we examine the constitutions of the various states, we find in them a constant recognition of religious obligations. **_Every Constitution of every one of the forty four states contains language which, either directly or by clear implication, recognizes a profound reverence for religion, and an assumption that its influence in all human affairs is essential to the wellbeing of the community._** [Emphasis added]

This recognition may be in the preamble, such as is found in the Constitution of Illinois, 1870:

> *"We, the people of the State of Illinois, grateful to Almighty God for the civil, political, and religious liberty which He hath so long permitted us to enjoy, and looking to Him for a blessing upon our endeavors to secure and transmit the same unimpaired to succeeding generations," etc.*

It may be only in the familiar requisition that all officers shall take an oath closing with the declaration, "so help me God." It may be in clauses like that of the Constitution of Indiana, 1816, Art. XI, section 4:

> *"The manner of administering an oath or affirmation shall be such as is most consistent with the conscience of the deponent, and shall be esteemed the most solemn appeal to God."* . . .

Or, as in sections 5 and 14 of Article 7 of the Constitution of Mississippi, 1832:

> *"No person who denies the being of a God, or a future state of rewards and punishments, shall hold any office in the civil department of this state. . . . Religion morality, and knowledge being necessary to good government, the preservation of liberty, and*

> *the happiness of mankind, schools, and the means of education, shall forever be encouraged in this state."*

Or by Article 22 of the Constitution of Delaware, (1776), which required all officers, besides an oath of allegiance, to make and subscribe the following declaration:

> *"I, A. B., do profess faith in God the Father, and in Jesus Christ His only Son, and in the Holy Ghost, one God, blessed for evermore, and I do acknowledge the Holy Scriptures of the Old and New Testament to be given by divine inspiration."*

Even the Constitution of the United States, which is supposed to have little touch upon the private life of the individual, contains in the First Amendment a declaration common to the constitutions of all the states, as follows: "Congress shall make no law respecting an establishment of religion, or prohibiting the free exercise thereof," etc., and also provides in Article I, Section 7, a provision common to many constitutions, that the executive shall have ten days (Sundays excepted) within which to determine whether he will approve or veto a bill.

The foregoing brief excerpts from the court record provide far more than a history lesson. It is evidence submitted in a court of law to be used in consideration of a final verdict. The Supreme Court, at the end of the discussion, summarizes what this means legally.

> *There is no dissonance in these declarations. There is a universal language pervading them all, having one meaning. They affirm and reaffirm that this is a religious nation. These are not individual sayings, declarations of private persons. They are organic utterances. They speak the voice of the entire people. While, because of a general recognition of this truth, the question has seldom been presented to the courts . . .*

In other words the Court is saying, this evidence is unanimous – you cannot point to a single situation or place in this country where Christianity was not the foundation of the society and the law. And, by the way, this has never really come up before in the courts because it is so obvious.

At this point the decision goes on to cite case law prohibiting un-Christian acts, particularly blasphemy against God or against Jesus Christ. The Court quotes from the famous 1811 case in the New York Supreme Court, *People v. Ruggles*, in which a Mr. Ruggles was charged and convicted of blasphemy:

> *And in People v. Ruggles, 8 Johns. 290, 294-295, Chancellor Kent, the great commentator on American law, speaking as Chief Justice of the Supreme Court of New York, said:*
>
>> "*The people of this state, in common with the people of this country, profess the general doctrines of Christianity as the rule of their faith and practice, and to scandalize the author of these doctrines is not only, in a religious point of view, extremely impious, but, even in respect to the obligations due to society, is a gross violation of decency and good order...*"
>
> *The free, equal, and undisturbed enjoyment of religious opinion, whatever it may be, and free and decent discussions on any religious subject, is granted and secured; but to revile, with malicious and blasphemous contempt, the religion professed by almost the whole community is an abuse of that right. Nor are we bound by any expressions in the Constitution, as some have strangely supposed, either not to punish at all, or to punish indiscriminately the like attacks upon the religion of Mahomet or of the Grand Lama, and for this plain reason, that the case assumes that we are a Christian people, and the morality of the country is deeply engrafted upon Christianity, and not upon the doctrines or worship of those impostors.*"

The Supreme Court here is quoting, with approval, the esteemed jurist James Kent. Justice Kent was a friend of Justice Joseph Story, and the two together were regarded as the greatest jurists of their time. Kent, like Story, also wrote a much used legal textbook, the multi-volume *Commentaries on American Law*.

The *Ruggles* decision, and the use of it by the U.S. Supreme Court is significant. Notice what Justice Kent is saying in convicting Ruggles of blasphemy against God, and I paraphrase, "Yes, we have freedom of religion in this country. Everyone has the freedom to worship as conscience dictates. However, that freedom does not extend to blaspheming God, and this blasphemy of Ruggles is so onerous against God and the Christian religion as to be legally unacceptable. Those laws which are established to prevent blasphemy of this type are completely legal. Although we are all equally guaranteed freedom of religion, we are under no obligation under the law to, in like manner, punish those who may speak against Mohammed or the Grand Lama," because, and here I quote directly, "the morality of the country is deeply engrafted upon Christianity, and not upon the doctrines or worship of those impostors."

The Supreme Court then moves on to the present, or the state of the nation, as of the writing of this decision in 1892.

> *If we pass beyond these matters to a view of American life, as expressed by its laws, its business, its customs, and its society, we find every where a clear recognition of the same truth. Among other matters, note the following: the form of oath universally prevailing, concluding with an appeal to the Almighty; the custom of opening sessions of all deliberative bodies and most conventions with prayer; the prefatory words of all wills, "In the name of God, amen;" the laws respecting the observance of the Sabbath, with the general cessation of all secular business, and the closing of courts, legislatures, and other similar public assemblies on that day; the churches and church organizations which abound in every city, town, and hamlet; the multitude of charitable organizations existing every where under Christian auspices; the gigantic missionary associations, with general*

support, and aiming to establish Christian missions in every quarter of the globe.

These, and many other matters which might be noticed, add a volume of unofficial declarations to the mass of organic utterances that this is a Christian nation. [emphasis added] *In the face of all these, shall it be believed that a Congress of the United States intended to make it a misdemeanor for a church of this country to contract for the services of a Christian minister residing in another nation?*

The term "organic utterances" refers to founding documents, coming from the same root, to *organize*. The Supreme Court is unanimously declaring these truths, that the founding documents speak with one voice, the lives of the people speak with the same voice, our court precedents speak with the same voice, and by the way, we have just scratched the surface of all the evidences which concur, all virtually shouting the same refrain, "This is a Christian nation!" We do not recognize all religions as being equal. We do not give legal parity to all religions. We are Christian. We prefer Christianity. We support Christianity. Christianity enjoys a privilege under the law that other religions do not enjoy.

The court decision concludes with this hypothetical challenge:

Suppose, in the Congress that passed this act, some member had offered a bill which in terms declared that if any Roman Catholic church in this country should contract with Cardinal Manning to come to this country and enter into its service as pastor and priest, or any Episcopal church should enter into a like contract with Canon Farrar, or any Baptist church should make similar arrangements with Rev. Mr. Spurgeon, or any Jewish synagogue with some eminent rabbi, such contract should be adjudged unlawful and void, and the church making it be subject to prosecution and punishment. Can it be believed that it would have received a minute of approving thought or a single vote? Yet it is contended that such was, in effect, the meaning of this statute.

In other words, suppose the legislature were to be presented with a law which prohibited the ministers of any Jewish or Christian denomination from coming to this country as ministers in a church or synagogue. Does anyone think such a law would receive *any* favorable discussion? Does anyone believe that such a law would garner *a single vote* in the Congress? So how can anyone imagine that such could be the intent of this law that is before us?

> *The construction invoked cannot be accepted as correct. It is a case where there was presented a definite evil, in view of which the legislature used general terms with the purpose of reaching all phases of that evil, and thereafter, unexpectedly, it is developed that the general language thus employed is broad enough to reach cases and acts which the whole history and life of the country affirm could not have been intentionally legislated against. It is the duty of the courts under those circumstances to say that, however broad the language of the statute may be, the act, although within the letter, is not within the intention of the legislature, and therefore cannot be within the statute.*
>
> *The judgment will be reversed, and the case remanded for further proceedings in accordance with this opinion.*

The clear, indeed the only, interpretation of this court case is that the United States of America, in 1892, held exclusively to a Judeo/Christian world view, and according to the court that was the case from the very beginning of the colonial era. That world view was woven into the entire fabric of the country. They intended that always to be the case. In the chapters that follow you will see just how deeply Christianity is woven into the original American fabric.

With apologies, and with all due respect to President Barack Hussein Obama, if *stare decisis* has any practical application at all, then we are still a *Christian* nation, and no other kind. And so it is ordered, in a legal proceeding of the highest court in the land, *The United States Supreme Court.*

Chapter 3
America's Early School System

Our fathers were pious, eminently so. Let us then forever venerate and imitate this part of their character. When the children of the pilgrims forget that Being who was the pilgrim's Guide and Deliverer, when the descendants of the Puritans cease to acknowledge, and to obey, and love that Being, for whose service the Puritans forsook all that men chiefly love, enduring scorn and reproach, exile and poverty, and finding at last a superabundant reward; when the sons of a religious and holy ancestry fall away from its high communion, and join themselves to the assemblies of the profane, they have stained the luster of their parentage. They have forfeited the dear blessings of their inheritance, and they deserve to be cast out from this fair land without even a wilderness for their refuge. No! Let us still keep the ark of God in the midst of us. Let us adopt the prayer of the wise monarch of Israel, "The Lord our God be with us, as he was with our fathers: let him not leave us, nor forsake us; that he may incline our hearts unto him, to walk in all his ways, and to keep his commandments, and his statutes, and his judgments, which he commanded our fathers. [Character of the Pilgrim Fathers of New England, by Francis William Pitt Greenwood; excerpt from a public school reading book, 1837, Eclectic Fourth Reader, William H. McGuffey]

As we saw in *Vidal v. Girard's Executors*, our public school system in the mid-1800s was characterized by religious instruction. That was the case long before Vidal, and was true from the earliest moments of our founding. It remained true in many parts of the country through the mid-1900s.

Much of what we know of the earliest schools comes from the Massachusetts Bay Colony. The "Colony" was represented and supported by the Massachusetts Bay Company, which was the legal governing entity back in England. This Colony existed in skeletal form in the late 1620s surrounding Salem, Massachusetts, led by one of the original investors who served as the Colony's Governor, John Endecott. Most members of the Massachusetts Bay Company were still living in England at that time.

Back in England the Massachusetts Bay Company, made up of many prominent English citizens, were seeking a royal charter, one signed by the King. This they were able to obtain. Their charter, presented by Charles I himself, allowed the Company's government to reside in New England, in contrast to charters for other settlements which required the government of those colonies to remain in England.

This provision allowed the Company to make some changes in their plans. Other colonies were governed from England. These were like-minded Puritans, all of whom were seeing and feeling the growing religious persecution of Puritans in their homeland. With the charter not requiring the government to reside in England, those members of the Company who could not or would not relocate to New England willingly sold their shares to those willing to emigrate, allowing for 100% ownership of the Company to reside in the Colony, and making them one and the same.

In 1630 the Massachusetts Bay Company moved its entire ownership and its royal charter across the ocean to New England. A fleet of eleven ships containing more than 700 people landed at Salem, Massachusetts that summer. Among them were various necessary skilled tradesmen which would provide the infrastructure for a modern English settlement. The flagship of the fleet, the *Arbella*, carried Governor John Winthrop, Thomas Dudley, and a number of other substantial men who were now owners of the enterprise. (Either Winthrop, Dudley, or Endecott would be elected to serve as Governor for 33 of the first 37 years of the Colony.)

The *Arbella* carried with it the royal charter, and with it the seat of government. The profits from the Company, rather than helping a rich investor back in England to build an elegant estate, all went into building up the Colony itself. And the government – well it could be whatever they chose.

It was a unique time in human history – a new land full of resources, mostly empty of inhabitants, settled by a group of like-minded people who were free to form whatever type of government they believed would suit them best. Their charter was out of the easy reach of future kings to revoke or to revise.

Just 40 miles to the south, a struggling Plymouth Colony would at times render assistance and at other times benefit from this larger, better organized Massachusetts Bay Colony to the north. There was much interaction between these colonies; initially Plymouth sent its physician to assist in a time of epidemic. Also, the northern Massachusetts Bay Colony had the benefit of William Bradford's years of experience in the new world. Bradford had experimented with various forms of government from communal living to free, private enterprise, and had discovered that free enterprise left the Plymouth Colony with plenty, whereas communal living (socialism) had left them starving.

The settlers in the northern Colony were different from those in the south. The Plymouth Colony was settled primarily by a Separatist church group. These were those who had severed ties with the Church of England to form their own church. As such, they were initially inclined more toward a communal type of settlement. Yes, they had brought some people along that had skills they needed who were not part of the Separatist church, but mainly they were simple, religious people coming out of a culture in which enterprise was not predominant. In Holland they had had to settle for whatever occupation could provide them with a living. Their voyage to Plymouth aboard the Mayflower was poorly planned and furnished with inadequate resources. By landing in Plymouth right at the beginning of winter, they lost half of the group to starvation the first year.

While most of the Plymouth Colony consisted of small farmers just trying to survive, in contrast, a great number of those who were part of the Massachusetts Bay Company were businessmen – entrepreneurs who were accustomed to good planning and hard work, and in turn, accustomed to reaping the rewards of those efforts. Many of the investors in the Massachusetts Bay Company were involved in enterprise and foreign trade within just a few short years after their arrival, and many thrived financially.

The continued persecution of Puritans and Separatists in England, and the great English Civil War that resulted from it, led to a large migration of these religious refugees out of England. Many of these emigrated to Ireland

and even to the Caribbean Islands. This great migration added population to all of the American colonies, and most of these came to New England due to the Puritan sympathies of Massachusetts Bay, Plymouth, and Connecticut. By the early 1640s the migration had snowballed to about 30,000 refugees arriving in New England. (A great number of these returned to England in the 1640s to assist Oliver Cromwell in his war against King Charles I and the royalists.) This influx of new settlers in Massachusetts Bay led to an increasingly involved government, concerned with the well-being of the Colony from both an economic and spiritual point of view.

As the English Civil War waged through the 1640s, it became apparent that Oliver Cromwell and his Puritan backers were gaining the upper hand. After Cromwell won and Charles I was beheaded, the English government under Cromwell became as severe toward traditional Anglicans as the government under Charles had been toward Puritans. This led to a wave of traditional Anglican immigrants in areas of Colonial America where Anglicans were welcomed, particularly Virginia. Thus, Virginia and several other parts of the South, New York, and New Jersey experienced an influx of new Anglican refugees. Among the English Anglicans who arrived in Virginia in this wave in the mid-1600s were the ancestors of George Washington. Thus was Virginia settled a solidly Anglican State, while New England was predominately Puritan, later to be known as Congregationalists.

The provisions of the original Massachusetts Bay Company charter provided for a government which was comprised of a Governor, a Deputy Governor, and initially twelve (later eighteen) Assistants. This "General Court" as it was called, presided over the legislative, judicial, and religious particulars of the Colony. (Interestingly, that name has stuck to the extent that today the Massachusetts legislature goes by the name Massachusetts General Court.) The three prominent men, Winthrop, Dudley, and Endecott were all strict Puritans, usually uncompromising and often cruel toward those of different faiths.

The idea of religious freedom was foreign at the time, both in England and to those men who settled in the new world. They believed that they had come to New England to practice true Christianity, and they were not about to allow it to become polluted by heresy or unbelief, and they believed that was of particular importance with the huge migration of new people coming over from England.

The new Massachusetts Bay Colony did not consider the government tactics that had been used to persecute them in England to be wrong. To the contrary, they thought government should keep people strictly in line theologically. They just believed that the theology in England had been wrong and theirs was right. So they applied the same severe, heavy hand to those who disagreed with them on religion that had been applied to them in England, even to the point of executing some of the Quaker immigrants between 1659-1661.

At the "town" level, local government was run by "selectmen" which were chosen by the people of that town. Some of the General Court served as selectmen in the towns where they lived. The selectmen, much as today's town or city councils, ran the day-to-day affairs of the town, but they also oversaw and provided funding for the local church. If they encountered difficult questions about a specific pastor or controversy, they would usually refer it to the General Court. Church and government were one and the same, and pastors were paid out of the local public treasury. The local church building was built with public funds, and it functioned as the local meeting place for civil, religious, and educational functions alike.

In the early years of the colonies, most young people were schooled in their homes. Clergymen assisted where parents were incapable of teaching their children, but by the early 1640s it became apparent that too many children were being raised illiterate. This led to the original Massachusetts Bay School Law (1642), the first education law in the colonies passed by the General Court. (See Appendix A for full text).

Evidently this law did not give the Colony all the results that it had hoped, and in 1647 the Colony passed a second education law which was more specific. Today that law is known as *"The Old Deluder Satan Law"* because it states at the beginning that illiteracy and ignorance are goals of Satan to keep people from the Bible. (See Appendix A for full text).

This act implemented specific public infrastructure where the 1642 law was more subjective in nature. When a town grew to 50 families or more, the law required that they hire a teacher to begin a formal education program with the town's children. Then, when a town grew to over 100 families, the town was required to build and staff a school for all the children to attend.

Both laws remained in effect, and both were eventually copied, to varying degrees, by the other colonies. As in Massachusetts, so also among the other colonies, the public school system which sprang from these laws was very oriented toward teaching Bible and Protestant catechism.

The practical effect of these laws was that the smaller towns usually held school in the local church/meeting house, often with the local clergyman the teacher. Younger children usually learned reading, writing, and elementary Protestant catechism in what were called "dame schools," and these were taught by a woman, usually in her home. The larger towns which could afford a separate school building generally had a non-clergy school master, but even then the clergy, often the highest educated man in the town, was usually involved in the oversight of these schools.

In the early days of the colonies school textbooks were primitive if they existed at all. The main textbook was the Bible, and that was used for learning to read as well as for religious instruction. There were few other books, although homemade "hornbooks" were used extensively. Hornbooks were generally a single page of instruction mounted on a paddle shaped piece of wood with a transparent cover over the paper to make it more durable. Hornbooks for younger children might contain the alphabet or simple language rules or arithmetic.

In 1690 the first school textbook was printed in Boston, called the New England Primer, and published specifically for use in New England schools. None of the earliest editions of the primer remain today, but descriptions from advertisements describe a book very much like later editions of which there remain numerous copies from the mid-1700s and beyond.

The *New England Primer* contained reading exercises and lots of theology, including Reverend John Cotton's elementary catechism, titled *Spiritual Milk for Boston Babes*. Later versions drew Protestant doctrine from the "Westminster Shorter Catechism." The alphabet was learned using Protestant theology as a base. For example, the youngest students learned their ABC's by memorizing such child poems as, *"A – In Adam's fall, we sinned all; B – Heaven to find, the Bible mind; C – Christ crucify'd, for sinners dy'd; D – the Deluge drowned the Earth around; . . ."* and so on through the entire alphabet.

As children progressed to being able to read, another series of alphabet prompters was included for their memory work. Like the earlier alphabet, it employed Bible verses and principles, but which were more advanced. "A - A wise son maketh a glad father, but a foolish son is the heaviness of his mother.

B – Better is a little with the fear of the Lord than great treasure & trouble therewith. C – Come unto Christ all ye that labor and are heavy laden and he will give you rest. D – Do not the abominable thing which I hate saith the Lord; . . ." and on through the entire alphabet

The *New England Primer* contained far more than spelling and grammar. It also contained the "Westminster Confession of Faith" and "The Shorter Catechism of the Westminster Assembly of Divines." The catechism took the form of a series of questions and answers, such as, "Question 1 – What is the chief end of man? Answer – Man's chief end is to glorify God and enjoy him forever. Q. 2. What rule hath God given to direct us how we may glorify and enjoy him? A. The word of God which is contained in the scriptures of the old and new testaments is the only rule to direct us how we may glorify God and enjoy him. . ." The catechism contained a total of 107 such questions.

The *New England Primer* was by far the most popular reading primer through the American War for Independence and well into the 1800s. Beginning in the mid-1700s schools in the colonies began to make use of a "speller" by Reverend Thomas Dilworth in England. This was more of a reading primer and was used extensively to supplement, in some cases replace, the *New England Primer*. One of Dilworth's earliest reading lessons was as follows:

> *Some early Lessons on the foregoing Tables, consisting of Words not exceeding Three Letters.*
>
> *Lesson I*
> *No Man may put off the Law of God.*
> *The Way of God is no ill Way.*
> *My Joy is in God all the Day.*
> *A bad Man is a Foe to God.*
>
> *Lesson II*
> *To God do I cry all the Day.*
> *Who is God, but our God?*
> *All men go out of the Way of thy Law.*
> *In God do I put my Joy, O let me not sin.*

Lesson III
Pay to God his Due.
Go not in the Way of bad Men.
No Man can see God.
Our God is the God of all Men.

Lesson IV.
Who can say he has no Sin?
The Way of Man is ill, but not the Way of God.
My son, go not in the Way of bad Men.
No Man can do as God can do.

Lesson V
Let me not go out of thy Way, O God.
O do not see my Sin, and let me not go to the Pit.
Try me, O God, and let me not go
out of the Way of thy Law.

Lesson VI
The Way of Man is not as the Way of God.
The Law of God is Joy to me.
My Son, if you do ill, you can not go to God.
Do as you are bid, but if you are bid, do no ill.

Beginning in 1783, Noah Webster added his spelling and grammar books, a three volume set which included a spelling book (1783), later to be known popularly as the *Blue Backed Speller* which was more extensive than the *New England Primer*. Volume Two was a grammar text (1784), and volume three was a reading book (1785). The Webster speller and grammar books began to cut into the *New England Primer's* sales and influence, and it virtually eliminated the Dilworth text. However, the *New England Primer* was still a popular reading text all the way through the 1800s in many schools, and new editions were printed throughout the 1800s.

Those schools in the late 1700s that opted for Noah Webster's spelling and grammar books were treated to a less direct spiritual experience than the *New England Primer* or the Dilworth speller. Initially there was no

Protestant catechism in the Webster texts. Webster believed that Dilworth overused the name of God, making this revered word too commonplace in the minds of children. Indeed, in the above excerpt, Dilworth used the name "God" nineteen times in just twenty-four lines. Webster, in the introduction to the first edition went to great length to explain his reasons for relying less on Scriptural passages than the competing texts, particularly the New England Primer.

> *It will be observed, that in all the easy lessons, taken from scripture, the name of Deity is generally omitted. The reason of this omission is important and obvious. Nothing has greater tendency to lesson the reverence which mankind ought to have for the Supreme Being, than a careless repetition of his name upon every trifling occasion. Experience shows that a frequent thoughtless repetition of that sacred word, which, in our Spelling Books, often occurs two or three times in a line, renders the name as familiar to children as the name of their book, and they mention it with the same indifference. To prevent this profanation, such passages are selected from scripture, as contain some important precepts of morality and religion, in which that sacred name is seldom mentioned. Let sacred things be appropriated to sacred purposes.*

In brief, Webster's reason for not including a lot of references to the name of God in his *Blue Backed Speller* was because he held Scripture, and the God of the Bible, in such high regard that he did not want God's name to become routine by school children and as such, treated with indifference or irreverence. In contrast, recall from the Introduction, secularist historian Joseph Ellis, in his book *After the Revolution*, quoted only the very last sentence of the above quote, "Let sacred things be appropriated to sacred purposes," leaving the preceding explanation out and substituting his own flawed explanation.

By omitting the reason Webster gave for toning down the religious content in the first few editions, Ellis was able to claim to those who did not have access to Webster's actual statement that it was his intent to publish a set of textbooks that were secular in nature, as contrasted with contemporary,

Bible-based textbooks such as the Dilworth speller and the *New England Primer*. Ellis described the speller, grammar, and reading texts as follows:

> ... [I]n October of 1783 the Hartford firm of Hudson and Goodwin printed 5,000 copies of a 119-page book entitled *A Grammatical Institute, of the English Language, Comprising An easy, concise and systematic Method of Education, Designed for the Use of English Schools in America. In Three Parts. Part I.* It sold for fourteen cents a copy. Known soon after as *The American Spelling Book* or "the Blue-Backed Speller," it was destined to become the best-selling book ever written by an American and one of the most profitable ventures in American publishing history.
>
> Part of the book's appeal to late-eighteenth-century Americans lay in Webster's bold and distinctive brand of patriotism. The introduction to the first edition of the speller – there would be 385 editions in Webster's lifetime – was a skillful polemic. He reminded Americans that before the recent Revolution "the king, the constitution, the laws, the commerce, the fashions, the books and even the sentiments of Englishmen were implicitly supposed to be the best on earth Not only their virtues and improvements but their prejudices, their errors, their vices, and their follies were adopted by us with avidity." Now, however, most Americans "stand astonished at their former delusion and enjoy the pleasure of a final separation from the insolent sovereigns..."
>
> ... The speller concluded with two pages of important dates in American history, beginning with Columbus's discovery and ending with the battle of Yorktown. This litany of national names and dates replaced any mention of God, the Bible, or sacred events. "Let sacred things be appropriated for sacred purposes," wrote Webster. In place of Christian myths, Webster began to construct a secular catechism to the nation-state. Here was the first appearance of "civics" in American schoolbooks. <u>In this sense, Webster's speller was the secular successor to *The New England Primer* with its explicitly biblical injunctions.</u>" [emphasis added]

This "secular" characterization of Webster's early textbooks is at least inaccurate, and is arguably dishonest, given Ellis's well-documented history of being truth-challenged. Ellis here ignores Webster's own rationale for his work. Nor could it be more inaccurate when we look at what Webster actually wrote in his speller, and here the influence of Dilworth is striking. As you can see, the word "God" is used sparingly compared to Dilworth, but it is used along with numerous pronoun references to God. And the spiritual content is very similar to the content contained in the Dilworth speller.

TABLE XIII.

Lessons of easy Words, to teach Children to read, and to know their Duty.

LESSON I.
No man may put off the law of God.
My joy is in his law all the day.
O may I not go in the way of sin.
Let me not go in the way of ill men.

II.
A bad man is a foe to the law.
It is his joy to do ill.
All men go out of the way.
Who can say he has no sin?

III.
The way of man is ill.
My son, do as you are bid.
But if you are bid, do no ill.
See not my sin, and let me not go to the pit.

[Notice that in the first three exercises all words are 3 letters or less. Beginning with Lesson IV the words grow increasingly complex.]

IV.

Rest in the Lord, and mind his word.
My son, hold fast the law that is good.
You must not tell a lie, nor do hurt.
We must let no man hurt us.

V.

Do as well as you can, and do no harm.
Mark the man that doth well, and do so too.
Help such as want help, and be kind.
Let your sins past, put you in mind to mend.

VI.

I will not walk with bad men; that I may not be
cast off with them.
I will love the law and keep it.
I will walk with the just and do good.

VII.

This life is not long, but the life to come has no end.
We must pray for them that hate us.
We must love them that love not us.
We must do as we like to be done to.

VIII.

A bad life will make a bad end.
He must live well that would die well.
He doth live ill that doth not mend.
In time to come we must do no ill.

IX.

No man can say that he has done no ill.
For all men have gone out of the way.
There is none that doth good: no, not one.
If I have done harm, I must do it no more.

X.
Sin will lead us to pain and woe.
Love that which is good and shun vice.
Hate no man, but love both friends and foes.
A bad man can take no rest day nor night.

XI.
He that came to save us will wash us from all sin; I will be glad in his name. A good boy will do all that is just; he will flee from vice; he will do good, and walk in the way of life. Love not the world, nor the things that are in the world; for they are sin. I will not fear what flesh can do to me; for my trust is in him who made the world. He is nigh to them that pray to him, and praise his name.

XII.
Be a good child: mind your book; love your school, and strive to learn. Tell no tales; call no ill names; you must not lie, nor swear, nor cheat, nor steal. Play not with bad boys; use no ill words at play; spend your time well; live in peace; and shun all strife. This is the way to make good men love you, and save your soul from pain and woe.

XIII.
A good child will not lie, swear nor steal. He will be good at home, and ask to read his book, when he gets up, he will wash his hands and face clean; he will comb his hair, and make haste to school; he will not play by the way, as bad boys do.

XIV.
When good boys and girls are at school, they will mind their books, and try to learn to spell and read well, and not play in time of school. When they are at church, they will sit, kneel or stand still; and when they are at home, will read some good book, that God may bless them.

XV.

As for those boys and girls that mind not their books, and love not church and school, but play with such as tell tales, tell lies, curse, swear and steal they will come to some bad end, and must be whipt till they mend their ways.

Let's assume, for sake of argument, that Joseph Ellis wrote the above characterization of the Webster speller having never actually read it, so he was just ignorant of the explicit religious nature of the book. That would represent a rather glaring oversight for such an esteemed historian, not really plausible in my mind. No, I think we must assume that Ellis had read the *Blue Backed Speller* himself and was aware of its content. Anything less would be an academic crime. As we can clearly see, this textbook was anything but "secular" in content.

In *After the Revolution,* Ellis never sets the record straight – that with the first major revision of the Webster speller in 1787 the speller had become even more religious in character rather than increasingly secular, with Bible and doctrine throughout. The following is a typical reading exercise which comes from a Webster speller published following the 1787 revisions. I have included much lengthier portions of the Webster speller than I might otherwise have done, if not for the inaccurate characterization of Joseph Ellis. I want you to see for yourself what the Webster speller was all about – certainly not in any respect a secular work as implied by Ellis:

TABLE XL.

The History of the Creation of the WORLD.

IN six days God made the world, and all things that are in it. He made the sun to shine by day; and the moon to give light by night. He made all the beasts that walk on the earth, all the birds that fly in the air, and all the fish that swim in the sea. Each herb, & plant, & tree, is the work of his hands. All things both great and small, that live and move, and breathe in this wide world, to him do owe their birth, to him their life.

And God saw that all things he had made were good. But as yet there was not a man to till the ground, so God made man of the dust of the earth, and breathed into him the breath of life, and gave him rule over all that he had made.

And the man gave names to all the beasts of the field, the fowls of the air, and the fish of the sea. But there was not found an help meet for man; so God brought on him a deep sleep, and then took from his side a rib, of which he made a wife, and gave her to the man, and her name was Eve; and from these two came all the sons of men.

All things are known to God, and though his throne of state be far on high, yet doth his eye look down to use in this lower world, and see all the ways of the sons of men.

If we go out he marks our steps: and when we go in, no door can shut him from us. While we are by ourselves, he knows all our vain thoughts, and the ends we aim at; and when we talk to friend or foe, he hears our words, and views the good or harm we do to them or to ourselves.

When we pray he notes our zeal. All the day long he minds how we spend our time, and no dark night can hide our works from him. If we play the cheat, he marks the fraud, and hears the least word of a false tongue.

He sees if our hearts are hard to the poor, or if by alms we help their wants; if in our breast we pine at the rich, or if we are well pleased with our own estate. He knows all that we do; and be we where we will he is sure to be with us.

> The Lord who made the ear of man,
> Must needs hear all of right;
> He made the eye, all things must then
> Be plain in his clear sight.
> The lord doth know the thoughts of man,
> His heart he sees most plain,
> And he, on high, man's thoughts doth scan,
> And sees they are but vain.
> But oh! that man is safe and sure,

> *Whom thou dost deep in awe;*
> *And that his life may be most pure,*
> *Dost guide him in thy law:*
> *For he shall live in peace and rest,*
> *He fears not at his death;*
> *Love fills his heart, and hope his breast,*
> *With joy he yields his breath.*

But the religious content in public school textbooks was scrapped right after the U.S. Constitution was implemented (1788) and the First Amendment was ratified (1790), right? Wrong, of course. If anything the religious content, after the first amendment was ratified, was stronger than that found in previous textbooks. To understand why the First Amendment did not eliminate the overtly Christian nature of America's public school textbooks, you will need to digest Chapter 9.

In 1790, and thereafter, was added "The Federal Catechism" which was about four pages of questions followed by answers concerning the American government. Of this, historian Joseph Ellis might accurately say that civics had been specifically introduced into the speller. In 1794, and thereafter, was added a section called "The Moral Catechism," also a series of questions followed by answers concerning moral and religious themes, filled with Christian theology, which Ellis failed to mention in his own description of Webster's work. For sake of space I have not included it here, but please see Appendix B for an excerpt of Webster's moral catechism.

The foregoing selections are representative of the whole speller, and there is no excuse for trying to characterize it as a secular text. Later in his life, when publishing the first edition of the Webster Dictionary in 1828, Noah Webster described in the preface of the dictionary his reasons for including Christian themes in his books.

> *In my view, the Christian religion is the most important and one of the first things in which all children, under a free government ought to be instructed... No truth is more evident to my mind than that the Christian religion must be the basis of any government intended to secure the rights and privileges of a free people.*

As the Webster texts were gaining strength as the textbooks used most in American classrooms, schools in the late 1830s were given yet another option in textbooks. At this time both the *New England Primer* and the Webster grammar and *Blue Backed Speller* were in common use, or a combination of the two. It was in 1836 William H. McGuffey published the first volume of what would become the best-selling school textbooks in American history.

William H. McGuffey was an ordained Presbyterian minister, and at the time of the original publication of his readers from 1836-38 he was the President of Cincinnati College. Like Webster, McGuffey was a professional educator. And, as we will see in the next chapter, the colleges in America at that time were led primarily by clergy.

The McGuffey Readers, as they came to be called, consisted of an elementary primer, a pictorial primer, a speller (written by Alexander McGuffey, William's brother), and four graded reading books. Later there was a fifth reader added and then a sixth, both compiled by Alexander McGuffey. The McGuffey Readers set was used extensively into the mid-1900s, and it shaped American education like no other educational force in its time. Between 1836 and the mid-1900s an estimated 120 million copies were sold.

The McGuffey speller which competed directly with the Webster speller had numerous references to Christianity and the Bible. One selection that caught my attention, especially because of its relevance today, is the following reading exercise for older children:

> *"Pa!" said James Wake "how do we know that there is a God who takes care of us?*
>
> *"If you should find a watch," said his father "would you not suppose that someone had made it?"*
>
> *"Yes sir," said James.*
>
> *"Then," said his papa "if we see every day around us a great many things more perfect than a watch, must we not think that they too have been made?"*
>
> *"Certainly," said James.*
>
> *"Now," said his papa "in every blade of grass there is more to admire than in anything which man can make.*

> *Its maker then must be wiser than we are.*
>
> *The grass could not happen to be as it is, any more than the watch.*
>
> *And if we admire the skill of the watchmaker, who should much more admire the wisdom of God, who has done all things well.*
>
> *How happy are they who have this wise and great God, for their friend.*

In thumbing through the McGuffey speller, I counted sixteen exercises which were devoted to Christian or religious themes which invoked the name of God as creator and sustainer. The Christian theme is even more evident in the graded readers. Bear in mind, this is among the first set of reading books for schools which had multiple volumes, each volume becoming increasingly more difficult to read. Each of the graded readers is full of Bible stories and moral themes.

The selection quoted at the beginning of this chapter, urging Americans of the mid-1800s to embrace the Christian faith of their fathers, is from the fourth reader and is intended for youth in the 11-12 year range. The third reader similarly invokes numerous religious themes, and I have included excerpts of the Bible doctrine section in Appendix C for your further study. *Please take the time to review these excerpts.* You will be amazed at the overtly Christian message, and you might be amazed that a child of 9 or 10 could master this material.

I will cite a short example from Appendix C, McGuffey's Third Reader so that you will understand the spirit of McGuffey's graded reading books.

1. *The design of the Bible is evidently to give us correct information concerning the creation of all things by the omnipotent word of God, to make known to us the state of holiness and happiness of our first parents in paradise, and their dreadful fall from that condition by transgression against God, which is the original cause of all our sin and misery.*
2. *It is also designed to show us the duty we owe to Him, who is our almighty Creator, our bountiful Benefactor, and our righteous Judge; the method by which we can secure His eternal friendship, and are prepared for the possession of everlasting mansions in His glorious kingdom.*

William H. McGuffey died in 1873. By the time of his death the McGuffey Readers were still being published under his name, but he was neither involved, nor did he approve of the revisions that took place after the first few printings of his readers. Much of the religious content, particularly the strict Calvinist Presbyterian doctrine, was replaced with other materials, good moral materials, but not Bible or Bible doctrine.

In the latter 1800s the country was changing, being populated with tens of thousands of immigrants from all over Europe, many of them Roman Catholics. As we saw in Chapter 1, the issue of Protestant Christianity being taught in the schools was resisted by many of the schools in the larger cities which were a harbor for immigrants of all religious persuasions. By the late 1800s the public school textbooks had evolved to more general religious themes – non-sectarian Christian teachings that could be embraced by all types of Christians, not just Protestant Calvinists. The public schools remained defenders of general, nonsectarian Christianity well into the 1900s.

In my personal library are a number of old hymn books, one of which is a hymn book commissioned by and written for the public schools of Boston, Massachusetts in 1880. The complete title of the book: *The National Hymn and Tune Book; For Mixed Voices; A Collection of Unsectarian Hymns for Use in High and Normal Schools by L.W. Mason; Late Sup't of Music in the Public Schools of Boston, Mass.* This hymn book was a collection of nearly 400 Christian hymns which could be sung by all sects of Christianity. It includes many hymns which are sung today throughout Christendom: *O God, Our Help in Ages Past; O Worship the King; Jesus Shall Reign; Come Thou Almighty King; How Firm a Foundation;* many familiar Christmas carols, and on and on. These hymns were regularly sung in our public schools throughout the 1800s.

In the early 1900s the theory of evolution began to creep into America's public schools, replacing the story of creation by an omnipotent and omniscient God with the idea of something derived from nothing, totally by chance or accident. This led to philosophical battles throughout the country, first, in the more populated cities and eventually creeping into the rural areas as well. In the infamous Scopes Monkey Trial in 1925 in Dayton, a rural area of Tennessee, teacher John Scopes was fined $100 for teaching evolution.

Many schools, especially in the southern part of the country, continued to teach the truth of the Bible, until the Supreme Court declared, in the early 1960s, that Bible reading and prayer were unconstitutional. This notion would have certainly been foreign to the founders who actually wrote the U.S. Constitution, the Bill of Rights, and particularly those who ratified the Northwest Ordinance in 1789. As we have noted, the Northwest Ordinance recognized the importance of teaching the next generation Christian morals and Biblical truth – that these were to be essential if America was to experience "good government" and "happiness" in the years to come.

Chapter 4
America's Early Colleges

Ball Town Springs Wednesday August 21, 1799

My Dear Mrs. Willard,

Yesterday afternoon, after a week's excursion to lakes George and Champlain, I returned to this place mended in my health and gratified with my journey, in many respects. I had the additional pleasure of finding at the Post Office a letter from you, in the 5th instant, giving me an account of your health and that of the family. But alas! How soon were my pleasures most dreadfully marred by a packet delivered me by Mr. Foster, put into his hands by Mr. Kirkland, who was here in my absence? There I found the extremely painful news of the death of our son Augustus. How shocking is the stroke, to have him cut down in the bloom and vigor of life, with so short a warning, and when his prospects seemed to be smiling around him! ...

My dear partner of my joys and sorrows, let us not sink under this heavy loss, but consider that the affliction is brought upon us by an all-wise, unerring, and gracious Being, who doth not afflict willingly nor grieve the children of man; that he has the best designs in all that he lays upon us, and can determine what is for our good, infinitely better than we can ourselves. Let us repair for our consolation to the excellent religion of the blessed Jesus, which affords a healing balm for every woe, and under every kind of affliction, affords that well-grounded and *solid support, which <u>mere philosophy</u> [emphasis in original] can never give. The more we imbibe the spirit of this heavenly plan of grace, and follow the example of its divine Author, the more largely shall we receive, from our Father in Heaven, those comforts under our sorrows, which the world can neither give nor take away, and the more disposed shall we be to bless the hand which has chastised us. Let it be our constant prayer to the Father of mercies and God of all grace, that He would enable us so to improve this very sorrowful bereavement, that it may work for us the peaceable fruits of righteousness, so that we may have reason to say "that it is good for us that we have been thus afflicted". May this and every other sorrow which we may be called to endure further us in our way to the heavenly Zion, that blessed place, where sickness and death can never enter, and all tears shall be wiped away from the eyes...*

Thus begins a long and touching letter from a man to his wife – a man far away from home, with broken health, alone, convalescing at a well-known health spa, and sharing with his beloved wife a searing, common grief at the loss of a young son. The man who wrote this letter was Joseph Willard, President of Harvard University. The stresses of his job and the pace of his life had so impacted him that he had found himself jaundiced and with rapidly declining health. It had been recommended to him, by the Board of Overseers at Harvard, to spend the summer at the spa in northeastern New York with the hope that he might recover his strength.

Reverend Joseph Willard had been the President of Harvard since his appointment in 1781, toward the end of the War for Independence. He had guided Harvard through the last months of the war and restored the school after many disruptions and interruptions that the war had brought on, including the suspension of classes and the shrinking of the student body. Now Harvard was enjoying a time of growth, prosperity, and health, but the health of President Willard was at a breaking point. And then he received the "packet" from Mr. Kirkland informing him of the death of his son.

It is at a time like this when the true character of a man is seen, and it is clearly seen in Rev. Willard's letter to his wife. It demonstrates a clear-eyed, practiced, solid faith which "<u>mere philosophy</u> can never give." Rev.

Willard exemplified all that was good in Harvard University with its long tradition of Godly clergy-led education, preparing young men for civic duty and ministry. At that time, at the close of the century, Harvard was still a shining light, spreading the gospel of Jesus Christ throughout Boston and New England as it had since its founding more than 160 years earlier. This letter, written by its President, illustrates by extension the religious spirit of what Harvard was originally intended to stand for.

Rev. Willard represents somewhat of a final exclamation point at Harvard. He was the last of a long line of conservative clergy to run the school. It is during his tenure that the university, once the main source of ministers in New England, was beginning to look sympathetically at a new, more liberal trend within the Congregational churches. This trend would wrest control of Harvard from the more conservative clergy and entrust it to those who embraced the Unitarian doctrines of Henry Ware, Samuel Webber, and William Ellery Channing, truly a transition from faith to "mere philosophy."

Rev. Willard went on to experience for himself the "heavenly Zion" in 1804, after years as a pastor and even many more years leading America's foremost university. His death, and that of Harvard University's conservative Hollis Professor of Theology, David Tappin, one year earlier, led to a major shake-up in the religious philosophy of the school. Soon after the death of Rev. Willard, liberal theologian Henry Ware was appointed to assume the position of the Hollis Theology chair, and in 1806, liberal minister Samuel Webber was installed as President.

These changes led Rev. Henry Morse (father of inventor Samuel Morse), one of the overseers of Harvard, along with a few like-minded conservative pastors to form a new, conservative Congregational seminary, Andover Theological Seminary. With the more orthodox pastors from the Boston area pulling their support and their influence from Harvard, the school was free to veer quickly toward Unitarianism.

One hundred years after the inspiring spiritual leadership of Joseph Willard, another Harvard President, Charles William Eliot wrote this:

> *The true reformer is not he who first conceives a fruitful idea: but he who gets that idea planted in many minds and fertilizes it there through the power of his personality. Such a reformer was*

> *Jesus... His memory was surrounded by clouds of marvel and miracle during the four or five generations which passed before the Gospels took any settled form. The nineteenth century has done much to disengage Him in the Protestant mind from these encumbrances; and the twentieth will do more to set Him forth simply and grandly as the loveliest and best of human seers, teachers, and heroes. Let no man fear that reverence and love for Jesus will diminish as time goes on. The pathos and the heroism of His life and death will be vastly heightened when He is relieved of all supernatural attributes and powers...*

And thus, God the Son, Creator and Redeemer of mankind is reduced to folk hero at Harvard. The Unitarianism of the early 1800s had led ultimately to skepticism in the mid-1800s. By the turn of the next century it was full-blown infidelity which characterized Harvard University. Harvard had slid from the faith of Joseph Willard in 1800 to the folly of Charles William Eliot in 1900. But I am getting ahead of myself...

Originally Harvard was never intended to be a secular college, let alone a bastion of infidelity. It was formed in 1636 and began actual classes in 1638 for one purpose, and only one – to train ministers of the gospel. As mentioned in the previous chapter, the founders of the Massachusetts Bay Colony were men of means, and many were well educated. For the first few years after the arrival of the Winthrop fleet in 1630, several educated ministers arrived in the Colony as well. Notable among these were ministers Roger Williams, John Cotton, and John Harvard.

As young men in the Colony grew into manhood in the early years, the brightest were singled out for advanced education. However, there was no formal education available to them in Massachusetts, and several were shipped back to England for their formal education. Some of them returned eventually to Massachusetts, and some decided to remain in England.

In addition to this problem, there were more towns being formed than there were educated men to serve as ministers. Within the first years of the development of the Colony, the leaders of the Colony understood that they would need to provide for the education of clergy in their own country, otherwise the education and quality of ministers would cause the Colony to decline spiritually.

On September 8, 1636, the General Court passed a resolution to appropriate 200 pounds the following year to commence building a college, with the promise that an additional 200 pounds would be paid to the builder once the building was finished. In his *History of Harvard University*, published in 1840 in two volumes, Josiah Quincy, then President of Harvard University, describes the founding:

> *The year ensuing (1637), the General Court appointed twelve of the most eminent men of the Colony "to take order for a college at Newtown." All of them names dear to New England, on account of their sacrifices, their sufferings, and virtues. Among these, there were, of the clergy, Shepard and Cotton and Wilson; of the laity, Stoughton and Dudley; and above all, Winthrop, the Governor, the guide and the good genius of the Colony. Soon afterward the General Court changed the name of the town from Newtown to Cambridge; a grateful tribute to the transatlantic literary parent of many of the first emigrants, and indicative of the high destiny to which they intended the institution they were establishing should aspire.* [There were by far more graduates from Cambridge in England among the Massachusetts Colonists than from any other European University.]

The following year Rev. John Harvard the Puritan minister from Charlestown died. His will directed that one half of his estate would go to the new college in Newtown, and that all 260 volumes in his library would also go to the new college. His library was extremely valuable, containing a host of theological and scientific volumes, including numerous volumes from the church fathers, Calvin, Luther, Beza, and Bacon and a host of classical and linguistic volumes as well – just the wide range of knowledge that a college would need. The generosity of Harvard, and the immense value placed on his gift, led the General Court soon after to name the college after him.

In late 1641 three pastors from Massachusetts were commissioned by the General Court to travel to England to raise support for the Colony and particularly the new Harvard College. The three were Hugh Peter of Salem, Thomas Weld of Roxbury, and William Hibbens of Boston.

Once in England, the three commissioned a London printer and book seller to print promotional materials to facilitate their mission. The promotional pamphlet that resulted was titled, *New England First Fruits* and was divided into two parts. The first part was a description of the New England area, its Indian inhabitants, and relations with these natives. The second part was a promotion of Harvard College as a great place to learn, or for those of means, to invest for the glory of God. While many of the oldest records for Harvard College were lost in a fire, this pamphlet printed in England preserves a general description of the purpose of the college.

The second section of the pamphlet first described the reasons for establishing the college (the spellings, punctuation and emphasis are all in the original.)

> After God had carried us safe to *New England,* and wee had builded our houses, provided necessaries for our livelyhood, rear'd convenient places for God's worship, and settled the Civill Government: One of the next things we longed for, and looked after was to advance *Learning* and perpetuate it to Posterity; dreading to leave an illiterate Ministry to the Churches, when our present Ministers shall lie in the Dust. And as wee were thinking and consulting how to effect this great Work; it pleased God to stir up the heart of one Mr. *Harvard* (a godly Gentleman, and a lover of Learning, there living amongst us) to give the one halfe of his Estate (it being in all about 1700. l.) towards the erecting of a Colledge: and all his Library: after him another gave 300 l. others after them cast in more, and the publique hand of the State added the rest: the Colledge was, by common consent, appointed to be at *Cambridge,* (a place very pleasant and accommodate) and is called (according to the name of the first founder) *Harvard College.*
>
> The Edifice is very faire and comely within and without, having in it a spacious Hall; (where they daily meet at Commons, Lectures) Exercises, and a large Library

with some Bookes to it, the gifts of diverse of our friends, their Chambers and studies also fitted for, and possessed by the Students, and all other roomes of Office necessary and convenient, with all needful Offices thereto belonging: And by the side of the Colledge a faire *Grammar* Schoole, for the training up of young Schollars, and fitting of them for *Academicall Learning*, that still as they are judged ripe, they may be received into the Colledge of this Schoole: Master *Corlet* is the Mr., who hath very well approved himselfe for his abilities, dexterity and painfulnesse in teaching and education of the youth under him.

Over the Colledge is master *Dunster* placed, as President, a learned conscionable and industrious man, who hath so trained up, his Pupills in the tongues and Arts, and so seasoned them with the principles of Divinity and Christianity, that we have to our great comfort, (and in truth) beyond our hopes, and beheld their progresse in their publique declamations in *Latine* and *Greeke,* and Disputations Logicall and Philosophicall, which they have beene wonted (besides their ordinary Exercises in the Colledge-Hall) in the audience of the Magistrates, Ministers, and other Schollars, for the probation of their growth in Learning upon set dayes, constantly once every moneth to make and uphold ...

Over the Colledge are twelve Overseers chosen by the generall Court, six of them are of the Magistrates, the other six of the Ministers, who are to promote the best good of it and (having power of influence into all persons in it) are to see that every one be diligent and proficient in his proper place.

After this prefatory section describing the reasons for the college and a brief description of the facilities and faculty, an exact list of the rules for students at Harvard is included for the advantage of would-be students or financial donors.

1. *When any Schollar is able to understand Tully, or such like classicall Latine Author extempore, and make and speake true Latine in Verse and Prose, suo ut aiunt Marte; And decline perfectly the Paradigm's of Nounes and Verbes in the Greek tongue: Let him then and not before be capable of admission into the Colledge. [Interestingly, today we might expect a scholar to graduate from a masters or PhD program with the ability to understand, read and write Greek and Latin. Early students at Harvard had to have mastered that ability to be admitted in the first place.]*

2. *Let every Student be plainly instructed, and earnestly pressed to consider well, the maine end of his life and studies is, to know God and Jesus Christ which is eternall life, Joh. 17. 3 and therefore to lay Christ at the bottome, as the only foundation of all sound knowledge and Learning. And seeing the Lord only giveth wisedome, Let every one seriously set himselfe by prayer in secret to seeke it of him, Prov 2, 3.*

3. *Every one shall so exercise himselfe in reading the Scriptures twice a day, that he shall be ready to give such an account of his proficiency therein, both in Theroretticall observations of the Language, and Logick, and in Practicall and spirituall truths, as his Tutor shall require, according to his ability; seeing the entrance of the word giveth light, it giveth understanding to the simple, Psalm. 119. 130.*

4. *That they eschewing all profanation of Gods Name, Attributes, Word, Ordinances, and times of Worship, doe studie with good conscience, carefully to retaine God, and the love of his truth in their mindes, else let them know, that (notwithstanding their Learning) God may give them up to strong delusions, and in the end to a reprobate minde, 2 Thes. 2. 11, 12. Rom 1. 28.*

5. *That they studiously redeeme the time; observe the generall houres appointed for all the Students, and the speciall houres for their owne Classis: and then diligently attend the Lectures, without any disturbance by word or gesture. And if in any thing they doubt they shall enquire, as of their fellows, so, (in case of Non Satisfaction) modestly of their Tutors.*

6. *None shall under any pretence whatsoever, frequent the company and society of such men as lead an unfit, and dissolute life. Nor shall any without his Tutors leave, or (in his absence) the call of Parents or Guardians, goe abroad to other Townes.*

7. *Every Schollar shall be present in his Tutors Chamber at the 7th. Houre in the morning, immediately after the sound of the Bell at his opening the Scripture and prayer, so also at the 5th. houre at night, and then give account of his owne private reading, as aforesaid in Particular the third, and constantly attend Lectures in the Hall at the houres appointed? But if any (without necessary impediment) shall absent himself from prayer or Lectures, he shall bee liable to Admonition, if he offend above once a weeke.*

8. *If any Schollar shall be found to transgresse any of the Lawes of God, or the Schoole, after twice Admonition, she shall be liable, if not adultus, to correction, if adultus, his name shall be given up to the Overseers of the Colledge, that he may bee admonished at the publick monethly Act.*

Early Harvard College graduates were mostly preachers, and from the above rules it is easy to understand why. The education, while in great part classical, was primarily theological, with much Bible study demanded. As the years went by, various new departments were added such as botany, mathematics, medicine, and law, but the Christian emphasis remained unchanged through the first nearly 200 years of Harvard's existence. In fact, from the founding of Harvard through the 1820s only one of the first fourteen Harvard presidents, John Leverett (1708-1724), was *not* a Christian minister. Yet as a notable attorney, Leverett was also known for his Christian piety.

A letter written by Leverett while Harvard President illustrates his heart for the advancement of the Christian churches. It was written to the Rev. Benjamin Coleman in London, in an effort to urge him to accept the position of pastor of a Boston church which Leverett was instrumental in founding. "... I am heartily pleased with the motion they have made towards yourself, because I shall exceedingly rejoice at your return into your country. We want persons of your character. You will, I doubt not, let the name of your country have a weight in the balance of your consideration. The affair offered to you is great, and of great moment. I pray almighty God to be your director in it. It is he that thrusts laborers into his harvest, and bounds the habitations of the sons of Adam..."

Early in Harvard's history, the popular college seal was designed which shows a shield containing three books, each book containing a part of the Latin word *veritas*, or *truth*. That part of Harvard's great seal exists to this day, with two notable exceptions. On the original seal of the University, below the shield with the *veritas* inscription, you would see these words inscribed in decorative scroll, *Christo et Ecclesiae*, or, *Christ and Church*. Putting that entire inscription together then, we have Harvard's original motto, *Truth for Christ and the Church*. In the mid-1800s, the phrase *Christo et Ecclesiae* was eliminated from the seal, leaving Harvard's motto simply *Veritas*, or "truth."

Another change in the seal is informative as well. The original seal has two books opened facing up, and below those is a single book opened but facing down, or laying flat on the surface of the seal face-down. This was said to symbolize the fact that book-learning has its limits, and that there are times where you simply must proceed by faith apart from intellectual pursuits. It was designed to picture the important mingling of faith and academics. Today's Harvard seal has all three books opened and facing up signifying that there is no limit to academic pursuit – it is all sufficient.

I have included quite a bit of information about the early Harvard College to serve as an example of all of the early American colleges. Each of the schools founded before the American War for Independence has its own similar story; each one was founded primarily to train Christian ministers. Harvard was founded by members of the Congregational denomination as was Yale in 1701 and Dartmouth in 1769, for the main purpose of training ministers of the gospel.

In the same way, the College of William & Mary, founded in 1693 in Williamsburg, Virginia, was founded to train Anglican ministers. It original charter stated, "... that the Church of Virginia may be furnished with a seminary of ministers of the gospel, and that the youth may be piously educated in good letters and manners, and that the Christian faith may be propagated amongst the Western Indians, to the glory of Almighty God..."

In 1701 Yale University was formed with the motto *Lux et Veritas*, or, *Light and Truth*. Yale's stated purpose was summarized in its original charter as "... upholding and propagating of the Christian Protestant Religion by a succession of learned and orthodox ministers..."

The College of New Jersey, later Princeton, was founded by four Presbyterian pastors. It was established in 1746 under the motto *Under God's Power She Flourishes*. One of the Princeton founders wrote, "Though our great Intention was to erect a seminary for educating Ministers of the

Gospel, yet we hope it will be useful in other learned professions - ornaments of the State as well as the Church."

In 1754 Kings College (now Columbia University) was founded in New York City by the Anglican Church with the motto from the Bible, *In Thy light shall we see light*, taken from Psalm 36:9. The purpose statement read, "The chief thing that is aimed at in this college is to teach and engage the children to know God in Jesus Christ, and righteousness of life ..."

In 1764 the College of Rhode Island was formed (now Brown University) under the motto *In God we hope*. The college was founded explicitly for the training of Baptist ministers. Early notes concerning the college in the college archives contain this description, "... at every commencement [Rev. James Manning, first president] gave a solemn charge to his scholars, never to presume to enter into the work of the ministry until they were taught of God, and had reason to conclude that they had experienced a saving change of heart."

1766 witnessed the formation of Queens College (now Rutgers University) for the purpose of training ministers of the Dutch Reformed faith; its motto, *Sun of righteousness, shine upon the West also*. Its purpose statement read, "For the education of the youth of said Province and the neighboring colonies in true religion and useful learning, and particularly for providing an able and learned Protestant Ministry ..."

As we mentioned, Dartmouth College was formed in 1769 by New England Congregationalists. Interestingly, Dartmouth's unique emphasis was to train Indians and others with a special focus on a missionary effort to reach the Indians in northern New England with the gospel of Jesus Christ. The Dartmouth motto was taken from the Bible description of John the Baptist, *The voice of one crying in the wilderness.*

All of the colonial colleges were founded specifically to train ministers – that is all but one, the Academy of Pennsylvania (now University of Pennsylvania). Founded in 1740, the Academy of Pennsylvania was created to fill a void in American education. All of the other schools were primarily training ministers, and the Anglican Church recognized a need to train men in secular professions as well. It was important to them that the training be Christian and Biblical, just as though they were studying for ministry. As a result, they founded this college, "... that the said academy through the blessings of Almighty God would prove a nursing of wisdom and virtue and be the means of raising up men of dispositions and qualifications beneficial to the public in various occupations of life..." While the University of Pennsylvania was founded primarily to train laymen in the various professions, even this college trained numerous ministers of the gospel.

I have used Harvard University as the prime example for another reason also, other than just as an example of the detail that went into the formation of these American colleges. I use it because Harvard, of all the colonial colleges of America, fell into unbelief far earlier than the others. As uniquely Christian as Harvard was at its beginning, it had become a bastion of skepticism and atheism by the early 1900s, in contrast to Princeton University, which was, of all of the aforementioned institutions, the most orthodox at that time – still strongly upholding the Bible and Christianity into the 1900s.

As all of these schools, including Princeton, dropped one by one into secular unbelief, and as America's universities and Bible Colleges continue to do so, they were replaced by new Christian institutions and seminaries, some of which continue the American tradition of Christian education up to the present day. Conservative Christian schools like Pensacola Christian College, or Bob Jones University, or Liberty University, or Crown College, or The Masters College, or others too numerous to mention, today teach the exact same gospel that was taught up through most of the 1800s at all of the Ivy League schools in early America.

This brings us to The University of Virginia, founded in 1819. The U of V took a different approach from the other colleges, all of which were run by a particular Christian denomination, but it was a Bible college none-the-less. It simply was not established as a denominational institution as were the others. It was Christian, but it was trans-denominational, and this approach was purposeful in order to avoid denominational disputes. It was attended by students from a wide variety of Christian sects, and there they received Bible training and Christian worship, similar to what existed in all the other colleges of the time.

I realize how popular it is for dishonest secular historians to claim that in the University of Virginia, Thomas Jefferson established the first purely secular college in America, consistent with his own non-religious character. Secular historians love to claim that the U of V was founded by Jefferson intentionally as a strictly secular college because he distrusted, perhaps even despised the religious training that characterized the other colleges. They love to claim that the professors were intentionally chosen because they were secularists, deists, or Unitarians and that there were no chaplains at the college.

Each one of these erroneous charges (I would have to also use the term *dishonest* charges because most secular historians know better) have been carefully researched and debunked using original sources from Jefferson's own writings and from college records. I will not take up a lot of space here to challenge these false claims other than to refer you to David Barton's excellent work, *The Jefferson Lies*, published in 2012 by Thomas Nelson Publishers, Nashville, Tennessee.

To my leftist secular critics: yes, I fully understand you have made David Barton's research on Jefferson controversial with your dishonest attacks on this scholarly work. I challenge you, if you think Barton got it wrong, ignore the text of Barton's book and just look at the hundreds of footnotes to original source documents and follow them – do some honest research of your own, if you are capable of that. You will recognize the truth in the original sources, if you are at all inclined to embracing truth.

Barton explains the trans-denominational character of the University of Virginia as follows:

> This nondenominational approach caused Presbyterians, Baptists, Methodists, and others to give the university the friendship and cooperative support necessary to make it a success. Consider Presbyterian minister John Holt Rice as an example.
>
> Rice was a nationally known evangelical leader with extensive credentials. He founded the <u>Virginia Bible Society</u>, started the <u>Virginia Evangelical and Literary Magazine</u> to report on revivals across the country, was elected national leader of the Presbyterian Church, and offered the presidency of Princeton (but instead accepted the chair of theology at Hampden-Sydney College). Rice fully supported and promoted the University of Virginia, but this would not have been the case had the university been perceived to have been affiliated with just one denomination.

> As Rice explained: "The plan humbly suggested is to allow Jews, Catholics, Protestants, Episcopalians, Methodists, Baptists, any and all sects, if they shall choose to exercise the privilege, to endow professorships, and nominate their respective professors.... [T]he students shall regularly attend Divine worship, but in what form should be left to the direction of parents; or in failure of this, to the choice of the students. In addition to this, the professors in every case must be men of the utmost purity of moral principle and strictness of moral conduct."

Barton goes on to successfully debunk the notion that all the faculty were deists and Unitarians – in fact *none* were initially. He also shows that once the University was well established, it had paid chaplains who performed religious services for the students, usually in the University Rotunda. The chaplain position was intentionally rotated among the four main denominations serving Virginia at that time: Baptist, Presbyterian, Anglican, and Methodist.

The Bible exposition was taught by professors of the various Biblical languages. Christian evidences were taught, not by professors of divinity but, in order to avoid inter-denominational disputes, by professors of ethics. As Barton points out, quoting from Jefferson's own written instructions on the issue,

> Jefferson personally directed that the teaching of "the proofs of the being of a God, the Creator, Preserver, and Supreme Ruler of the Universe, the Author of all the relations of morality and of the laws and obligations these infer, will be within the province of the Professor of Ethics."

The numerous stories of the Christian but non-sectarian nature of State established colleges through the 1800s are similar from State to State. The University of Michigan, for example, was established as a "non-sectarian" college. But non-sectarian was by no means non-religious or non-Christian. The U of M's first two presidents were prominent Protestant ministers. The third president was non-clergy, but in his inaugural address in 1871 expressed, "the Christian spirit, which pervades the law, the customs, and the life of the State shall shape and color the life of the University, that a lofty, earnest, but catholic and unsectarian Christian tone shall characterize the culture which is here imparted."

Similarly, every college in America through at least the mid-1800s and more likely into the twentieth century, was a Christian college, comparable to modern day Christian colleges. In the introduction of his 1994 book, *The Soul of the American University; From Protestant Establishment to Established Nonbelief*, George M. Marsden writes:

> *In the late nineteenth century, when American universities took their shape, the Protestantism of the major northern denominations acted as a virtual religious and cultural establishment. This establishmentarian outlook was manifested in American universities, which were constructed not, as is sometimes supposed, as strictly secular institutions but as integral parts of a religious-cultural vision. The formal strength of such nonsectarian Protestantism was evidenced by the continuing place of religious activities on most campuses. In the 1890s, for instance, almost all state universities still held compulsory chapel services and some required Sunday church attendance as well. State-sponsored chapel services did not become rare until the World War II era. In the meantime, many of the best private universities maintained Christian divinity schools and during the first half of the twentieth century built impressive chapels signaling their respect for their Christian heritages. As late as the 1950s it was not unusual for spokespersons of leading schools to refer to them as "Christian" institutions.*

Understanding the formation of America's early colleges helps us to better understand the story behind *Vidal v. Girard's Executors* in the first chapter – why Justice Story would write in his opinion in 1844, "It is unnecessary for us, however, to consider what would be the legal effect of a devise in Pennsylvania for the establishment of a school or college, for the propagation of Judaism, or Deism, or any other form of infidelity. Such a case is not to be presumed to exist in a Christian country..."

Part II
The Way We Thought

Where did our founders get their philosophy? What constituted the foundation of their unique thinking? What were the foundational concepts that they embraced, and who were the philosophers and writers behind American Independence and ultimately behind America's unique form of government?

Chapter 5
Our Charter of Freedom

When in the Course of human events, it becomes necessary for one people to dissolve the political bands which have connected them with another, and to assume among the powers of the earth, the separate and equal station to which the Laws of Nature and of Nature's God entitle them, a decent respect to the opinions of mankind requires that they should declare the causes which impel them to the separation.

We hold these truths to be self-evident, that all men are created equal, that they are endowed by their Creator with certain unalienable Rights, that among these are Life, Liberty and the pursuit of Happiness.—That to secure these rights, Governments are instituted among Men, deriving their just powers from the consent of the governed, -- That whenever any Form of Government becomes destructive of these ends, it is the Right of the People to alter or to abolish it, and to institute new Government, laying its foundation on such principles and organizing its powers in such form, as to them shall seem most likely to effect their Safety and Happiness. Prudence, indeed, will dictate that Governments long established should not be changed for light and transient causes; and accordingly all experience hath shewn, that mankind are more disposed to suffer, while evils are sufferable, than to right themselves by abolishing the forms to which they are accustomed. But when a long train of abuses and usurpations, pursuing invariably the same Object evinces a design to reduce them under absolute Despotism, it is their right, it is their duty, to throw off such Government, and to provide new Guards for their future security.— Such has been the patient sufferance of these Colonies; and such is now the necessity which constrains them to alter their former Systems of Government. The history of the present King of Great Britain is a history of repeated injuries and usurpations, all having in direct object the establishment of an absolute Tyranny over these States. To prove this, let Facts be submitted to a candid world.

So begins *The unanimous Declaration of the thirteen united States of America,* dated July 4, 1776. No other founding document gives us an insight into the thinking of our founders like this document. In getting into this section of the book – how our founders thought – I believe this is the place to start. We will learn in subsequent chapters where these ideas came from. Suffice it to say at the outset, the ideas of American independence came ultimately from the Bible. All of the men who were influential in the thinking of our founders were Bible believing students of theology - men like Sir Francis Bacon, Rev. Samuel Rutherford, Sir Isaac Newton, John Locke, Charles Montesquieu, Sir William Blackstone, etc.

While our founders had many differences in their approach to various issues, they all thought alike in the one area that mattered most; they all held an identical world view. And what was that world view? It was the Judeo-Christian view that God exists, that the Bible is true, that we, and everything around us, are here by a special act of creation whereby God assigned to His creation the laws that would govern the physical and moral universe. As we have already seen, this world view played a key role in our court decisions and in our educational system.

The unanimous Declaration of Independence, which was supported by all thirteen of the former colonies, now States, spelled out the ideas, the foundational philosophy that these States all shared in common and embraced in 1776. These new States proclaimed in the Declaration that they believed in the God of Creation, that He had created them free and equal, and that they were ultimately bound by His law above all else. Make no mistake, the Declaration of Independence contains a lot of theology.

The language of the Declaration illustrates that common world view as nothing else could. First, it must be pointed out that the "self-evident" fact that, "all men are created equal, that they are endowed by their Creator with certain unalienable Rights," is an indication that these men did not hold this view as a mere religious principle. No, they believed it to be an obvious, observable fact. In Jefferson's first draft he used the language, "we hold these truths to be sacred." That was later amended from the word "sacred," a religious concept, to "self-evident," a non-debatable, obvious fact of natural law. Even those founders who are claimed today to have been less "religious," Jefferson and Franklin, still believed in the existence of God the Creator as self-evident truth.

Indeed, they all proclaimed that the very authority that they acted on in declaring independence from Great Britain was, "the laws of nature and of nature's God." In so declaring, they were also declaring that they were not a secular, but rather a God-honoring people, and that they were willing to implement the law of God as the highest possible authority of a government. They believed that, "the laws of nature and of nature's God," were higher than the authority of the King of England or the British Parliament, and they were willing to stake their very lives, fortunes, and sacred honor on that distinction. In the next chapter we will discuss the whole idea of natural law and of its role in this and other founding documents.

Our founders, all very well versed in the concept of natural law, appealed to natural law not only as the authority for their actions but also as the source of their fundamental rights. Referring to this idea of natural law, the Declaration of Independence goes on to say, "We hold these truths to be self-evident, that all men are created equal, that they are endowed by their Creator with certain unalienable Rights, that among these are Life, Liberty and the pursuit of Happiness.--That to secure these rights, Governments are instituted among Men, deriving their just powers from the consent of the governed..."

What does it mean when they write that, "all men ... are endowed by their Creator with certain unalienable Rights . . ."? It means that under natural law our rights and our laws are part of the Created Order. It means that God is the giver of life and liberty, because life and liberty are part of

God's holy character. It means that because God gives us life and liberty, it is absolute, far above the reach of government. It means that government must give priority to God. It means that God's laws are higher than the laws established by any human government. (This, by the way, is why there is a concerted effort on the part of secular academia to view the U.S. Constitution as our founding document rather than The Declaration of Independence.)

In 1776 this was not just some quirky theological theory or an offhanded rationalization for rebellion. This was the legal, operating understanding of all of the signers of the Declaration, and later, for all of the signers of the U.S. Constitution for that matter. This is how our founders understood and viewed the world, and it was the main distinguishing difference between the American Revolution and the French Revolution. The American Founders embraced a Judeo-Christian world view. The French revolutionaries embraced various forms of a materialistic world view. And the differences in outcome were predictable and understandable.

This might be a good time to get a better understanding to the God-given right enumerated by our founders, "the pursuit of happiness." That word "happiness" was used frequently in many writings of that era. Washington used the words "happy" and "happiness" five times in his farewell address. In the first chapter we discussed the Northwest Ordinance which states, "Religion, morality and knowledge being necessary to good government and the happiness of mankind, schools and the means of education shall forever be encouraged." Education was necessary to achieve the "happiness" of mankind. What did that mean? And what is this "pursuit of happiness" all about?

It is interesting to observe how words change over time. The meaning of some words tends to evolve through the centuries. When I was young and I heard the phrase "pursuit of happiness" I always thought of the word "happiness" as we use it today. The founders seemed to be saying that we have a natural right to pursue whatever makes us happy at the moment, almost a right to pursue any temporary pleasure; to play golf, to go fishing, to go to the movies etc. Of course linking that sort of trivial concept to the deep importance of life and liberty is a monumental mismatch.

Words, and their meanings, change over time. Today's usage of the word *happiness* is shallow compared to the deep meaning people attached to it two hundred years ago. The word *felicity* was also much used during that era, and *felicity* was generally synonymous with *happiness*. Both *felicity* and *happiness* can be found many times in our founding documents and in letters and speeches of our founding fathers.

Both the words *happiness* and *felicity* were used liberally in the seventeenth and eighteenth centuries to describe a particular state of being. The reason for the confusion is that today the word happiness is almost never used to describe a state of being, but rather, is almost always used to describe a state of mind.

Let me repeat that because it is critical to understanding the difference in today's usage compared to the common usage in the late 1700s, and therefore, to understanding the Declaration of Independence and the Northwest Ordinance, among other contemporary documents. Happiness today usually refers to ***a state of mind.*** Happiness in the late 1700s almost always referred to ***a state of being*** – huge difference.

Probably the word in general use today that would come the closest to expressing the old usage of the word happiness is the word *success*. Today we could say that a certain person is successful but not happy. We would all understand what that means. We have seen a lot of people who had a great state of being but not a great state of mind i.e. wealthy but miserable. Back in the 1700s you would not say that a person was successful but not happy because both the word happiness and the word success carried much the same meaning, both a description of a state of being.

In 1755 an Englishman by the name of Samuel Johnson published *A General Dictionary of the English Language*. In this early work Johnson defined *success* as "The termination of any affair happy or unhappy. Success without any epithet is commonly taken for good success." Interestingly, the word epithet back then simply meant adjective. In other words Johnson defined success as achieving *the state of happiness*, unless of course there was an epithet (adjective) which described the success otherwise, such as bad success or poor success.

In that same 1755 dictionary Johnson defined *happiness* as follows:

Happiness
1. Felicity; state in which the desires are satisfied.
Happiness is that estate whereby we attain, so far as possibly may be attained, the full possession of that which simply for

itself is to be desired, and containeth in it after an eminent sort the contentation of our desires, the highest degree of all our perfection. Hooker [Richard]
Oh! Happiness of sweet retir'd content,
To be at once secure and innocent.
Denham [Sir John]
The various and contrary choices that men make in the world, argue that the same thing is not good to every man alike: this variety of pursuits shews, that every one does not place his happiness in the same thing.
Locke [John]
2. Good luck; good fortune.
3. Fortuitous elegance; unstudied grace.

Each of these definitions from 1755 describe a state of being, very different from the American Heritage College Dictionary in 2002 which doesn't even define happiness separately but has it as a noun form of *happy*. Happy is defined as "1. Characterized by good luck; fortunate. 2. Enjoying, showing, or marked by pleasure, satisfaction, or joy. See syns at *glad*." The second definition is the one today most associated with the word happiness, which is generally a state of mind – how one *feels* regardless of circumstances. It is synonymous with such other states of mind as satisfaction or contentment. That is why we can say today that a man is successful but not happy, and why you would not say that back in 1776.

So exactly what were the founders trying to say when they said that we are endowed by God Himself with certain inalienable natural rights, one of which is "the pursuit of happiness?" What the founders were saying was that each person has the right to pursue success or fulfillment as he sees fit. As John Locke is quoted in Johnson's Dictionary, ". . . the same thing is not good to every man alike: this variety of pursuits shews, that every one does not place his happiness in the same thing."

In the agrarian culture of eighteenth century America, most persons equated the pursuit of happiness with the right to go out and purchase property, buy or build a homestead, harvest crops, increase livestock, and ultimately to personally enjoy the fruit of their labors. Or perhaps happiness to another man was becoming a tradesman or a merchant or the owner of a large plantation. To another it might mean the personal fulfillment of being a minister and attending to the special needs of parishioners. It incorporated the right to acquire education, the necessary property (both real and personal) or professional tools, to realize your view of success, to acquire wealth – sometimes great wealth, and the right to hold and enjoy those fruits.

From the concept that all men are created equal, the natural right to pursue happiness carried with it the equal right of each person to better oneself, spiritually and materially. In the original state of nature people were not born with social status. There were no hereditary lords, no serfs such as permeated European history. In America each person was to realize the God-given right to seize opportunity and chart his own course. Indeed, liberty and the pursuit of happiness are two sides of the same coin. Liberty does not exist where an individual's pursuit of happiness is prevented or curtailed.

There is another aspect of this concept that we must not miss. The founders believed that we have a God-given right to *pursue* happiness, but not a God-given right to *have* happiness, as many utopian schemes would presume to provide. A right to *have* happiness would imply that our neighbors must give us the material means to be happy (successful), which is the object of socialistic societies. No, this is the right to an opportunity – to the pursuit of success or fulfillment.

This is why the Declaration does not list property along with life and liberty, as has often been done (life, liberty, property as in the Fifth and Fourteenth Amendments to the U.S. Constitution). Simply put, life and liberty are both at the same time rights as well as possessions. Property itself is not a right, but only a possession. Thus it is not listed among God-given rights.

We have a right to life, but we have no right to property. We have a right to liberty which makes us free to attempt to acquire property, but we have no fundamental right to property itself. The pursuit of happiness (personal success) is a right which incorporates the acquisition and ownership of property as an opportunity. Once that opportunity has been exercised, we have the right to acquire, and hold as a possession, property that we have obtained lawfully. Such acquired property is a possession, just as life and liberty are possessions, which cannot be encroached by government without due process of law. Property cannot be taken by government without government paying a fair price for it, or "just compensation."

It was that opportunity to work to acquire property – that opportunity society that America was famous for through the 1800s, which brought thousands of immigrants from various countries to our shores. Unlike many immigrants today, they didn't flock here for free stuff or entitlements. There was no welfare state back then. They came because America provided every person with opportunity. They had heard that in America a person had the right to pursue happiness, and yes, even to acquire great wealth. Our founders believed that pursuit to be a God-given right.

The second of the great ideas that were proclaimed in the Declaration of Independence was the idea of the *social compact*. The social compact is simply the idea that a group of people have a fundamental, God-given, natural right to voluntarily join together to form governments for their mutual support and protection. In doing so, the individual agrees to submit in some respects to that government, voluntarily forfeiting some of his personal prerogatives, in exchange for a greater level of security and welfare.

So, the founders stated the sole purpose of a people forming a social compact in the first place, the securing of God-given rights: "That to secure these rights, Governments are instituted among Men, deriving their just powers from the consent of the governed..." In other words, under God's laws, governments are created specifically to protect God-given rights, and governments are accountable to the people, not the other way around.

The Declaration also stated that those same people have a natural and fundamental right to disband the government they have formed should the government become oppressive and cease to function in the way it was originally intended. "But when a long train of abuses and usurpations, pursuing invariably the same Object evinces a design to reduce them under absolute Despotism, it is their right, it is their duty, to throw off such Government, and to provide new Guards for their future security."

Lincoln understood the value of the Declaration of Independence as our founding legal document, and he constantly campaigned to have it respected and recognized as fundamental law. In a campaign speech in 1858 Lincoln pleaded with the nation to "come back" to the principles of the Declaration of Independence. Lincoln went on,

> *Now, my countrymen, if you have been taught doctrines conflicting with the great landmarks of the Declaration of Independence; if you have listened to suggestions which would take away from its grandeur and mutilate the fair symmetry of its proportions; if you have been inclined to believe that all men are not created equal in those inalienable rights enumerated by our chart of liberty, let me entreat you to come back. Return to the fountain whose waters spring close by the blood of the Revolution. Think nothing of me — take no thought for the political fate of any man whomsoever — but come back to the truths that are in the Declaration of Independence.*

In 1861 Lincoln wrote in a letter, "... Freedom is the natural condition of the human race, in which the Almighty intended men to live. Those who fight the purpose of the Almighty will not succeed..."

Part of the Lincoln legacy was that beginning with the resolution which made Nevada our 36th state, in 1864, all States since that time including Alaska and Hawaii, in their original enacting resolutions, have been required to form a State government which is "not repugnant to the U.S. Constitution or to the principles of the Declaration of Independence" thus giving the principles of the Declaration of Independence the force of law in these States.

To summarize then, if you look closely at the text of the Declaration of Independence, you will see several clear principles that these founders embraced in common:

1. There is a Creator God who created mankind and to whom all mankind are accountable. *[... the Laws of... Nature's God... endowed by their Creator...]*
2. There is a higher, universal law, given by God, that transcends the laws and edicts of kings or parliaments. *[... the Laws of Nature and of Nature's God...]*
3. Because of these higher laws, the laws of nature and of nature's God, we have the natural right, or entitlement, to enter into social compacts with others for our mutual protection. *[... to assume among the powers of the earth, the separate and equal station to which the Laws of Nature and of Nature's God entitle them...]*

4. All men are created equal by birth into the human race. *[We hold these truths to be self-evident, that all men are created equal...]*
5. All men are given by God their Creator certain rights, the three most fundamental of which are listed in the Declaration. *[...they are endowed by their Creator with certain unalienable Rights, that among these are Life, Liberty and the pursuit of Happiness.]*
6. Since these rights come from God, they predate and transcend human government and are, therefore, out of the reach of human government.
7. The fundamental purpose of human government is to protect God-given rights. *[That to secure these rights, Governments are instituted among Men...]*
8. No human government is valid if not consented to by the people under it. *[That to secure these rights, Governments are instituted among Men, deriving their just powers from the consent of the governed...]*
9. People in a society have the right to change any government that has become abusive. *[That whenever any Form of Government becomes destructive of these ends, it is the Right of the People to alter or to abolish it...]*
10. People have a right and a *duty* to throw off a government that has become tyrannical. *[But when a long train of abuses and usurpations, pursuing invariably the same Object evinces a design to reduce them under absolute Despotism, it is their right, it is their duty, to throw off such Government, and to provide new Guards for their future security.]*

So now, what is the popular, modern opinion of the Declaration of Independence? The answer to that question is, unfortunately, that the Declaration is viewed today by most academics as a quaint, philosophical statement which was politically useful in energizing the masses to support the War of Independence. The *real* founding document, they opine, is the Constitution, and the Constitution, which includes the Bill of Rights, established a completely secular government, instituting a complete separation from religion.

The National Archives in Washington DC is very influential in determining, or perhaps reflecting, how our founding documents are perceived today. It is within this shrine that these founding documents are displayed to the modern world. And this is how the official website of the National Archives describes these "Charters of Freedom."

> *The Rotunda for the Charters of Freedom is the permanent home of the Declaration of Independence, Constitution of the United States, and Bill of Rights. These three documents, known collectively as the Charters of Freedom, have secured the rights of the American people for more than two and a quarter centuries.*
>
> - *The Declaration announced to the world on July 4, 1776, that thirteen British colonies in North America were leaving Great Britain to form a separate nation, called the United States of America. In justifying the revolution, the Declaration asserted a universal truth about human rights.*
> - *The Constitution, drafted in 1787 after a hard-won victory in the War for Independence, codified the spirit of the Revolution into an ingenious practical scheme of government to promote the welfare of all its citizens.*
> - *The Bill of Rights, added to the Constitution in 1791 as the first ten amendments, explicitly protected freedom of speech, of the press, of religion, and of assembly, among many other rights.*

These descriptions of the Declaration of Independence and of the Bill of Rights are popular ideas but historically inaccurate. The Declaration of Independence was *not* issued to form a new nation at all. It was the mutual, simultaneous declaration of thirteen separate colonies that they were now thirteen, separate, independent States. The word "united" throughout the Declaration of Independence is never capitalized, whereas the word States is capitalized. The words "united States" thus was not an official title but rather a signal to the King of England of the thirteen independent States' willingness to all stand together against the British Empire.

As we will see in Chapter 9, the first ten amendments (the Bill of Rights) were not ratified by the States in order to establish these rights under a federal government. These enumerated rights were already guaranteed and enforced by the individual States to whatever degree they determined best for them. These ten amendments were ratified to prevent mission creep on the part of the federal government. These were not declarations of a list of rights, but rather, a firewall to prevent the federal government from trespassing or interfering in all these areas which were powers already in place and jealously protected by the individual States.

As we shall see in Chapter 9, a better title for the Bill of Rights would be the "Bill of Restrictive Clauses" ("restrictive clauses" is the wording used to describe these amendments in the preamble to the Bill of Rights) or perhaps "Bill of Prohibitions" which prevented the federal government from interfering in these enumerated areas, plus any other areas that they had not thought to enumerate (Ninth Amendment). The Tenth Amendment makes it clear that the powers of the federal government are to extend only to areas specifically enumerated in the Constitution, and no further. Thus, these areas of concern: religion, press, speech, assembly, bearing arms, taking of property, etc. were areas where States could manage very well without the input of the federal government, thank you very much.

Not long ago I visited the National Archives in Washington D.C. I have been there probably at least 6-8 times over the years and have been mindful of the changes that have been made. During my first visit in 1968 I found the display of the Declaration of Independence and the U.S. Constitution just as the pictures in my school textbooks illustrated. The Declaration of Independence was in the central place of honor – elevated and mounted on the wall in almost altar-like positioning, with the Constitution centrally displayed in glass beneath the Declaration of Independence. To the sides, in glass casements, were other, lesser founding documents.

Over the years I found the display largely unchanged. But during a visit in 2005, I noted that the rotunda had been remodeled and the display had changed dramatically. The remodeling design has a decidedly secular/liberal influence. No longer was the Declaration of Independence in its former place of honor. It had been relegated off to the side, to the left of the Constitution, which was now all alone in the central place of honor.

This new design reflects the modern view, that the Constitution stands alone as our true founding document. The Declaration of Independence, still situated in a place of honor but no longer the central document in the display, now bows to the superiority of the Constitution which is the *real* founding document.

It is worth pointing out that since the First Continental Congress there have been three different governments associated with the thirteen original colonies, each government with its own particular founding documents. The uniting document for the First Continental Congress was the October 14, 1774, Declaration and Resolves.

For nearly two years the colonies viewed themselves as loyal British subjects just trying to get along with the mother country but united in opposition to the treatment Americans were receiving from King and Parliament. The Continental Congress amounted to an ad hoc committee which had very little real authority. Its main goal was to maintain a united front for dealing with England and to speak with a singular voice.

Everything changed in July, 1776. With the signing of the Declaration of Independence, the colonies put England on notice that they were no longer colonies of Britain or the King. They were henceforth thirteen independent, sovereign States, but united in their opposition to England. The Continental Congress at that time began to take on the form of government in naming a commanding general of the Continental army and of beginning to assume debts on behalf of the war effort.

A few years later, in 1782, the States formed a more formal governmental agreement under the Articles of Confederation. The Articles spelled out which State prerogatives were to be subsumed by the federal government for the sake of increased security. The Articles of Confederation, *however*, never assumed any preeminence over the Declaration of Independence. Indeed, the Declaration was simply our "statement of faith" if we might apply a church term to founding documents. The Articles of Confederation were our by-laws – literally how we worked out our statement of faith in practical terms.

However, the Articles of Confederation were too weak to be effective, and it was soon obvious that for the States to maintain order and to maintain an international presence which rivaled the European powers, the States needed to grant additional State powers and prerogatives to the general government. Thus, the States met in Convention during the summer of 1787 to outline what improvements were needed to make the Articles of Confederation effective. The result of that Constitutional Convention was a draft for a new proposed Constitution which would result in a more powerful general government, but not an all-powerful general government.

Nothing in that effort changed anything relative to the Declaration of Independence. All the States still believed in all the principles of the Declaration. All still shared a Biblical Judeo-Christian world view. The Declaration was still our "statement of faith." The Constitution simply changed the bylaws so that the principles of the Declaration could be realized in a more secure manner.

And indeed, the validity of these principles was acknowledged in the final lines of the new Constitution, "Done in Convention by the Unanimous Consent of the States present the Seventeenth Day of September in the Year of our Lord one thousand seven hundred and Eighty seven and of the Independence of the United States of America the Twelfth. In Witness whereof We have hereunto subscribed our Names."

Two thoughts come to mind in reviewing this subscript. First, Congress places the date "in the Year of our Lord one thousand seven hundred and Eighty-seven," a clear reference to how these men regarded the religious significance of that date. Second, Congress refers to the Declaration of Independence, "and of the Independence of the United States of America the Twelfth.[year]" This is an indication that Congress believed the Declaration to be the founding document, and that their efforts were a continuum of the governmental process under that philosophy, being merely a better set of by-laws.

Indeed, apart from Holy Scripture, the Declaration of Independence is perhaps the single most profound and amazing philosophy of government ever penned by mankind. Did Thomas Jefferson and Ben Franklin and John Adams and the 53 other delegates who signed this document think all this up on their own? No, the principles contained therein were well-known by the founders, who were well-read, well-educated leaders of the American Colonies. So, where did these ideas come from?

Chapter 6
Natural Law, The Created Order

When in the Course of human events, it becomes necessary for one people to dissolve the political bands which have connected them with another, and to assume among the powers of the earth, the separate and equal station to which the Laws of Nature and of Nature's God entitle them, a decent respect to the opinions of mankind requires that they should declare the causes which impel them to the separation.

In this chapter we are going to try to discover the concepts of natural law and natural rights that our founders embraced. Indeed, in declaring their independence from Great Britain, the founders used "the laws of nature and of nature's God" as their authority for such an action which might otherwise be considered brash and reckless, not to mention illegal and treasonous. By using "the laws of nature and of nature's God" as their authority, the founders were relying on the then universally known concept of natural law, the highest of all laws, and a law that is higher than the laws of Great Britain or any other country.

We don't discuss natural law much today. Today's academic experience, with a very few exceptions, is almost totally bankrupt concerning the concept of a universal, natural law. This is because the idea of natural law presupposes an absolute authority or lawgiver to which we are accountable, a concept which is unthinkable to the materialistic secular mind. Taking that a step further, it is only through the recognition that there is a Creator/

Supreme Ruler of the universe that absolute universal, natural laws and rights are possible in the first place.

Since the mid-1900s, in some cases the early 1900s, leaders of academia have embraced a different world view from that of our founders, one of materialism. While there are numerous philosophical approaches to a materialistic world view, in general, they are all variations of a common idea – that there is no God to believe in who created or controls mankind. There is no original lawgiver; the only thing we can see and experience for certain, and thus truly put our faith in, is matter. There is no absolute morality.

Thus, there are really only two world views: the theistic world view in which God exists as creator and sovereign lawgiver, and the materialistic world view in which there is no certain and knowable God. Put another way, the two general world views are "God Created Man" vs. "Man Created God." Many will argue that there are other world views besides these two, but I would respond that all can be condensed into these two categories: theistic and materialistic, ultimately depending on what you truly put your faith in, and *not* on what you give lip-service to. Our founding fathers, with the possible exception of Thomas Paine, all embraced a theistic world view, believing that there is a Creator/Lawgiver/Ruler to whom we owe our ultimate reverence and obedience.

So, what is natural law? To our founders, natural law was an essential part of that world view. Natural law is the reflection of God's nature and His moral attributes. The Judeo-Christian world view is this: since God is absolute holiness, His creation is bound by certain absolute laws of morality which reflect His holy character. And just as God assigned certain physical laws to His creation such as gravity, inertia, and thermodynamics, so also God assigned certain moral laws to His creation which are consistent with his character. In other words, God's laws, whether physical or moral, are universal and supreme over His creation, whatever human laws we might concoct.

This was not a new idea with the founders. Quite to the contrary, the idea of universal laws of morality go back for millennia, at least as far back as Plato and to his student Aristotle. Aristotle saw the injustice in pure Athenian democracy in which 51% of the citizen voters could do any injustice to any minority by a simple vote. By a simple vote justly earned wealth could be confiscated on behalf of the majority. By a simple vote, persons could be deprived of life or liberty. He knew intuitively that there was a better way, a better law which the majority must acknowledge and respect so that injustice could not flourish at the hands of the majority.

Aristotle wrote, "Universal Law is the law of Nature. For there really is, as everyone to some extent divines, a natural justice and injustice that is binding on all men, even on those who have no association or covenant with each other." Aristotle's view of God was imprecise, although he described god-like "movers" as living, eternal, unchanging, and supreme, with both intelligence and will. And from one "unmoved mover," or today we might say "uncaused cause," flowed a universal, binding law.

Just a few decades before Jesus Christ became man, Cicero, one of the founders' favorite philosophers, spoke of a timeless, universal law when he wrote in *De re publica (The Republic)*,

> *True law is correct reason congruent with nature, spread among all persons, constant, everlasting. It calls to duty by ordering; it deters from mischief by forbidding. Nevertheless it does not order or forbid upright persons in vain, nor does it move the wicked by ordering or forbidding. It is not holy to circumvent this law, nor is it permitted to modify any part of it, nor can it be entirely repealed. In fact we cannot be released from this law by either the senate or the people. No Sextus Aelius should be sought as expositor or interpreter. There will not be one law at Rome, another at Athens, one now, another later, but one law both everlasting and unchangeable will encompass all nations and for all time. And one god will be the common teacher and general, so to speak, of all persons. He will be the author, umpire, and provider of this law. The person who will not obey it will flee from himself and, defying human nature, he will suffer the greatest penalties by this very fact, even if he escapes other things that are thought to be punishments.*

Western civilization embraced the concept of natural law because it fit perfectly with the idea of a Sovereign Creator. In the fifth century, Saint Augustine wrote of natural law using the term "eternal law," and although his concept of eternal law was broader than how natural law was to be later defined, his eternal law included universal human morality. The idea behind "eternal" law is the idea that this law always has been and always will be because it is the manifestation of an eternal God.

In the thirteenth century Saint Thomas Aquinas wrote much about natural law, and even took it upon himself to clarify Augustine's eternal law. He wrote, "[natural law] is nothing else than the rational creature's participation in the eternal law."

Scottish churchman, Samuel Rutherford, wrote much about natural law in his watershed work *Lex Rex* in the mid-1600s, and John Locke further developed the idea in the late 1600s in his *Two Treatises on Government*. And finally, the man who, along with Locke, solidified this concept in the minds of America's learned men of the later 1700s and the 1800s more than any other was Sir William Blackstone, author of the famous *Blackstone Commentaries* (lit. *Commentaries on the Laws of England*).

We will discuss the development (and developers) of this concept in more detail in the next two chapters, but for the purpose of this chapter we need to firmly fix in our minds what the concept of natural law is, and why it is so important. Not to understand natural law makes understanding our founding experience impossible.

A helpful concept in understanding natural law is the often-used synonymous phrase, *the Created Order*. Natural law simply is this: all of the laws of physics, morality, humanity, music, and art which God created into the universe because of who He is – a reliable, immutable, holy God who is sovereign over His creation. Natural law declares a thing to be unjust regardless of its origin. Even an edict from a king can be wrong under natural law. A unanimous declaration by a legislature or a court can be wrong under natural law.

As was mentioned earlier, when God created the universe, He established certain physical laws to govern the natural world. God did not give us a written list of these laws – He left them for us to observe, experiment with, reason over, and thereby, to increase our understanding of the world around us. They simply exist as part of the Created Order, and mankind continues to discover and observe these laws and reduce them to mathematical precision so as to better understand them.

Because God is immutable (unchanging), we have come to understand that these laws have been built into creation, and that as long as creation exists we can rest assured that as part of the Created Order they will not change. These physical laws are knowable and predictable, and understanding these physical laws enables us to sail across the ocean in a massive ship, or to fly across the continent in only a few hours in a modern jet airplane.

Observing the laws of gravity and motion, in 1686 Isaac Newton published *Philosophiæ Naturalis Principia Mathematica*, which is Latin for "Mathematical Principles of Natural Philosophy" (generally referred to as simply the *Principia*). In *Principia* Newton attempted to put into mathematical terms certain laws such as gravity and inertia. As a result, when I was a boy in school, I was taught that Newton "discovered" gravity.

But Newton didn't discover gravity per se – rather he expressed it with a certain amount of mathematical precision which was, up to that point, not completely understood. Everyone knew about gravity naturally and instinctively before that. Before Newton, people still fell off of cliffs just as they did after Newton. Gravity was always there, but the details and understanding of gravity were subject to further discovery and explanation. Newton simply gave form, understanding, and detail to what everyone always recognized instinctively and experientially as a universal law.

In the same way, we apply certain universal laws of morality which are known instinctively by everyone, but codified in various ways by society. For instance, we are all born with the knowledge that murder is wrong, that stealing is wrong. We do not need a civil law to understand that, but in all civilized countries murder is recognized as wrong. In the most primitive village, completely separated from civilization, where no modern thinker or written language exists, if a stranger stumbles into the village dying of hunger and thirst, every villager knows in his innermost conscience that it is the right thing to do to give this stranger water and food.

These "instinctual" understandings are the result of a holy God placing into the hearts of each human person created in His image the knowledge of absolute right and wrong – something which is absent in the animal kingdom. These villagers may act in accordance with this inner voice by giving food and water to this desperate stranger, or they may decide to act against it and kill him, but each one knows from conscience what is the right thing to do.

This is what the Bible means when it says, *"For when the Gentiles, which have not the law* [the written law of Moses/ The Ten Commandments], *do by nature the things contained in the law, these, having not the law, are a law unto themselves: Which show the work of the law written in their hearts, their conscience also bearing witness, and their thoughts the mean while accusing or else excusing one another."* Romans 2:14-15

Thus, as everyone has a general, instinctive knowledge of gravity and of motion, though perhaps not a very complete understanding, so too everyone has a general, instinctive knowledge of absolute moral laws. And just as Isaac Newton expanded our knowledge about gravity and inertia, he did not invent gravity or inertia.

So also our natural human understanding of morality is expanded and clarified by the Bible as God's explanation of Himself and of His creation to man. The Bible does not establish morality - morality has always existed in the person of an eternal Creator God. And morality was therefore a part of God's creation – a reflection of God's essential morality. In a sense, the Bible is to morality what *Principia* is to gravity.

So, is murder wrong because the Bible says it is wrong? No, it is the other way around. The Bible says murder is wrong because it simply is naturally, fundamentally, morally wrong – it always has been wrong, because it is contrary to the nature of the Creator. From even before the original creation, murder has always been against the nature of God.

Murder was already wrong when Cain killed Abel. It was universally known to be wrong for the thousands of years between Cain and the written law of Moses which commands us, *Thou Shalt Not Kill*. As a part of the Created Order, these natural laws are an indispensable part of a holy God's creation – they have existed since the beginning, and these natural laws are there to be discovered as we learn more and more about the character of the Creator.

This is what Calvin Coolidge meant when he said, "Men do not make laws. They do but discover them." Nearly all human laws have a moral component. The old saying, "You can't legislate morality" is simply not true. Every law is an attempt to legislate morality in some way. For instance, by law I cannot drive faster than 25 MPH down a residential street. The moral reason for this is that in driving 60 MPH down that street, sooner or later I will injure or kill some innocent victim, which would be morally wrong and a violation of natural law. It is that speed limit which helps me to avoid a violation of natural law.

When I am asked to pay taxes it is for a moral reason. If I am experiencing the benefits and security of an orderly society, I am morally obligated to contribute my proportionate share to the cost of that society. If I simply let everyone else pay the cost for the value I receive, I am stealing from them, which is morally wrong. There are few human laws for which a moral component is not obvious.

In American history the whole concept of slavery was denounced repeatedly under natural law, particularly by Thomas Jefferson himself, but later by abolitionists and President Abraham Lincoln. Jefferson, who penned the draft of the Declaration which speaks of natural law, also wrote, "God who gave us life gave us liberty. Can the liberties of a nation be secure when we have removed a conviction that these liberties are the gift of God? Indeed I tremble for my country when I reflect that God is just, that his justice cannot sleep forever. Commerce between slave and master is despotism. Nothing is more certainly written in the book of fate than that these people are to be free."

Abraham Lincoln deferred to a higher law when he wrote, "In the early days of the world, the Almighty said to the first of our race 'In the sweat of thy face shalt thou eat bread... no good thing has been, or can be enjoyed by us, without having first cost labor... [all] such things of right belong to those whose labor has produced them... *some* have labored, and *others* have, without labor, enjoyed a large proportion of the fruits. This is wrong, and should not continue." In Lincoln's Gettysburg Address, Lincoln points out that our country was, "conceived in liberty and dedicated to the proposition that all men are created equal," which is the fundamental, natural law argument made by the founders in 1776.

This brings us to some more recent applications of natural law. One very important application of natural law was the trial of the Nazi leaders at Nuremberg. After World War II it was expressed by the allies, particularly the USA, England, and France, each of which profess to believe in the rule of law concept, that rather than just execute the Nazi leaders, they should first be tried in a legal proceeding. Otherwise the message to the world would simply be that "might makes right."

The problem with trying the Nazis was, on what basis of law do you charge them? As atrocious as the Nazi conduct was, under the laws of Germany that conduct was entirely legal. By the time of the "final solution" the laws of Germany permitted the extermination of the Jewish race. What law do you accuse the Nazis of breaking? The Nazis were not under any obligation to obey American laws, or the laws of England, or the laws of France, or, thankfully, the laws of the Soviet Union. Or is there some higher moral law that would demand a just penalty – a law higher than the laws of nations?

The Nazis were accused of breaking some international laws and treaties, but these are not capital crimes or the sort of violations which lead to wholesale execution of a country's leaders. No, the Nazis were guilty of far greater crimes, crimes which demanded the ultimate penalty. But those crimes were nowhere written in the laws of Germany.

The Nazis' legal defense team made that very clear – that these defendants had broken no laws. Yet everyone in the entire world, including the Nazis themselves, knew instinctively that the Nazis were guilty of a great evil that could not go unpunished. Everyone knew instinctively that just because a State allows a particular atrocity, that does not make it right or even allowable. There obviously is a higher, universal law.

US Supreme Court Justice Robert Jackson, the Chief U.S. Prosecutor for the allied prosecution made his opening statement, which included these words, "[The Nazi Leaders] took from the German people all those dignities and freedoms that we hold *natural and inalienable rights in every human being*... The Charter of this Tribunal evidences a faith that the law is not only to govern the conduct of little men, but that even rulers are, as Lord Chief Justice Coke put it to King James, '*under God and the law*.'" [emphasis mine]

It is interesting that Justice Jackson would use this well-known incident in English history to be included in his opening statement at Nuremberg. In 1608 Jurist Edward Coke (1552-1634) had written into one of his legal opinions, "The Law of Nature is that which God at the time of creation of the nature of man infused into his heart, for his preservation and direction; and this is *Lex Aeterna*, the moral law, called also the Law of Nature ... and written with the finger of God in the heart of man." Coke was a strong vocal proponent of the concept that English Common Law is based on natural law.

The confrontation between King James and Edward Coke is fascinating, particularly for the characters involved. King James had authored a book while king of Scotland, but prior to becoming king of England, on the divine right of kings. His book, *The True Law of Free Monarchies*, was written anonymously, obviously because James didn't want his fingerprints on such a self-serving concept.

The thesis of James's book was that it is God who appoints kings, and kings are the law – they cannot err. In appointing a king, God takes into consideration the needs of the country. If the country is deserving of blessing, God will appoint a good king. If the country is deserving of judgment, God will appoint a bad king – even a tyrant. Either way, the king is God's appointed ruler, and every subject is to be under strict obedience to the king, God's appointed sovereign. The king is law and above all laws.

So when Edward Coke confronted James and told him that he should be "under God and the law" James was furious. It was treasonous to confront a monarch in such a way, but Coke did not back down. He went on to quote the famous legal authority Lord Henry de Bracton (1210-1268) "the King shall not be under man, but under God and the Law." For his impudence Coke was demoted and eventually dismissed from his position. He would later become a member of Parliament and a strong voice of opposition to the King.

What Edward Coke was saying to King James, and what Justice Stephen Jackson was reinforcing at Nuremberg was the idea that King James, as well as every Nazi leader, as well as every man ever born, are all under a higher law – natural law – a law that takes precedence over national laws, law codes, and monarchs. Passing a law nullifying gravity does not make it possible to fly, nor does passing laws permitting murderous atrocities make it permissible to kill.

The final judgment at Nuremberg contained this profound observation, "... so far from it being unjust to punish [them], it would be unjust if [their] wrong[s] were allowed to go unpunished." In other words, this is a time when technical legal arguments to the contrary are obviously absurd. Justice of the highest authority (God Himself) demands punishment for such atrocities, however legal they might be under the laws of man or of a particular government.

An even more current application of natural law came with the civil rights movement under the leadership of Dr. Martin Luther King. King had often been challenged for being "lawless" and for refusing to obey democratically established laws. Dr. King explained his reasons for civil disobedience, declaring that there were indeed two types of laws, those which were just and those which were unjust. He stressed that it is important to obey legitimate laws, but laws which conflict with God's law are inherently unjust and are actually, quoting St. Augustine, "no law at all." He concluded that we have an obligation to disobey laws which conflict with God's law.

King, in explaining his reasons for civil disobedience argued the following in his famous *Letter From Birmingham Jail.*

> One may well ask: "How can you advocate breaking some laws and obeying others?" The answer lies in the fact that there are two types of laws: just and unjust. I would be the first to advocate obeying just laws. One has not only a legal but a moral responsibility to obey just laws. Conversely, one has a moral responsibility to disobey unjust laws. I would agree with St. Augustine that "an unjust law is no law at all."
>
> Now, what is the difference between the two? How does one determine whether a law is just or unjust? A just law is a man made code that squares with the moral law or the law of God. An unjust law is a code that is out of harmony with the moral law. To put it in the terms of St. Thomas Aquinas: An unjust law is a human law that is not rooted in eternal law and natural law. Any law that uplifts human personality is just. Any law that degrades human personality is unjust.[1]

Ronald Reagan summarized the risk in departing from natural law when he said, "Freedom prospers when religion is vibrant and the rule of law under God is acknowledged. . . . Our natural, inalienable rights are now considered to be a dispensation from government, and freedom has never been so fragile, so close to slipping from our grasp as it is at this moment."

We will discuss the influence of William Blackstone in a later chapter in some detail, but for now it is timely to mention that Blackstone was convinced of the importance of understanding natural law. Indeed, virtually

---

[1] Reprinted by arrangement with The Heirs to the Estate of Martin Luther King Jr., c/o Writers House as agent for the proprietor New York, NY.

Copyright: © 1963 Dr. Martin Luther King Jr. © renewed 1991 Coretta Scott King

all of our founders, as great admirers of Blackstone, embraced the philosophy of this great thinker to the degree that they made it a part of our founding document.

Much of Blackstone's philosophy seems to come from his predecessor, John Locke. In his *Commentaries on the Laws of England,* which became the foundation of American jurisprudence, Blackstone explained the two foundations of law in general. He said that any municipal law must necessarily be based on these two foundations, natural law and revealed law (the Bible), and that any law not based on these fundamental pillars is illegitimate, just as those laws that allowed the persecution and murder of Jews by the Nazis were universally recognized as illegitimate. Blackstone wrote:

> ...As therefore the creator is a being, not only of infinite power, and wisdom, but also of infinite goodness, he has been pleased so to contrive the constitution and frame of humanity, that we should want no other prompter to inquire after and pursue the rule of right, but only our own self-love, that universal principle of action. For he has so intimately connected, so inseparably interwoven the laws of eternal justice with the happiness of each individual, that the latter cannot be attained but by observing the former...

Notice Blackstone mentions that God, in creating mankind, created him with a fundamental attribute – self-love – which he describes as "that universal principle of action." In other words, God programmed man on purpose with the desire to live, to survive, and to pursue happiness (happiness as the word was commonly defined in the late 1700s – not as the word is commonly used today). Self-love is a principle of action that can be found on virtually every page of the Bible and on every page of human history. It is part of the Created Order, or the natural law.

As the Bible explains, "For no man ever yet hated his own flesh; but nourisheth and cherisheth it..." (Ephesians 5:29). Further, in establishing the two most fundamental of commandments, Jesus Christ tells us that, one, we must love God with all our hearts, and two, we must love our neighbor as ourselves. He does not criticize us for self-love – to the contrary, He assumes it to be the natural condition of mankind.

Because of self-love we feed ourselves when we get hungry, we drink water when we are thirsty. We engage in many different actions, some voluntary, some involuntary such as breathing or reflexive action, to preserve our lives. We have natural inclinations to love our families and to protect them from harm. We have natural inclination to protect our lives and property and the means of our survival or betterment.

Our whole created being focuses on our personal well-being. Blackstone tells us that our self-love is inseparably interwoven with the universal moral law to the degree that true happiness (well-being) can only come about through an environment of fundamental justice. Because of self-love we hate being wronged. We don't want to be murdered. We don't want to be stolen from. We hate being lied to.

As Jesus instructs us in the golden rule, if we hate being wronged ourselves, then we should hate inflicting such injustice on others, and we should hate it when others are unjustly abused. This makes the murder of innocents wrong *always and everywhere*. This makes theft from innocents wrong *always and everywhere*. Thus, even if government allows the infliction of murder or theft on innocents, it is still wrong under natural law because it transgresses the character of the holy Creator and ultimate law giver.

Blackstone well describes self-love as "that universal principle of action" the driving force behind free enterprise and the betterment of the individual. That is simply because free enterprise, energized by self-love, compels us to work and then to enjoy the fruit of our own labor.

Because of self-love a man will work a twelve-hour day to receive personal reward in the form of pay or profit. Without pay or profit he would usually not do it unless there was some other motivating factor such as a whip. We do not have to be forced to work a twelve-hour day – we are willing to work hard so long as sufficient reward is the likely outcome. As a result of this personal initiative, society is benefited. In a free-enterprise society people are inventive because it leads to some form of personal betterment or profit.

Understanding natural law and the principle of self-love allows us to understand why socialism, in all of its forms, destroys wealth and initiative, and is generally unworkable. Pure socialism forces us to work without any direct personal benefit – for the greater good. Few of us are really interested in laboring for the greater good rather than for our own direct benefit, and as a result only external force will produce labor for no personal benefit, and that labor will be inefficiently performed with only enough effort as required to escape retribution.

We will not voluntarily offer inventiveness "for the greater good" unless there is some personal incentive. Only politicians and tyrants promote such unworkable concepts as socialism – those who themselves are able to live like kings under such an arrangement, themselves proving in a perverse way the universal law of self-love. Socialism or any social norm which goes contrary to natural law will be generally unworkable as it is in conflict with the creator and His wise design for humanity.

Franklin Roosevelt's famous "Four Freedoms" speech declared that everyone has a fundamental freedom from want. The United Nations, in establishing the Universal Declaration of Human Rights, in 1948 declared that all persons have a fundamental right to life's material necessities. They did not declare that these rights come from God as our founders declared of life, liberty, and pursuit of happiness. Are these things (medical treatment, food, clothing, housing, a good paying job, etc. etc.) "rights" in the same sense of the word that life, liberty, and the pursuit of happiness are rights?

Herein lies a fundamental misunderstanding of natural law. The rights that our founders listed in the Declaration and the Constitution (life, liberty, pursuit of happiness, security in our persons and papers, self-defense, speech, religion, etc.) are all rights that cost no other person anything except proper respect. They do not require labor. Once you begin to add material rights you have created a new question, one which socialists and Biblicists answer quite differently.

Before we get into the details of that question, it is important to recognize the most fundamental and obvious natural law of economics – that is: All goods or services must be worked for. The acquiring of property (food, clothing, housing) requires work. Food must be harvested by someone. Clothing must be manufactured by someone. Housing must be built by someone, the components fabricated or purchased by someone. In each case labor multiplied by time is required to produce all these expected goods.

If I have an absolute right to food, even though I refuse to work, that means that I can expect someone else to provide the labor necessary to supply this right. If I have an absolute right to medical care, I can expect someone else to work hard to obtain the necessary education and experience to provide this to me efficiently. Whatever amount of work is involved to pay for this service, it is the responsibility of someone else to provide that labor. If it is a right, then some individual(s) in society has an obligation to provide the necessary labor.

That expectation we used to call slavery. Morally speaking, as Lincoln said in his Second Inaugural Address, "It may seem strange that any men should dare to ask a just God's assistance in wringing their bread from the sweat of other men's faces . . ." stealing labor is no more acceptable when a poor man steals labor from a rich man than when a rich man steals labor from a poor man. It is stealing either way, a violation of God's law.

It has only been within the last century that the concepts of natural law have become so perverted, and that socialism has taken hold to such a widespread extent. Material things are assumed to be absolute rights, and in every case it has, or ultimately will, lead to a diminishing of wealth and living standard. This is to be expected when we begin to concoct rights which are not supportable from either natural law or the Bible.

It also must be noted that most of this change is attributable to politics, not compassion. Liberal politicians recognize that one of the surest means of maintaining their cushy life style and retirement benefits is to capture large voting blocks, and a growing voting block is comprised of those who are dependent on government. Whether food stamps, Obamacare subsidies, or housing subsidies, these altogether represent security to the politician who is generous with other people's money. As Margaret Thatcher once observed, "The problem with socialism is that eventually you run out of other people's money."

From the pen of King Solomon, Ecclesiastes 5:18-19, "Behold that which I have seen: it is good and comely for one to eat and to drink, and to enjoy the good of all his labor that he taketh under the sun all the days of his life, which God giveth him: for it is his portion. Every man also to whom God hath given riches and wealth, and hath given him power to eat thereof, and to take his portion, and to rejoice in his labor; this is the gift of God."

When Solomon says, "It is his portion," he is simply saying that it is his natural right. In contrast, it is a perverted form of self-love which allows an able-bodied man to refuse to work in a society which will otherwise feed him. Solomon, in the book of Ecclesiastes in at least a half dozen places, writes something like those words found above. In each case the message is simply this: a man has a God-given right to have and to possess those things he has worked for or as Jefferson might have said it, every person has been equally given by God the right to pursue happiness.

In an opportunity society such as the United States, it takes only modest effort for most people to provide for one's food, clothing, shelter, and even medical care. In a socialist society which believes that these necessities of life are human rights, a great number of people will allow all the others in society to provide these needs for them. This inevitably leads to general poverty in a society. Ironically, under socialism fewer people ultimately will have access to these "rights" than those in an opportunity society.

Our founders were students of the Bible, and recognized the truth, not to mention the wisdom of the Apostle Paul's admonition, "If a man work not, neither should he eat," and "... if any provide not for his own, and specially for those of his own house, he hath denied the faith, and is worse than an infidel." There is nothing which motivates a common man to spectacular success quite like hunger. Modern western society has taken hunger, this greatest of motivations, out of the equation, and we as a society are no longer allowed to benefit from it.

Does this mean we do not feed the hungry or clothe the naked or give shelter to the homeless? No, not at all. However, as the Apostle Paul was quoted above, there are some basic guidelines. First, a man able but unwilling to work should be allowed to go hungry. He will not starve – eventually he will go to work. Second, a man should be required to provide for his own (his extended family), and especially for the members of his own house (immediate family). Family has the first obligation to provide for those unable to provide for themselves.

Yet throughout the Bible, with these principles in mind, people of faith are morally (not legally) obligated to feed the hungry, clothe the naked, and give shelter to the homeless. Christian ministries throughout our country's history have provided these things to those who were unable to provide for themselves. Throughout the world it has been Christian ministries, not communists, not socialists, who expended multiplied billions of dollars to distribute food to the hungry, and clothing to the naked. Most hospitals worldwide were founded originally by Christian ministries. However, in each case supplying social needs, it was performed out of love and a moral compulsion, not a legal one.

So, let's review Blackstone's logic. First, he argues that God is creator and that He created us intentionally in His own image with a love of self; that this love of self results in positive action leading to personal betterment. Self-love, like all of mankind's created attributes, was originally created to be a positive, energizing force. Self-love, combined with the golden rule, eliminates transgression against any innocent person. It explains the natural love of life, liberty, and the pursuit of happiness and the emphasis of those values in a society.

Blackstone further explains that our reason, while a useful gift from God, is not always enough in and of itself to fully comprehend what natural law is. So, God gave us His Word, the Bible, to explain right and wrong in a more accurate and detailed way than our reason might itself conclude.

> *But every man now finds ... that his reason is corrupt, and his understanding full of ignorance and error.*
>
> *This has given manifold occasion for the benign interposition of divine providence ... to discover and enforce its laws by an immediate and direct revelation. The doctrines thus delivered we call the revealed or divine law, and they are to be found only in the holy scriptures...*
>
> *Upon these two foundations, the law of nature and the law of revelation, depend all human laws; that is to say, no human laws should be suffered to contradict these...*

Indeed, the concepts of God's natural law – the Created Order – the universal law – the eternal law – as augmented and explained by the Bible gave Americans their founding philosophy and their understanding of fundamental rights. If these "laws of nature and of Nature's God" are not legitimate, then our founding is illegal, and in fact treasonous, and our founding document incomprehensible.

From Locke and Blackstone, to Jefferson, to all the founders, to Abraham Lincoln, to the American prosecutors at Nuremburg, to Martin Luther King, to Ronald Reagan, the great Americans and their influencers in every age have understood and embraced a law which is higher than the law of any nation, or even an International Law endorsed by every nation. It is the simple acceptance of God-ordained, absolute morality, right vs. wrong, good vs. evil.

We don't have to agree that everyone believing in natural law always gets every detail right in every case, but we will rarely be far off from true morality. It is also true that someone embracing a materialistic world view will seldom get it right, morally speaking. And how could we expect them to when they do not believe that anything can be intrinsically, universally, and absolutely moral in the first place?

Chapter 7
On the Shoulders of Giants

What Des-Cartes did was a good step. You have added much several ways, and especially in taking the colors of thin plates into philosophical consideration. If I have seen further it is by standing on the shoulders of Giants. [Letter from Sir Isaac Newton to fellow-scientist Robert Hooke, 1676]

The above quote from a letter by Isaac Newton represents the use of a common word picture that went back at least to the twelfth century. The word picture helps to explain how sometimes simple men are able to build upon the thinking and the discoveries of previous generations, sometimes upon the ideas of great men, to advance learning or culture or political thinking far beyond their own creative capacity, or as the metaphor goes, "We are dwarfs, standing on the shoulders of giants."

While our founders were not exactly dwarfs, they were not the originators of most of their foundational thinking. They were well educated in the classics and were acutely aware of enlightenment thinking, both theistic and atheistic. They studied government in all of its forms, reading carefully the writings of all of the various advocates of this approach or of that one. As Benjamin Franklin stated in his most famous speech at the Constitutional Convention in 1787, "We have gone back to ancient history for models of government, and examined the different forms of those Republics which, having been formed with the seeds of their own dissolution, now no longer exist. And we have viewed Modern States all around Europe, but find none of their Constitutions suitable to our circumstances."

Our Founders applied themselves to learning the various theories of government and philosophy, and particularly theological concepts. By understanding who these founders admired, who they believed to be most correct in their philosophy of government, we can better understand how our founders thought and what their intentions were in constructing the United States and its government.

On January 16, 1811, Thomas Jefferson wrote a letter to Dr. Benjamin Rush in Philadelphia, one of the signers of the *Declaration of Independence* and a close friend of Jefferson. The subject of the letter was to respond to Dr. Rush's efforts to reconcile Thomas Jefferson with John Adams. These two great founders had been the principals in a divisive presidential election in 1800. This election had resulted in bitter feelings between these two titanic rivals, particularly on the part of Adams.

(Eventually these two rivals were reconciled and carried on a correspondence of letters until their deaths on the same day, July 4, 1826, exactly 50 years after the country was founded in which each played a leading role.)

Jefferson's letter contained two deep insights into the mind of Jefferson, one reflecting his religious sentiments, the other reflecting his values – who he considered to be the tallest giants on whom to stand. The first reference at the beginning of the letter was to convey his condolences to Dr. Rush on a personal tragedy that Rush had recently suffered. Jefferson wrote, "I had before heard of the heart-rending calamity you mention, and had sincerely sympathized with your afflictions. But I had not made it the subject of a letter, because I knew that condolences were but renewals of grief. Yet I thought, and still think, this is one of the cases wherein we should 'not sorrow, even as others who have no hope.'"

From the context of the letter we do not know the specifics of the calamity that Jefferson refers to, but it appears from the letter more to suggest a case where a family member of Dr. Rush had experienced a complete loss of sanity rather than a death. Whatever the calamity, Jefferson here quotes from the Bible, I Thessalonians 4:13, a familiar passage referring to those who have died as believers ("them, also, which sleep in Jesus"), where Paul writes that our hope of the resurrection of the body keeps us from the type of sorrow experienced by non-believers, "that ye sorrow not, even as others who have no hope."

Jefferson, in his letter uses quotation marks around the phrase, "not sorrow, even as others who have no hope," indicating that he is knowingly quoting Scripture. As such Jefferson was offering comfort to a friend of a spiritual nature from a hope they shared in common, a resurrection and restoration of mind and body, separating himself and Dr. Rush from those unbelievers who do not have such hope.

The second insight that this letter contains is Jefferson's characterization of the men he most admired. Jefferson described in this letter a dinner he had hosted at Monticello at the request of President Washington, and some of the subjects of conversation at that dinner. His letter continues:

> *While he [Adams] was Vice President, and I Secretary of State, I received a letter from President Washington, then at Mount Vernon, desiring me to call together the Heads of departments, and to invite Mr. Adams to join us (which, by-the-bye, was the only instance of that being done) in order to determine on some measure which required despatch; and he desired me to act on it, as decided, without again recurring to him. I invited them to dine with me, and after dinner, sitting at our wine, having settled our question, other conversation came on, in which a collision of opinion arose between Mr. Adams and Colonel Hamilton, on the merits of the British constitution, . . .*
>
> *Another incident took place on the same occasion . . . The room being hung around with a collection of the portraits of remarkable men, among them were those of Bacon, Newton and Locke, Hamilton asked me who they were. I told him they were my <u>trinity of the three greatest men the world had ever produced,</u> naming them.* [emphasis added]

There is a story behind this comment that goes back to Jefferson's term as the American Ambassador in Paris, France, in the late 1780s. In a world before photography, portraits were common in varying degrees of skill. There were a great many artists in the portrait business, each commanding a price commensurate with their ability to produce a life-like reflection of the subject.

In 1789 Jefferson initiated an effort to have his "trinity" of great men reproduced on canvas, along with three other men Jefferson admired:

Algernon Sidney (1622-1683), John Hampden (1594-1643), and Shakespeare. He wished to have these six portraits shipped home and displayed at Monticello. He wrote a letter to American artist John Trumbull who was in London at the time, "What would it cost to have them copied by some good young hand, who will do them well and is not of such established reputation as to be dear?"

Trumbull responded, "I have made enquiry about the pictures for which you enquire. Several of them exist, and are to be got at: and a young man whom I know and who will do these Copies as well as most copiers: undertakes to do them for three Guineas each ... I do not think tolerable copies can be procur'd for less."

Jefferson then responded, "I will put off till my return from America all of them except Bacon, Locke, and Newton, whose pictures I will trouble you to have copied for me: and as *I consider them as the three greatest men that have ever lived, without any exception, and as having laid the foundation of those superstructures which have been raised in the Physical and Moral sciences . . .*" [Emphasis added]

So as Jefferson sat at dinner with John Adams, Alexander Hamilton, and the other cabinet members, the portraits of these three giants, displayed in the room in which they dined, became the topic of discussion as the "trinity of the three greatest men the world had ever produced." Because Jefferson admired these men and esteemed them so highly, we have to assume that he was in general agreement with what they thought and wrote.

Jefferson says that these men "laid the foundation of those superstructures which have been raised in the Physical and Moral sciences." So, what did we get from Bacon, Newton, and Locke, and why did Jefferson admire them so much? One thing that needs to be pointed out about all three of these men is that they were all strictly Bible believing Christians in their world view. All three wrote theological works, all of these works were strictly Christian and orthodox in nature.

Among his writings is Bacon's *Confession of Faith*, which is precisely that, a personal statement of his religious beliefs. Bacon's *Confession* begins,

> *I Believe that nothing is without beginning, but God; no nature, no matter, no spirit, but one, only, and the same God. That God, as he is eternally almighty, only wise, only good, in his*

nature; so he is eternally Father, Son, and Spirit, in persons. I believe that God is so holy, pure, and jealous, as it is impossible for him to be pleased in any creature, though the work of his own hands; so that neither angel, man, nor world, could stand, or can stand, one moment in his eyes, without beholding the same in the face of a Mediator; and therefore, that before him, with whom all things are present, the Lamb of God was slain before all worlds; without which eternal counsel of his, it was impossible for him to have descended to any work of creation; but he should have enjoyed the blessed and individual society of three persons in Godhead for ever.

But that, out of his eternal and infinite goodness and love purposing to become a Creator, and to communicate to his creatures, he ordained in his eternal counsel, that one person of the Godhead should be united to one nature, and to one particular of his creatures: that so, in the person of the Mediator, the true ladder might be fixed, whereby God might descend to his creatures, and his creatures might ascend to God: so that God, by the reconcilement of the Mediator, turning his countenance towards his creatures, though not in equal light and degree, made way unto the dispensation of his most holy and secret will; whereby some of his creatures might stand, and keep their state; others might possibly fall, and be restored; and others might fall, and not be restored to their estate, but yet remain in being, though under wrath and corruption: all with respect to the Mediator; which is the great mystery and perfect centre of all God's ways with his creatures, and unto which all his other works and wonders do but serve and refer.

That he chose, according to his good pleasure, man to be that creature, to whose nature the person of the eternal Son of God should be united; and amongst the generations of men, elected a small flock, in whom, by the participation of himself, he purposed to express the riches of his glory; all the ministration of angels, damnation of devils and reprobates, and universal administration of all creatures, and dispensation of all times, having no other end, but as the ways and ambages of

> *God, to be further glorified in his saints, who are one with their head the Mediator, who is one with God....*

Likely what Jefferson most admired in Bacon was his development of the scientific method. Jefferson was a man much interested in science and discovery, and we have seen his reference to these three as providing "... the foundation of... the Physical and Moral sciences..." Bacon's writings had advanced the inductive Baconian method, later known as the scientific method. However, even in the realm of science, Bacon's discoveries had a theological purpose. Bacon wrote of learning, "Knowledge is the rich storehouse for the glory of the Creator and the relief of man's estate ... A little philosophy inclineth man's mind to atheism, but depth in philosophy bringeth men's minds about to religion."

Bacon's last will and testament included this final prayer, "When I thought most of peace and honor, thy hand [was] heavy on me, and hath humbled me, according to thy former loving kindness. ... Just are thy judgments upon my sins. ... Be merciful unto me for my Savior's sake, and receive me into thy bosom."

Isaac Newton was the second of Jefferson's "trinity." We all know him as a man of science who, in a giant leap forward, greatly expanded our knowledge of science, particularly the laws of color, mathematics, gravity, and motion. Isaac Newton was also a man of faith, much like Bacon. As Charles E. Hummel wrote in the periodical *Christian History* in April, 1991,

> ... Even in Newton's lifetime, his contemporaries' adulation verged on worship. Following his death in April 1727, Newton lay in state in Westminster Abbey for a week. At the funeral, his pall was borne by three earls, two dukes, and the Lord Chancellor. Voltaire observed, "He was buried like a king who had done well by his subjects." No scientist before or since has been so revered and interred with such high honor...
>
> For Newton the world of science was by no means the whole of life. He spent more time on theology than on science; indeed, he wrote about 1.3 million words on biblical subjects. Yet this vast legacy lay hidden from public

view for two centuries until the auction of his nonscientific writings in 1936.

So what was Newton's world view? His writings make it clear. He believed in a literal creation, a Created Order, a literal interpretation of the Bible, particularly Bible prophesy. In his work *Principia* which was referred to in the preceding chapter Newton wrote, "... This most beautiful system of the sun, planets, and comets could only proceed from the counsel and dominion of an intelligent and powerful Being. And if the fixed stars are the centres of other like systems, these, being formed by the like wise counsel, must be all subject to the dominion of One."

In 1832 the prominent Scottish physicist Sir David Brewster published *The Life of Sir Isaac Newton*. Brewster, an esteemed scientist in his own right, wrote from the standpoint of science, but he also wrote from the standpoint of a Christian in describing not only Newton's scientific achievements but also his theological contributions.

Late in the book Brewster includes a chapter on the theology of Newton, beginning the chapter with the following, "The history of the theological studies of Sir Isaac Newton will ever be regarded as one of the most interesting portions of his life. That he who among all the individuals of his species possessed the highest intellectual powers was not only a learned and profound divine, but a firm believer in the great doctrines of religion, is one of the proudest triumphs of the Christian faith."

Brewster discussed at length Newton's commentaries on the prophetical Biblical books of Daniel and the Apocalypse. This work, *The Observations on the Prophesies of Daniel and the Apocalypse of St. John,* makes clear that Newton expected a literal fulfillment of all of these prophetic predictions, and he strove to write just how that fulfillment would look.

Interestingly, Brewster includes a letter from Newton to John Locke, in 1690, in which Newton discusses with Locke his ideas on how to interpret some of the difficult parts of Daniel's prophesy. Wrote Newton to Locke, "... The Son of Man, Dan vii, I take to be the same with the Word of God upon the White Horse in Heaven, Apoc. xii, for both are to rule the nations with a rod of iron; but whence are you certain that the Ancient of Days is Christ? Does Christ anywhere sit upon the throne? ... Know you the meaning of Dan. x. 21.[?] There is none that holdeth with me in these things but Michael the prince." It is fascinating to contemplate these two great theologians exchanging letters in which they contend back and forth over how to interpret various Scriptures.

Brewster next describes how Newton entered into the debate over two difficult passages in the New Testament (I John 5:7 and I Timothy 3:16), and published a pamphlet about the subject, *Historical Account of Two Notable Corruptions of Scripture*. In this pamphlet Newton wrote a paraphrase of the John 5 text in question, italicizing the words of the actual text, and using the non-italicized words as explanation.

> *Who is he that overcometh the world, but he that believeth that Jesus is the Son of God,* that Son spoken of in the Psalms, where he saith, "thou are my Son; this day have I begotten thee." *This is he that,* after the Jews had long expected him, *came,* first in a mortal body, *by* baptism of *water,* and then in an immortal one, by shedding his *blood* upon the cross and rising again from the dead; *not by water only, but by water and blood;* being the Son of God, as well by his resurrection from the dead (Acts xiii. 33), as by his supernatural birth of the virgin (Luke i. 35).
>
> *And it is the Spirit* also *that,* together with the water and blood, *beareth witness* of the truth of his coming; *because the Spirit is truth;* and so a fit and unexceptionable witness. *For there are three that bear record* of his coming; *the Spirit,* which he promised to send and which was since shed forth upon us in the form of cloven tongues, and in various gifts; *the* baptism of *water,* wherein God testified 'this is my beloved Son;' *and the* shedding of his *blood,* accompanied with his resurrection, whereby he became the most faithful martyr, or witness, of this truth.
>
> *And these three,* the spirit, the baptism, and passion of Christ, *agree* in witnessing one and the same thing (namely, that the Son of God is come); and therefore their evidence is strong: ...

Brewster describes how this pamphlet was used to accuse Newton of not believing in the Trinity. He then goes on to debunk that theory, pointing out that Newton was only interested in sound Biblical scholarship, not in any way attacking this cardinal doctrine. (It is interesting to note that accusations against Newton of this sort persist to this day, being embraced by religious skeptics and secularists who would love to find some way to have Newton on their side. It should also be noted that these two texts are hotly debated to this day among those who embrace an unshakable faith in the Trinity.)

Brewster then goes on to describe the nature of the physical world as being similar to the nature of the theological sphere, the truth of both being not apparent on the surface, but both being capable of study and of finding out upon the application of sound study and reasoning. He concludes the chapter with this comment, "If such, then, is the character of the Christian faith, we need not be surprised that it was embraced and expounded by such a genius as Sir Isaac Newton. Cherishing its doctrines, and leaning on its promises, he felt it his duty, as it was his pleasure, to apply to it that intellectual strength which had successfully surmounted the difficulties of the material universe."

We could certainly understand if someone wanted to make the case that what Jefferson admired in Bacon and Newton was strictly scientific. Jefferson had stated that these three men developed the foundation of the physical and moral sciences. Both Bacon and Newton were most noted for their scientific contributions.

However, the third member of Jefferson's trinity of the three greatest men the world has produced was John Locke. Locke was not at all known for scientific discovery. He was a Christian philosopher of the enlightenment – that is what he is noted for. We can safely assume that when it came to the foundation of *moral* sciences, Jefferson was *at least* referring to Locke, although it should be pointed out that the world views of all three were identical.

While some secularists have ascribed deism to Locke, none have so described him which have actually read his writings. It is easy for someone to say that Locke was a deist if all that one does is parrot what is being said by some other secularist who is trying to paint Jefferson as a deist. But no one who has read Locke's *The Reasonableness of Christianity* would ever, no, *could* ever, call Locke a deist.

If Jefferson embraced the moral foundations of his trinity, then we must assume that what these men believed as to morals was what Jefferson also believed. Anyone who has read Locke has had to conclude that he, like Bacon and Newton, was a devout Christian man who would fit well in most conservative evangelical churches today.

John Locke is best known for two books, *Two Treatises of Government* (1689) and *The Reasonableness of Christianity; as Delivered in the Scriptures* (1695). We will be focusing mostly on the former, which was, for the most part, a reply to a book written by Robert Filmer (1588-1653) published under the title *Patriarcha*, in 1680, long after Filmer's death. Filmer's work supported the idea of monarchy, the divine right of kings, and the divine right of hereditary entitlement.

In the *Two Treatises* Locke develops in detail the concept of natural law which was discussed in the previous chapter. Much of Locke's ideas on natural law came, no doubt, from Samuel Rutherford's watershed work, *Lex Rex* published in 1644. *Lex Rex* was written at the only time in English history, up to that point, that such a book could be safely published. The very title was Latin for *The Law is King*, which virtually screamed out against the prevailing theory of the time: *The King is Law*.

With the English civil war raging in England and Scotland, and Charles having lost control of Scotland, Samuel Rutherford, a renowned Scottish theologian, published a book which at any other time would have gotten him tried, convicted, and executed for treason. It was a book that shredded the idea that kings ruled by divine right and could do no wrong. It replaced that notion with the idea, found in the Bible in Deuteronomy 17, that kings and subjects are all equally under the Law of God. It further promoted the idea that humans had a natural right to decide what type of government best suited their needs for security, and who should run it. (Rutherford referred to Deuteronomy 17 a total of 79 times in *Lex Rex*.)

Rutherford talked much about natural law, and the fact that all law has its authority ultimately in the Creator, "What is warranted by the direction of nature's light is warranted by the law of nature, and consequently by a divine law; for who can deny the law of nature to be a divine law?"

He then took that thinking to the next level, proclaiming that natural law superseded the king, and that the king was as obligated to this law as anyone else, "As the king is under God's law both in commanding and in exacting active obedience, so is he under the same regulating law of God, in punishing or demanding of us passive subjection, and as he may not command what he will, but what the King of kings warranteth him to command, so may he not punish as he will, but by warrant also of the Supreme Judge of all the earth."

This was not all that controversial in and of itself. Great men like de Bracton and Coke had advocated that the king was under the law of God prior to Rutherford. However, a step too far was Rutherford's idea that the law of nature gave ultimate political power to the people, not the king, and if the people didn't like the king they were free to dismiss him and install another: ". . . Power is not an immediate inheritance from heaven, but a birthright of the people borrowed from them; they may let it out for their good, and resume it when a man is drunk with it. . . By way of limitation: because no law in its letter hath force where the safety of the subject is in hazard; and if law or king be destructive to the people they are to be abolished. This is clear in a tyrant or a wicked man."

And an even greater stride into political heresy was Rutherford's contention that the form of government was not that important, that democracy and aristocracy were just as valid forms of government as monarchy, provided that is what the people believe will tend to their safety the most. Needless to say, Rutherford was not popular with monarchists.

Rutherford was charged with treason and summoned before the Scottish Parliament immediately after the Restoration in 1660 of Charles II, but his health did not permit him to go. He died shortly thereafter in 1661. A copy of *Lex Rex* was burned in a public ceremony by the official executioner at Edinburgh, and he was convicted of treason post mortem. However, *Lex Rex* had been popular throughout England and Scotland, and although it was banned after the Restoration, the toothpaste was out of the tube, and the role of monarchy was fair game for discussion.

The next great opportunity to safely publish anti-monarchy thought was immediately following the Glorious Revolution in 1688. With the replacement of the tyrant James II by William and Mary, and the official Parliamentary discussion of a formal Bill of Rights, John Locke published his *Two Treatises of Government* in 1689. His arguments were pretty much the same as those in *Lex Rex*, but more detailed and expansive.

In part one of the *Two Treatises* Locke attacks Filmer head on over the idea of monarchy, divine right of prerogatives, and divine right of hereditary succession, basing his arguments, for the most part, on the Bible. In the second part of the *Two Treatises*, Locke writes in detail his own philosophy of government.

Locke begins the second treatise with a detailed discussion of some great concepts ancillary to government: in whom does political power ultimately reside?; mankind in his natural state, absent government; slavery; property. He then begins to develop his ideas of natural law, how and why governments are formed, and where the authority to form or abolish government comes from. Locke makes it clear that there is a Natural Law based on the Creator.

> *The state of Nature has a law of Nature to govern it, which obliges every one, and reason, which is that law, teaches all mankind who will but consult it, that being all equal and independent, no one ought to harm another in his life, health, liberty or possessions; for men being all the workmanship of one omnipotent and infinitely wise Maker; all the servants of one sovereign Master, sent into the world by His order and about His business; they are His property, whose workmanship they are made to last during His, not one another's pleasure.*
>
> *... Thus the law of Nature stands as an eternal rule to all men, legislators as well as others. The rules that they make for other men's actions must ... be conformable to the law of Nature— i.e., to the will of God, of which that is a declaration, and the fundamental law of Nature being the preservation of mankind, no human sanction can be good or valid against it...*
>
> *... the legislative or supreme authority cannot assume to itself a power to rule by extemporary arbitrary decrees, but is bound to dispense justice and decide the rights of the subject by promulgated standing laws...*

[At the end of this clause is a footnote number 9, which footnote, following, is a quote from Hooker.]

> *9. "Human laws are measures in respect of men whose actions they must direct, howbeit such measures they are as have also their higher rules to be measured by, which rules are two: the law of God and the law of Nature; so that laws human must*

> be made according to the general laws of Nature, and without contradiction to any positive law of Scripture, otherwise they are ill made.' Hooker, Eccl. Pol. iii. 9

Understand what Locke is saying here. He says there is a state of nature governed only by natural law. He describes that law as being the law of the Creator eternal, and he quotes Hooker to say that it must be consistent with Divine Scripture.

Space does not permit me to quote Locke's entire work here, but it is well worth reading. It is available for speedy download on the internet – free for the effort. I encourage you to download and to read all of Locke's writings, especially if you have been misled to believe that Locke was a deist. However, for those who will not take advantage of this opportunity, I will quote here some additional thoughts by Locke. The more you read of Locke, the more you will recognize him in our Declaration of Independence, originally drafted by Thomas Jefferson.

Locke writes at length of the "state of nature" into which every man is born. Picture a land where there are few inhabitants and no government. Man is born free, by nature, king of his own affairs. He has the natural right of liberty, and, by the same logic, he has no right to make a slave of another man since that man is also born equally free. He is the sole arbiter of what he does and how he interacts with other men who have equal sovereignty.

He has the right to take from nature and to expend his labor in order to improve the value of natural things, such as wood or metals. He has a right of ownership over those things that his labor has improved for any purpose. Thus he has a natural right to property by virtue of the labor he has expended.

In the state of nature he has the right to set aside as much land as he needs for himself and his family to survive, provided it is not in use by another man and has no prior claim on it. He has the right to expend labor on that land to cultivate and improve it. He has a right by virtue of that labor and the resulting improved state of that land, to have it for his own property. Property is, by natural right, the product of a man's labor.

So why, in such a state of natural freedom, would any man want government? Locke explains:

123. If man in the state of Nature be so free as has been said, if he be absolute lord of his own person and possessions, equal to the greatest and subject to nobody, why will he part with his freedom, this empire, and subject himself to the dominion and control of any other power? To which it is obvious to answer, that though in the state of Nature he hath such a right, yet the enjoyment of it is very uncertain and constantly exposed to the invasion of others; for all being kings as much as he, every man his equal, and the greater part no strict observers of equity and justice, the enjoyment of the property he has in this state is very unsafe, very insecure. This makes him willing to quit this condition which, however free, is full of fears and continual dangers; and it is not without reason that he seeks out and is willing to join in society with others who are already united, or have a mind to unite for the mutual preservation of their lives, liberties and estates, which I call by the general name—property.

124. The great and chief end, therefore, of men uniting into commonwealths, and putting themselves under government, is the preservation of their property; to which in the state of Nature there are many things wanting.

Firstly, there wants an established, settled, known law, received and allowed by common consent to be the standard of right and wrong, and the common measure to decide all controversies between them. For though the law of Nature be plain and intelligible to all rational creatures, yet men, being biased by their interest, as well as ignorant for want of study of it, are not apt to allow of it as a law binding to them in the application of it to their particular cases.

125. Secondly, in the state of Nature there wants a known and indifferent judge, with authority to determine all differences according to the established law. For every one in that state being both judge and executioner of the law of Nature, men being partial to themselves, passion and revenge is very apt to carry them too far, and with too much heat in their own cases, as well as negligence and unconcernedness, make them too remiss in other men's.

126. Thirdly, in the state of Nature there often wants power to back and support the sentence when right, and to give it due execution. They who by any injustice offended will seldom fail where they are able by force to make good their injustice. Such resistance many times makes the punishment dangerous, and frequently destructive to those who attempt it.

127. Thus mankind, notwithstanding all the privileges of the state of Nature, being but in an ill condition while they remain in it are quickly driven into society. Hence it comes to pass, that we seldom find any number of men live any time together in this state. The inconveniencies that they are therein exposed to by the irregular and uncertain exercise of the power every man has of punishing the transgressions of others, make them take sanctuary under the established laws of government, and therein seek the preservation of their property. It is this that makes them so willingly give up every one his single power of punishing to be exercised by such alone as shall be appointed to it amongst them, and by such rules as the community, or those authorised by them to that purpose, shall agree on. And in this we have the original right and rise of both the legislative and executive power as well as of the governments and societies themselves.

Men being, as has been said, by nature all free, equal, and independent, no one can be put out of this estate and subjected to the political power of another without his own consent, which is done by agreeing with other men, to join and unite into a community for their comfortable, safe, and peaceable living, one amongst another, in a secure enjoyment of their properties, and a greater security against any that are not of it. This any number of men may do, because it injures not the freedom of the rest; they are left, as they were, in the liberty of the state *of Nature. When any number of men have so consented to make one community or government, they are thereby presently incorporated, and make one body politic, wherein the majority have a right to act and conclude the rest...*

This last paragraph is representative of Locke's concept that no change in a man's government can be rightly made apart from his own consent. He has a basic natural right to consent to moving from a state of nature into a commonwealth, and the purpose of that consent is that he might receive in return a greater security for his life and property. In effect, he trades some of his freedom for the security of the commonwealth (a term which comes from *commonweal*, meaning a common well-being).

Now consider Jefferson's words in the Declaration of Independence, almost as though written by Locke himself:

We hold these truths to be self-evident, that all men are created equal, that they are endowed by their Creator with certain unalienable Rights, that among these are Life, Liberty and the pursuit of Happiness.--That to secure these rights, Governments are instituted among Men, deriving their just powers from the consent of the governed, -- That whenever any Form of Government becomes destructive of these ends, it is the Right of the People to alter or to abolish it, and to institute new Government, laying its foundation on such principles and organizing its powers in such form, as to them shall seem most likely to effect their Safety and Happiness.

Prudence, indeed, will dictate that Governments long established should not be changed for light and transient causes; and accordingly all experience hath shewn, that mankind are more disposed to suffer, while evils are sufferable, than to right themselves by abolishing the forms to which they are accustomed. But when a long train of abuses and usurpations, pursuing invariably the same Object evinces a design to reduce them under absolute Despotism, it is their right, it is their duty, to throw off such Government, and to provide new Guards for their future security.

We can see the influence of Locke in the concepts and language he uses in drafting the Declaration of Independence. Indeed, Locke was the moral foundation of Jefferson's writings, as he himself described it.

I would be remiss if I did not include some of Locke's thoughts regarding God and the Christian faith. Locke truly did not fit into the Anglican world in which he was born. Nor would most Evangelical Christians of today. Locke was severely criticized by the religious authorities of his day because he did not embrace their view of sacramental faith. His was a pure and simple Christian faith.

Locke published another monumental work six years after his *Two Treatises*, this one titled *The Reasonableness of Christianity; as Delivered in the Scriptures* (1695). In it he argued that salvation – eternal life in heaven – is to be had by simple faith in Jesus as the Messiah, the Son of God. Locke wrote,

> *What we are now required to believe to obtain eternal life, is plainly set down in the gospel. St. John tells us, John iii. 36, "He that believeth on the Son, hath eternal life; and he that believeth not the Son, shall not see life." What this believing on him is, we are also told in the next chapter: "The woman said unto him, I know that the Messiah cometh: when he is come, he will tell us all things. Jesus saith unto her, I that speak unto thee, am he. The woman then went into the city, and saith to the men, come see a man that hath told me all things that ever I did: is not this the Messiah? and many of the Samaritans believed on him for the saying of the woman, who testified, he told me all that ever I did. So when the Samaritans were come unto him, many more believed because of his words, and said to the woman, We believe not any longer, because of thy saying; for we have heard ourselves, and we know that this man is truly the Saviour of the world, the Messiah." John iv. 25, 26, 29, 39, 40, 41, 42.*

Much of *The Reasonableness of Christianity*, is devoted to explaining the simple message of personal salvation – faith in Jesus Christ the Messiah and Son of God. Indeed, the personalized phrase "our Saviour" is used by Locke 350 times in the book in referring to Jesus Christ. Locke was a true believer in Jesus Christ as his own Savior. However, Locke had another important message contained in this writing, just in case he might not have made it clear enough before in his *Two Treatises:* a complete confirmation of the idea of natural law, and the idea that natural law comes ultimately from no other law giver – only through the Savior of mankind, Jesus Christ.

> *Though yet, if any one should think, that out of the sayings of the wise heathens before our Saviour's time, there might be a collection made of all those rules of morality, which are to be found in the Christian religion; yet this would not at all hinder, but that the world, nevertheless, stood as much in need of our Saviour, and the morality delivered by him. Let it be granted (though not true) that all the moral precepts of the gospel were known by somebody or other, amongst mankind before. But where, or how, or of what use, is not considered. Suppose they may be picked up here and there; some from Solon and Bias in Greece, others from Tully in Italy: and to complete the work, let Confucius, as far as China, be consulted; and Anacharsis, the Scythian, contribute his share. What will all this do, to give the world a complete morality, that may be to mankind the unquestionable rule of life and manners?...*
>
> *Whatsoever should thus be universally useful, as a standard to which men should conform their manners, must have its authority, either from reason or revelation. It is not every writer of morality, or compiler of it from others, that can thereby be erected into a law-giver to mankind; and a dictator of rules, which are therefore valid, because they are to be found in his books; under the authority of this or that philosopher. He, that any one will pretend to set up in this kind, and have his rules pass for authentic directions, must show, that either he builds his doctrine upon principles of reason, self-evident in themselves; and that he deduces all the parts of it from thence, by clear and evident demonstration: or must show his commission from heaven, that he comes with authority from God, to deliver his will and commands to the world.*
>
> *In the former way, no-body that I know, before our Saviour's time, ever did, or went about to give us a morality.*

> *It is true, there is a law of nature: but who is there that ever did, or undertook to give it us all entire, as a law; no more, nor no less, than what was contained in, and had the obligation of that law? Who ever made out all the parts of it, put them together, and showed the world their obligation? Where was there any such code, that mankind might have recourse to, as their unerring rule, before our Saviour's time? If there was not, it is plain there was need of one to give us such a morality; such a law, which might be the sure guide of those who had a desire to go right; and, if they had a mind, need not mistake their duty, but might be certain when they had performed, when failed in it.*
>
> *Such a law of morality Jesus Christ hath given us in the New Testament; but by the latter of these ways, by revelation. We have from him a full and sufficient rule for our direction, and conformable to that of reason. But the truth and obligation of its precepts have their force, and are put past doubt to us, by the evidence of his mission. He was sent by God: his miracles show it; and the authority of God in his precepts cannot be questioned. Here morality has a sure standard, that revelation vouches, and reason cannot gainsay, nor question; but both together witness to come from God the great law-maker.*

In other words, the power and miracles of Jesus Christ authenticate His message, that he came from God and was the true lawgiver. Also, the revealed Word, the Bible, is beyond question, the only true law of mankind.

It is no wonder that Thomas Jefferson, the author of America's most revered philosophical statement, attributed to his trinity of the three greatest men the world has ever produced – to Bacon, to Newton, to Locke – "as having laid the foundation of those superstructures which have been raised in the Physical and Moral sciences . . ." – especially the moral sciences of John Locke.

Chapter 8
More Giants

We have already looked in some detail at Thomas Jefferson's favorites, and indeed these three men, especially Locke, were admired by all of the founders. But were there other thinkers, philosophers, and writers that the founders looked to?

In the 1970s a study was made of the writings, letters, newspaper articles, political pamphlets, and speeches made during the time leading up to the War for Independence and through the founding of the nation at the close of the century. This study is described by Donald S. Lutz in his 1988 book *The Origins of American Constitutionalism*. Over 15,000 such original sources were considered in this study, and it gives us some good insights into where the thinking originated that culminated in our independence and our unique form of government - what it all was based upon.

The results of that study are not surprising if you understand the mindset and the world view of the founding era. The results are more difficult to accept if you are of the belief that our founding was a secular event by deists and skeptics, and secularists have expended a great deal of energy trying to explain or refute the findings of this study.

The study divided "source" origins from these writers or speechmakers into general categories. These categories were Bible, Enlightenment Thinkers, Whig Politicians, Common Law, and Classical Writers, with a category of *Other* for any source material that didn't fit into the other general categories. Overall, from the 1760s through 1805, the years considered in the study as our founding era, the Bible was the most often quoted source (34%), followed by Enlightenment Thinkers (22%), Whig Politicians (18%), Common Law (11%), Classical Writers (9%), and Other (6%).

Secular critics whine about the study because the study included sermons by religious leaders as well as essays and speeches by politicians. They would have us delete sermon pamphlets from the study as invalid. Sorry, secularists, but that is what people were reading back then. It was from Christian ministers that much of our philosophy of government and independence originated, and that is where the people (and politicians) were getting much of their thinking and all of their world view. Indeed, it would be censorship to exclude the single most fruitful source of thought from the founding era, although censorship is a common practice among liberal secularists today.

Beyond these more general categories of sources, the study was condensed down to individual writers, that is, which "Secular Thinkers" were the most often cited in discussions leading up to our independence and in the development of our organic documents. The four most cited "secular" giants on whom the founders stood were Enlightenment Thinkers: One, Charles Montesquieu (8.3% of all of the documents considered), a French philosopher and writer of the mid-1700s (1689-1755); Two, Sir William Blackstone (7.9%), an English jurist, lecturer, and writer from the mid-1700s (1723-1780); Three, John Locke (2.9%), an English Enlightenment Philosopher and writer from the late 1600s (1632-1704); and Four, David Hume (2.7%), a Scottish Enlightenment philosopher from the mid-1700s (1711-1776). Of these four, all but Hume maintained a Christian world view. He was more of an agnostic at least, and there is reason to believe he may even have been an atheist, and he wrote from that perspective. Number five on the list was the Greek historian Plutarch, the highest scoring classical writer in the study.

If we look more precisely at a timeline of the various stages of the development of our country we see an interesting shift. In the 1760s and early 1770s, the most cited authority was John Locke, from whom we quoted extensively in the previous chapter. After the Declaration of Independence through the development of the U.S. Constitution at the end of the 1780s, Charles-Louis de Secondat, Baron de La Brède et de Montesquieu (generally referred to as simply Montesquieu for obvious reasons) was the most often cited, and by a large margin.

As the founding period progressed however, William Blackstone became the most prominent source of our thinking. Blackstone's influence grew through the revolutionary timeframe, from 1% in the 1760s. That one percent is amazing when we consider that Blackstone's most influential contribution, *Commentaries on the Laws of England*, were not even published until 1766 (Vols. I-III), and not completed until 1768, and these were not printed in America until 1771. Blackstone was cited at 3% of all the citations in the 1770s, and increased to 7% of all citations in the 1780s. Beginning in the 1790s Blackstone is the most cited by a large margin (11%), and he is even more influential in the five years following at 15% from 1800 to 1805, becoming at the turn of the century by far the singular most popular authority of the founding fathers.

Another interesting side-note, as we mentioned above, is the agnostic skeptic David Hume which was cited fourth most (2.7%). Hume became more often cited beginning in the 1790s (6%) and in the 1800-1805 years (5%). Up through the ratification of the Constitution he didn't register above 1%. So, why would the founders refer so often to David Hume in their discussions, a man who held a world view contrary to the founders?

David Barton, in his book *The Jefferson Lies* explains the somewhat frequent citations of Hume in the founders' deliberations.

> *So why Hume? Because the Founders regularly cited him in order to refute his political theories rather than endorse them. John Adams described him as an atheist, deist, and libertine, James Madison placed him among "bungling lawgivers," and John Quincy Adams denounced Hume as "the Atheist Jacobite." Hume and his writings were also roundly criticized by other Founders, including John Witherspoon, Benjamin Rush, and Patrick Henry. But what about Jefferson? If Jefferson was indeed antireligious, then perhaps he would be drawn toward Hume as a kindred spirit. Such was definitely not the case. To the contrary, Jefferson found Hume "endeavoring to mislead, by either the suppression of a truth or by giving it a false coloring." He even regretted the early influence that Hume had once had upon him, candidly lamenting: "I remember well the enthusiasm with which I devoured it [Hume's work] when young, and the length of time, the research, and reflection which were necessary to eradicate the poison it had instilled into my mind."*

Generally speaking, then, the founders cited Montesquieu, Blackstone and Locke in a positive, authoritative way, and they cited Hume predominately as a good "bad example" of secular reasoning, one to be treated with caution.

We can add, then, to the giants of the previous chapter (Bacon, Newton and Locke) the names of Montesquieu and Blackstone as foundational to our thinking. And while those like Jefferson who were scientifically minded derived their science from Bacon and Newton, it is clear from the citations of the founders that it was Locke, Montesquieu, and Blackstone from which our political structure and philosophy came. Locke gave us the philosophical foundation of our independence, Montesquieu gave us the general structure of our Constitution, and Blackstone gave us the foundation of our jurisprudence. Each of these giants wrote from a Judeo/Christian perspective.

In the previous chapter we discussed in some depth the philosophy and world view of John Locke, and we will not duplicate that discussion here. Suffice it to say here that John Locke was the leading thinker behind the decision of the American founders to declare independence, and the authority for that decision was "the laws of nature and of nature's God" as described by Locke.

Once we moved beyond independence in 1776, the founders created a confederacy of States and bound them together by the Articles of Confederation. This loose agreement, as it turned out, was altogether too weak to maintain any united front relative to the powers of Europe, not to mention domestic tranquility. Coming up with a government which would give them the powers necessary to maintain their independence but would also preserve the cherished liberty that each State embraced was the challenge for the Constitutional Convention in Philadelphia in 1787. It was within this context that Montesquieu came to the forefront of the discussion.

Montesquieu's great work, *The Spirit of the Laws* (*De l'esprit des loix*), was a philosophical and historical work, written in French and first published in 1748. It was translated into English and printed in England in 1750. In 1751 it was banned by the Catholic Church. Montesquieu, like most Christian thinkers of the Enlightenment, began his work with a discussion of where laws come from. Concerning Natural Law he wrote, "God is related to the universe as creator and preserver: the laws by which he created all things are those by which he preserves them. He acts according to these rules, because he knows them; he knows them, because he made them; and he made them, because they are relative to his wisdom and power."

Montesquieu's great contribution to the American founding was his concept of separation of powers. Montesquieu wrote that there are basically three functions of government, whether that government be a monarchy, a republic, or of some other type. In any type of government, the citizens must be free from the fear of government in order for liberty to exist. In a nutshell, he explained his greatest idea.

> The political liberty of the subject is a tranquility of mind arising from the opinion each person has of his safety. In order to have this liberty, it is requisite the government be so constituted as one man need not be afraid of another. When the legislative and executive powers are united in the same person, or in the same body of magistrates, there can be no liberty; because apprehensions may arise, lest the same monarch or senate should enact tyrannical laws, to execute them in a tyrannical manner.
>
> Again, there is no liberty if the judiciary power be not separated from the legislative and executive. Were it joined with the legislative, the life and liberty of the subject would be exposed to arbitrary control; for the judge would be then the legislator. Were it joined to the executive power, the judge might behave with violence and oppression.
>
> There would be an end of every thing, were the same man, or the same body, whether of the nobles or of the people, to exercise those three powers, that of enacting laws, that of executing the public resolutions, and of trying the causes of individuals. Most kingdoms in Europe enjoy a moderate government, because the prince, who is invested with the two first powers, leaves the third to his subjects.
>
> In Turkey, where these three powers are united in the sultan's person, the subjects groan under the most dreadful oppression. In the republics of Italy, where these three powers are united, there is less liberty than in our monarchies. Hence

> their government is obliged to have recourse to as violent methods, for its support, as even that of the Turks; witness the state-inquisitors, and the lion's mouth into which every informer may at all hours throw his written accusations.
>
> In what a situation must the poor subject be, under those republics! The same body of magistrates are possessed, as executors of the laws, of the whole power they have given themselves in quality of legislators. They may plunder the state by their general determinations; and, as they have likewise the judiciary power in their hands, every private citizen may be ruined by their particular decisions.
>
> The whole power is here united in one body; and, though there is no external pomp that indicates a despotic sway, yet the people feel the effects of it every moment. Hence it is that many of the princes of Europe, whose aim has been leveled at arbitrary power, have constantly set out with uniting, in their own persons, all the branches of magistracy, and all the great offices of state.

Citing Montesquieu repeatedly, the founders developed a system which separated the government into these three distinct functions, executive, legislative, and judicial, and it disallowed any individual from exercising power in more than one of these areas so as to prevent any overlap of government roles. We all learned about this division in early civics classes and came to know it by the name <u>Separation of Powers</u>, as one of the foundation stones of our liberty.

Montesquieu wrote profusely about corruption in its different forms, and corrupting influences that come with power, especially when held in overlapping government functions. So, while Montesquieu was a great Christian historian and philosopher, his primary contribution to the American founding was more one of mechanics than a philosophical one. It is from Montesquieu that we get the very structure of the American government, and the most important safeguard against tyranny and corruption.

A rising star during the 1760s was Sir William Blackstone. His *Commentaries on the Laws of England*, generally to be known simply as *Blackstone's Commentaries*, provided both the philosophical and the mechanical framework for America's legal system. Blackstone's Commentaries were the product of a series of lectures that Sir William Blackstone delivered at the University of Oxford between 1753 and 1766, augmented by several pamphlets on various aspects of English law. The lectures and pamphlets were so popular that Blackstone was persuaded to commit them to book form so that posterity might benefit from his wisdom. *Blackstone's Commentaries* were popular in England, but they were even far more popular in America, likely because they, in no uncertain terms, exactly fit the American founding philosophy.

As we pointed out, by the early 1800s, Blackstone had become the most cited authority by our founders. However, his influence did not end with the founding era. The *Blackstone Commentaries* became the primary legal textbooks of our colleges throughout the 1800s and even into the 1900s. When Abraham Lincoln was asked by a young, would-be attorney how to prepare for a career in law, Lincoln advised him to read Blackstone, then adding, "read it twice." In other words, if you want to master the law, you need to master Blackstone.

Concerning the *Blackstone Commentaries* the *Encyclopedia Britannica* (2001) had this to say:

> *In England and America the Commentaries became the basis of University legal education... The fame of Blackstone in the 19th century was greater in the United States than in Blackstone's native land. After the American Revolution the Commentaries was the chief source of the knowledge of English Law in the American Republic.*

Blackstone, like Locke and Montesquieu wrote at length about where the ultimate authority for law comes from. And Blackstone spelled it out in as detailed a way as any of the enlightenment thinkers. He began his *Commentaries* by explaining where the source of municipal authority comes from – the source of all legal authority, the foundation of all man-made laws, God.

Blackstone was so universally embraced by our founders and ultimately by American academia throughout the 1800s that his writings provide the best reflection of how our country viewed things through the first 150 years of the republic. Because of its length I will not include here the entire quote of *Blackstone's Commentaries; Vol 1, Section Two, OF THE NATURE OF LAWS IN GENERAL,* but please take the time to review this remarkable document in one of the many places it is available online.

Let me paraphrase and summarize Blackstone's thoughts: God created everything. He established laws on which His Creation depended. Some of these laws were physical and some of these laws were moral in nature. These laws reflect the character of the Creator. Every man on earth at all times is subject to these laws. Since the Creator is good, His laws result in our well-being to a greater degree than any law we could devise ourselves. (See Chapter 6, *Natural Law*)

> Man, considered as a creature, must necessarily be subject to the laws of his creator, for he is entirely a dependent being... For as God, when he created matter, and endued it with a principle of mobility, established certain rules for the perpetual direction of that motion; so, when he created man, and endued him with freewill... he laid down certain immutable laws of human nature, whereby that freewill is in some degree regulated and restrained... These are the eternal, immutable laws of good and evil, to which the creator himself in all his dispensations conforms...
>
> As therefore the creator is a being, not only of infinite *power*, and *wisdom*, but also of infinite *goodness*, he has been pleased so to contrive the constitution and frame of humanity, that we should want no other prompter to inquire after and pursue the rule of right, but only our own self-love, that universal principle of action. For he has so intimately connected, so inseparably interwoven the laws of eternal justice with the happiness of each individual, that the latter cannot be attained but by observing the former... This law of nature... is of course superior in obligation to any other. It is binding over all the globe in all countries, and at all times; no human laws are of any validity, if contrary to this...

The natural, moral laws from God we can discover generally through reason, but our reason is very imperfect because of the fall of Adam and our resulting sin nature. For that reason, God gave us revealed law, the Bible, in case there might be questions concerning exactly what a particular natural, moral law is.

> But every man now finds the contrary in his own experience; that his reason is corrupt, and his understanding full of ignorance and error. This has given manifold occasion for the benign interposition of divine providence... to discover and enforce its laws by an immediate and direct revelation. The doctrines thus delivered we call the revealed or divine law, and they are to be found only in the holy scriptures.
>
> Upon these two foundations, the law of nature and the law of revelation, depend all human laws; that is to say, no human laws should be suffered to contradict these....

This is what our founders believed, and this is how our laws were established throughout the entire 1800s. To put things into perspective, Blackstone taught us that because of our imperfect reasoning ability, the law of revelation, the Bible, takes precedence over our reasoned opinion of what natural law is. Under Blackstone, then, and under the founders world view, the Bible was the highest law in the land, since "no human laws should be suffered to contradict" the Bible and natural law.

So the laws of these many Christian States were patterned exclusively after the Holy Scriptures. Where else but the Bible do we get human laws which compel us to treat one day of the week differently (actually we get that in the *U.S. Constitution* too), also known as "blue laws?" And on what basis were laws enacted against blasphemy against the God of the Judeo/Christian beliefs, or even our laws against adultery, homosexuality, bestiality, and pornography? Incidentally, since our laws were based upon the laws of the Bible, the Ten Commandments have a special place in our founding philosophy, because our founders believed them to be the highest, most authoritative laws of the land against which no human laws could be valid. This excellent condensation of our highest law should have just as prominent a place today.

Blackstone wrote that human laws should not be allowed to contradict the Bible. Our Founders agreed. And so it was at the beginning.

Chapter 9
Federalism, Safeguard of our Liberties

It is interesting to watch the argument back and forth questioning whether or not America was founded as a Christian nation, or, as secularists claim, as a secular nation. The question itself is problematic, perhaps even silly, as I shall try to explain.

It may surprise you when I say that I do not believe America was founded specifically to create a Christian nation, nor was it established to create a secular nation. Rather, it was founded to protect and to preserve what the States already were at the time, and to preserve their right to remain what they wanted to be, not to create within the States something new or different.

It should be remembered that prior to July 4, 1776, the States were not States at all but rather were 13 colonies subject to the laws of England. With the Declaration of Independence, each individual colony declared that it was now assuming all of the prerogatives of statehood.

What does that mean? A State is traditionally the fundamental unit of government sovereignty. For instance, the word "State" was used to describe the nations of Europe. England was a State. France was a State. Spain was a State. The colonies declared in 1776 that each one had every right to assume those exact same sovereign powers for themselves, or as they expressed it, "... to assume among the Powers of the Earth, the separate and equal Station to which the Laws of Nature and of Nature's God entitle them ..." that being statehood. They were each free and independent to act, trade, borrow, or declare war in pursuit of their own interests.

Thus the "united States of America" (I use the capitalization as used in the original Declaration), as an entity, was founded by thirteen sovereign

States which came together to continue their long, ongoing discussion about how to enhance their mutual welfare and security. Notice that the word "united" was in lower case, whereas the word "States" was capitalized. Note that it was not "the united State" (singular). The word "united" is an adjective which simply described the status of these States with respect to each other, not part of an official title. As sovereign, each State had every right to decide how much of its sovereignty it was willing to give up to the new general government in order to gain the benefits of union.

In America, following The American War of Independence, we were thirteen separate States, but it could be argued that we were one nation in that our backgrounds, language, values, and goals were all complimentary. And we had developed a working alliance among the States which gave us the resources and manpower to achieve victory over England. Thus Lincoln, at Gettysburg, was able to say that our Declaration of Independence "brought forth on this continent a new nation" but not a new State.

So the critical questions from this discussion are these: One, did the States in 1787 intend to create something new or different from what they already were with respect to religion? Two, were the States originally founded as Christian States? The answer to the first question is that in 1787 there was nothing in the new proposed Constitution which sought to change the essential philosophy or religious practices of any of the States. Moreover, as a condition of ratification of the U.S. Constitution by several of the States, the first ten amendments were added to prevent the federal government from impacting the essential domestic character of these individual, sovereign States.

To say that the U.S. Constitution established a secular government, or to say that it established a Christian government, either one, betrays a misunderstanding of American history. It *established* neither, and it was designed to establish neither. Rather it was designed to preserve something already in existence. It was designed to provide the security needed to preserve the nature and philosophy of the Christian States that gave it authority in the first place.

Some secularists argue that while the Declaration of Independence dealt with aspirational religious philosophy, when it came to drafting the U.S. Constitution the religious ideas of the former document were set aside in deference to a new, secular government. Nothing could be further from the truth.

As we mentioned in Chapter 5, the Declaration of Independence and the U.S. Constitution were meant to go hand in hand without contradiction or conflict. To use the church analogy, one is a *statement of faith,* the other is the *bylaws*. And they could hardly be in conflict as 36 of the delegates at the 1787 Constitutional Convention (65%) had also been delegates to the 1776 Continental Congress which drafted the Declaration of Independence in the first place. Their philosophy of government hadn't changed in the meantime.

While there are hints as to the philosophy represented by the U.S. Constitution, there is a lack of detail in the Constitution which makes the question at hand viable in the first place. To put it another way, it could be argued that there is nothing in the U.S. Constitution which would have changed the essential nature of the States had the States been entirely secular. Nor was there anything in the U.S. Constitution which would have changed the essential nature of the States had the States been entirely Christian, which they were.

Justice Antonin Scalia once described the U.S. Constitution as, "... a practical and pragmatic charter of government." He went on to write, "If you want aspirations, you can read the Declaration of Independence ... there is no such philosophizing in our Constitution." That is not to say that the founders had no philosophy of government. Clearly they did, and that philosophy was contained in the Declaration of Independence, the ultimate, organic document which can now be found on page one, volume one of the United States Code, in the section, "The Organic Laws of the United States."

(Just a side note here: it is important to point out that later generations under the leadership of President Abraham Lincoln sought to firm up the federal philosophy by making clear that the Declaration of Independence has the force of law. As we mentioned in Chapter 5 in the discussion of the Declaration of Independence, beginning with the resolution which made Nevada our 36th State in 1864, all States since that time, including Alaska and Hawaii, have been required by enacting resolution to form a State government which is "not repugnant to the U.S. Constitution or to the principles of the Declaration of Independence.")

The Declaration supported the right for individuals to enter into a social compact and to end it when they saw fit, and sovereign States had that same right of entering into social compacts with other States. So, these independent, sovereign States joined together in 1782 into a formal social compact which they believed would provide them greater individual security. This compact was called the Articles of Confederation. The Articles of Confederation were weak, lacking the power to compel taxation and mutual military support, among other things.

When the States recognized that the compact of 1782 was not producing the desired security or improvement in general welfare, they decided to rewrite the compact in a way that would produce a stronger government. (That is, twelve of the States decided to do that. Rhode Island did not support or attend the Constitutional Convention, which was their right as a sovereign State. Moreover, Rhode Island did not join the Union until a year after the U.S. Congress had assembled in early 1789.) The product of that rewrite in 1787 was a new proposed constitution, and it was submitted to the States in the fall of 1787 for their acceptance. After a lengthy series of debates throughout all of the thirteen States, the new constitution was ratified by the required number of States (nine) in mid-1788.

The original purpose of the U.S. Constitution was not to establish this or that particular philosophy. The States each individually already had a philosophy of government. Generally speaking, while the U.S. Constitution contained some general outlines concerning domestic commerce to avoid trade wars between the States, the U.S. Constitution mostly dealt with international issues. It was to provide mutual support and protection to each individual State, backed up by the other States. Ultimately, the purpose of the Bill of Rights was to tie the hands of the new federal government so that the nature and philosophy of the individual States would not be impacted. In the end, the First and Tenth Amendments reserved issues of religion as State issues. It prohibited the federal government from trespassing at all into this critical area.

In 1789 a new federal government was organized under this new constitutional structure, the same U.S. Constitution that has governed the actions of the United States Government since that inaugural year. This new U.S. Constitution represented a greater, more binding social compact in which the States yielded yet more of their sovereignty than they had yielded under the Articles of Confederation. This was done in exchange for achieving greater security and welfare. Although the States were willing to voluntarily yield a bit more of their sovereignty, they refused to yield any more than was absolutely necessary to achieve their goals.

In entering any social compact, the parties have the right to spell out in advance what they are willing to forfeit by way of prerogatives, and what they are not willing to forfeit. The Bill of Rights, and especially the Tenth Amendment, was the States' way of making sure that in establishing this federal government, they were limiting that new government from altering the fundamental character and philosophy that all the States held individually.

The States wanted as little change as possible from what was, at that time, well established in each of the States. These States were not all identical with respect to religion. In 1776 each State treated religious issues differently from the others. Some of the States had official State religions – some did not. Some of the State constitutions required their legislators to be exclusively Christian – some did not. When the States came together in 1789 under the new U.S. Constitution, one of the main concerns was to insure that this new federal government did not replace or usurp individual State sovereignty in a number of respects, but particularly with respect to religion.

We have already discussed in Chapter 2 the U.S. Supreme Court Decision, *Church of the Holy Trinity v. United States* (1892). Beyond what has already been discussed, however, it is important to point out that nearly all of the citations used in this decision to support the conclusion of the Court that "this is a Christian nation" come from charters, commissions, and constitutions of the various colonies and States as they were being formed. Yes, the court decision does refer to the Declaration of Independence and the U.S. Constitution as being in complete agreement with the State documents, but most of the discussion in this decision refers to the founding of specific States.

As we saw in Chapter 2, the history section in this important Court decision begins with the original commission given to Christopher Columbus. It goes on to cite the Virginia Charter of 1606 and the Mayflower Compact of 1620, applying to that early Plymouth Colony. Then the Court quotes from the *Fundamental Orders of Connecticut* (1639), and then goes on to say, "If we examine the constitutions of the various States, we find in them a constant recognition of religious obligations. Every Constitution of every one of the forty four States contains language which, either directly or by clear implication, recognizes a profound reverence for religion, and an assumption that its influence in all human affairs is essential to the wellbeing of the community."

The Court decision then goes on to cite quotations from the constitutions of Illinois, Indiana, Maryland, Massachusetts, Mississippi, and Delaware, each quote illustrating the unique Christian character and doctrine of the founders of these several States. Delaware, in particular, merits special notice because the court quotes from the oath which was required by the Delaware Constitution of 1776 which required this declaration of its legislators, "I, A. B., do profess faith in God the Father, and in Jesus Christ His only Son, and in the Holy Ghost, one God, blessed for evermore, and I do acknowledge the Holy Scriptures of the Old and New Testament to be given by divine inspiration."

Indeed, the constitutions of all of the other States could have been quoted by the Supreme Court just as well. One State constitution in particular, not quoted in the 1892 court decision, bears quoting here, that of the State of Pennsylvania, dated 1776 shortly after declaring independence. The reason this particular State constitution is especially relevant to this discussion is that the President of the convention which authored the Pennsylvania Constitution of 1776 was none other than that great "deist" and "secularist" Benjamin Franklin, and he was one of the drafters of the language that was ratified.

In Section 10 of the Pennsylvania Constitution of 1776, the section which outlined the duties of the State legislators, there was an oath prescribed for these elected lawmakers, "And each member, before he takes his seat, shall make and subscribe the following declaration, viz: I do believe in one God, the creator and governor of the universe, the rewarder of the good and the punisher of the wicked. And I do acknowledge the Scriptures of the Old and New Testament to be given by Divine inspiration."

We could indeed examine each and every State constitution right from 1776 through the early 1900s, and we would find that each one was founded on an explicitly and exclusively Christian world view and philosophy. To the Supreme Court it was the clear evidence of history that the philosophy and world view of the people of each of the States was exclusively Christian, and it is this evidence which gave the Supreme Court in 1892 the foundation to conclude, "This is a Christian nation."

So did these sovereign States during the ratification process in 1787-88 decide to give up their exclusively Christian views and form a secular government? NO, a thousand times NO. Many of the States ratified the new Constitution reluctantly, fearful that the new federal government, without added protections, would change the essential nature of their liberty, their sovereignty, and their religion.

We will not go into a lengthy discussion of the debates between Federalists and anti-Federalists that raged in speeches and newspaper articles, resulting in the Federalist Papers and the Anti-Federalist Papers. Suffice it to say, the States were concerned that the new Constitution was silent in too many areas, and they feared this silence would be seized upon by future tyrants in the federal government to rule over the States and rob them of their sovereignty and liberty. They were willing to give up some of their prerogatives, but not all or even most of them.

So State-by-State, there were heated debates concerning how much of a State's sovereignty could be traded for increased welfare and security. The ratifying conventions in the thirteen States were the culmination of these internal debates.

Following is a table of the original thirteen States in the order in which they ratified the new Constitution, along with the population (1790 census) of each of these States. Note that three of the early resolutions received no negative votes at all.

State	Ratification Date	Vote	Population	Rank
1 Delaware	December 7, 1787	30-0	59,000	13
2 Pennsylvania	December 12, 1787	46-23	434,000	2
3 New Jersey	December 18, 1787	38-0	184,000	9
4 Georgia	January 2, 1788	26-0	83,000	11
5 Connecticut	January 8, 1788	128-40	238,000	8
6 Massachusetts	February 6, 1788	187-168	379,000*	4
7 Maryland	April 28, 1788	60-11	320,000	6
8 South Carolina	May 23, 1788	149-73	249,000	7
9 New Hampshire	June 21, 1788	57-47	142,000*	10
10 Virginia	June 26, 1788	89-79	748,000	1
11 New York	July 26, 1788	30-27	340,000*	5
12 North Carolina	November 21, 1789	197-77	394,000	3
13 Rhode Island	May 29, 1790	34-32	69,000	12

* The 1790 census separates Vermont from New York and New Hampshire even though it was not yet a State. Vermont's 1790 population of 86,000 would have originally been split between New York and New Hampshire, giving both higher population totals. Also the District of Maine's 97,000 people in 1790 would have been citizens of Massachusetts even though the census treated Maine as a separate entity. These considerations would have made Massachusetts the second most populous State. It is possible that New York would have ranked the fourth most populous.

In late 1787 and early 1788 some States seemed in a hurry to ratify and did so with little debate on what might be problematic about the proposed Constitution. And so, by early January, 1788, first Delaware, then Pennsylvania, New Jersey, Georgia, and Connecticut had ratified the new Constitution. Their ratifying resolutions were short and contained little detail with no instructions to the new federal government on addressing any perceived shortcomings in the proposed Constitution.

However, after the first five States ratified quickly, a number of vital questions were being raised by the anti-Federalists which began to challenge the thinking of the remaining States. What if the suggested lack of specificity in the proposed Constitution eventually led to an all-powerful federal government that changed the character of the States and completely nullified their sovereignty? These questions, and the accompanying debates, began to slow the ratification process in the remaining States.

On February 6, 1788, the ratifying convention in Massachusetts passed a resolution which ratified the new Constitution, but the Massachusetts document was different from those of the preceding five States. This resolution recommended important changes in the text of the new Constitution. Massachusetts wanted a bill of rights added to the Constitution, and, specifically, the sovereignty of the individual States established in writing. "The Convention do therefore recommend that the following alterations & provisions be introduced into the said Constitution. *First,* That it be explicitly declared that all Powers not expressly delegated by the aforesaid Constitution are reserved to the several States to be by them exercised..." the proposals began.

This represented the beginning of what would follow – seven of the remaining eight States, Massachusetts being the first, would propose similar amendments which would later result in the Tenth Amendment to the U.S. Constitution. The Tenth Amendment reads, "The powers not delegated to the United States by the Constitution, nor prohibited by it to the States, are reserved to the States respectively, or to the people."

This Tenth Amendment was perhaps the single most important amendment in the view of the States. It is the only one of the first ten amendments which was suggested by a majority of the States in their ratifying documents, States representing over 65% of the total population. It came from a general caution and mistrust of government, and was designed to prevent future mission creep on the part of the federal government, which they knew could result in lost sovereignty for the States.

Under their social compact values, the States were willing to grant to the new federal government only the powers it needed to bring added security and increased welfare – no more than that. Beyond that, these sovereign States had no intention of allowing the federal government to usurp their sovereignty or alter their essential character.

After Massachusetts' ratifying resolution was passed on February 6, 1788, only one State failed to include conditions in their ratifying documents, that being Maryland, April 28, 1788, which was the next State to ratify the new Constitution. Following Maryland, all six of the remaining

States included the Massachusetts concept of preserving sovereignty in their ratifying resolutions.

South Carolina followed Maryland on May 23, 1788, with this statement, "This Convention doth also declare that no Section or paragraph of the said Constitution warrants a Construction that the States do not retain every power not expressly relinquished by them and vested in the General Government of the Union." It is important to note that this statement in the South Carolina resolution appears in the "Whereas" section, before any individual amendments are proposed in the "Resolved" section (which were three), clearly implying that this idea was not only being suggested as an amendment but also should be considered a "whereas" self-evident, obvious, existing truth. (At that time James Madison, Alexander Hamilton, John Jay, and others were actively assuring the States that this was indeed already the case, and that the new document should be read as assuming that to be the proper, indeed the only, interpretation.)

After South Carolina came the New Hampshire resolution on June 21, 1788, New Hampshire suggested twelve specific amendments to the new Constitution, but the very first was this, "First That it be Explicitly declared that all Powers not expressly & particularly Delegated by the aforesaid Constitution are reserved to the several States to be, by them Exercised."

A pattern was developing in which the States were in effect saying, "We are willing to go along with the new Constitution, but we expect some changes – guarantees of personal and State rights to be added to the text, and we expect the federal government to respect limits on its powers in deference to our State retained sovereignty. We do not trust the future to a document silent on our most important concerns. We declare at the outset that it must be understood by the federal government that, in matters where the new Constitution is silent, the federal government shall have no jurisdiction whatsoever. The States have ultimate authority unless the Constitution clearly reserves a specific power to the federal government."

New Hampshire was the first State to suggest that freedom of religion should also be incorporated into the Constitution, and a basic right to bear arms should be recognized. Thereafter, all four remaining State resolutions contained all three of these features: that the federal government's power be limited to what is specifically listed in the text of the Constitution, the remaining powers to be retained by the States or the people; that the right to worship according to one's conscience must be recognized; and that the right to bear arms must be recognized. (Also, beginning with Massachusetts, followed by five of the remaining States, several other rights were enumerated and urged on the federal government. Those would be later combined into our Bill of Rights, the first ten amendments to the U.S. Constitution.)

New Hampshire would be the ninth State to ratify. While the new Constitution required nine States to ratify before it would take effect, everyone knew that the larger States, Virginia and New York, held the key. If these large, influential States did not ratify, the new plan would not work despite its having been technically ratified by enough States. Both supporters and opponents focused much of their energies on trying to swing support in these two populous States where the decision to ratify was in doubt in both instances. A majority of the delegates in both Virginia and New York initially opposed ratification.

Virginia was the tenth State to ratify, on June 26, 1788. Its ratifying resolution began with a lengthy statement on the meaning of natural rights and of the concept of the social compact. The section began,

> *We the Delegates of the People of Virginia duly elected in pursuance of a recommendation from the General Assembly and now met in Convention having fully and freely investigated and discussed the proceedings of the Federal Convention and being prepared as well as the most mature deliberation hath enabled us to decide thereon Do in the name and in behalf of the People of Virginia declare and make known that the powers granted under the Constitution being derived from the People of the United States may be resumed by them whensoever the same shall be perverted to their injury or oppression and that every power not granted thereby remains with them and at their will: that therefore no right of any denomination can be cancelled abridged restrained or modified by the Congress by the Senate or House of Representatives acting in any Capacity by the President or any Department or Officer of the United States except in those instances in which power is given by the Constitution for those purposes . . .*

Following a lengthy background section was a list of proposed amendments to the new Constitution which began, "First, That each State in the Union shall respectively retain every power, jurisdiction and right which is not by this Constitution delegated to the Congress of the United States or to the departments of the Federal Government."

The story of the Virginia ratification is significant. It featured the Federalists, led by James Madison, arguing for the new Constitution and arguing strongly against any amendments. The anti-Federalists, led by Patrick Henry, George Mason, and James Monroe, argued against ratification of the new Constitution, which they regarded as a threat to their State sovereignty. They argued that the Constitution was fatally vague and contained no guarantees for the States or the people that the federal government would not eventually become all powerful and tyrannical, depriving the people of their God-given rights and the States of their sovereignty.

The lengthy ratifying resolution with its demanded alterations demonstrates the serious reservations the State had in signing on to the new government. The opening statement made it clear that Virginia believed that it was more *loaning* powers to the federal government rather than granting them.

A month later, July 26, 1788, New York weighed in with a similar statement, expressing exactly the same concerns as those expressed by Virginia a month earlier,

> *That all Power is originally vested in and consequently derived from the People, and that Government is instituted by them for their common Interest Protection and Security.*
>
> *That the enjoyment of Life, Liberty and the pursuit of Happiness are essential rights which every Government ought to respect and preserve.*
>
> <u>*That the Powers of Government may be reassumed by the People, whensoever it shall become necessary to their Happiness;*</u> *[emphasis added] that every Power, Jurisdiction and right, which is not by the said Constitution clearly delegated to the Congress of the United States, or the departments of the Government thereof, remains to the People of the several States, or to their respective State Governments to whom they may*

> have granted the same; And that those Clauses in the said Constitution, which declare, that Congress shall not have or exercise certain Powers, do not imply that Congress is entitled to any Powers not given by the said Constitution; but such Clauses are to be construed either as exceptions to certain specified Powers, or as inserted merely for greater Caution.

The New York resolution then advances twenty specific amendments to the new Constitution enumerating the rights which would later be incorporated into the Bill of Rights. Following this lengthy declaration of rights, the resolution concludes with an implied conditional support,

> Under these impressions and declaring that the rights aforesaid cannot be abridged or violated, and that the Explanations aforesaid are consistent with the said Constitution, And in confidence that the Amendments which shall have been proposed to the said Constitution will receive an early and mature Consideration: We the said Delegates, in the Name and in the behalf of the People of the State of New York Do by these presents Assent to and Ratify the said Constitution.

New York was serving notice that its ratification was conditional by declaring that these powers they were giving up to the federal government "may be reassumed by the People, whensoever it shall become necessary to their Happiness. . . And in confidence that the Amendments which shall have been proposed to the said Constitution will receive an early and mature Consideration... Do by these presents Assent to and Ratify the said Constitution."

So three of the largest, most influential States (Massachusetts, New York, and Virginia), upon which this entire proposed new government hinges, have made statements to a similar effect. They have gone on record as expecting the new government to amend the Constitution to *at least* limit the powers of the federal government to those specifically described in the document, and no more. In effect they were saying, "We are sovereign States. We agree to form a social compact made up of sovereign States, but forfeiting our sovereignty is not part of the deal."

After New York's ratification, the remaining two States, North Carolina (the third largest according to the 1790 census) and eventually Rhode Island, both created similar resolutions of ratification, each incorporating expectations for specific amendments similar to New York and Virginia. Both States expressed demands which included protection of State sovereignty, religious freedom, and the right to bear arms, among many other specified rights.

The North Carolina ratification was not finalized until after the new government was formed, November 21, 1789. The Bill of Rights, though proposed by that time, had not been approved by the States. So, North Carolina weighed in on the subject, beginning with a declaration of twenty specific rights that they believed were God-given and inalienable, the first three of which are as follows,

Declaration of Rights

1st That there are certain natural rights of which men, when they form a social compact, cannot deprive or divest their posterity, among which are the enjoyment of life, and liberty, with the means of acquiring, possessing, and protecting property, and pursuing and obtaining happiness and safety.

2d. That all power is naturally vested in, and consequently derived from the people; that magistrates therefore are their trustees, and agents, and at all times amenable to them.

3d. That Government ought to be instituted for the common benefit, protection and security of the people; and that the doctrine of non- resistance against arbitrary power and oppression is absurd, slavish, and destructive to the good and happiness of mankind.

These twenty declared rights were followed by a list of proposed amendments to the new Constitution which North Carolina believed were necessary to secure the list of declared rights. The list begins with what now would be a familiar theme, they being the sixth State to specify that this was of utmost importance to them.

AMENDMENTS TO THE CONSTITUTION

I. THAT each State in the union shall, respectively, retain every power, jurisdiction and right, which is not by this constitution delegated to the Congress of the United States, or to the departments of the Federal Government.

Rhode Island was the only State refusing to participate in the Constitutional Convention of 1787, and they were the last State to ratify the new Constitution. They did not join the union until their ratifying resolution was executed on May 29, 1790. In manner similar to the other States that ratified later in the process, Rhode Island began their resolution with a list of 18 enumerated rights, beginning as follows,

In That there are certain natural rights, of which men when they form a social compact, cannot deprive or divest their posterity, among which are the enjoyment of Life and Liberty, with the means of acquiring, possessing and protecting Property, and pursuing and obtaining happiness and safety.

2d That all power is naturally vested in, and consequently derived from the People; that magistrates therefore are their trustees and agents, and at all times amenable to them.

3d That the powers of government may be reassumed by the people, whensoever it shall become necessary to their happiness...

The eighteen enumerated rights were followed by a list of proposed amendments, very similar to the preceding three States: Virginia, New York, and North Carolina. Like several of the other States, Rhode Island left no question that its chief concern was State sovereignty, and like a majority of the States, it intended to limit the powers of the federal government to those specifically granted by the Constitution,

AMENDMENTS

1st The United States shall guarantee to each State its sovereignty, freedom and independence, and every power, jurisdiction and right, which is not by this constitution expressly delegated to the United States.

I believe it is safe to say that the five States which ratified the Constitution quickly and without much comment were just as concerned with State sovereignty as those who were slower to ratify. The first five that ratified rather quickly did so with the assurances of James Madison, Alexander Hamilton, and other leading Federalists that the new Constitution was not a threat to their rights or sovereignty. As Madison argued in January, 1788, in Federalist #45:

> *The powers delegated by the proposed Constitution to the Federal government, are few and defined. Those which are to remain in the State governments are numerous and indefinite. The former will be exercised principally on external objects, as war, peace, negotiation, and foreign commerce; with which last the power of taxation will, for the most part, be connected. The powers reserved to the several States will extend to all the objects which, in the ordinary course of affairs, concern the lives, liberties, and properties of the people, and the internal order, improvement, and prosperity of the State.*

Madison was explaining that under the proposed Constitution federal powers were *"few and defined"* and were essentially related to foreign affairs – *"... external objects, as war, peace, negotiation, and foreign commerce; with which last the power of taxation will, for the most part, be connected."* He went on to reassure the States that it was the intent of the new Constitution that the States' powers would be *"numerous and indefinite,"* and that these powers extended to virtually all domestic issues – *"... all the objects which, in the ordinary course of affairs, concern the lives, liberties, and properties of the people, and the internal order, improvement, and prosperity of the State."*

However, as the debate intensified through 1788, the anti-Federalists had raised significant enough questions so that States that ratified later put those concerns into their ratifying resolutions. They wanted Madison's assurances in writing. They wanted to make sure that the federal government served as their protector at the international level, not their dictator at the domestic level.

I have written all of this to illustrate that originally the Constitution provided for limited federal authority, that State sovereignty was a jealously guarded property right by all of the States. Further, within that State sovereignty resided matters pertaining to religion, and the States made that just as clear in their ratifying resolutions. Beginning with New Hampshire, and every State thereafter, the States made it clear that religion was within their jurisdictions, not the federal government's jurisdiction, and, as such, the new Constitution did not establish any particular federal position on religion, but rather a totally hands off approach.

New Hampshire stipulated in its resolution that religion was off limits to the federal government. Its list of proposed amendments included this, "Eleventh, Congress shall make no Laws touching Religion, or to infringe the rights of Conscience." Simply put, religion is our business, not that of the federal government. Bear in mind that New Hampshire, at the time of its ratification, had an official State church.

Virginia followed, having a bit more to say on the subject. Virginia's resolution began with a lengthy list of rights that they considered to be out of the reach of government, and the last of these enumerated rights, which it recommended to be incorporated into the Constitution, was as follows, "Twentieth, That religion or the duty which we owe to our Creator, and the manner of discharging it can be directed only by reason and conviction, not by force or violence, and therefore all men have an equal, natural and unalienable right to the free exercise of religion according to the dictates of conscience, and that no particular religious sect or society ought to be favored or established by Law in preference to others."

Years earlier, Virginia had come to the decision that there would be no religious preference within their State (no State church), and they wanted to make sure the new government did not alter that State decision. Virginia was a leader among the States in asserting that the federal government should take a hands-off approach to religion. Other States had far different views of the States' proper role in religion, as we shall see following.

New York followed Virginia with the following similar statement, "That the People have an equal, natural and unalienable right, freely and peaceably to Exercise their Religion according to the dictates of Conscience, and that no Religious Sect or Society ought to be favoured or established by Law in preference of others." Again, New York was saying that religion was a matter of conscience, outside the reach of government. They were also saying, in agreement with Virginia, that "establishment" meant preferring one Christian denomination over others.

North Carolina was next with this similar statement disconnecting religion from government, "That religion, or the duty which we owe to our Creator, and the manner of discharging it, can be directed only by reason and conviction, not by force or violence, and therefore all men have an equal, natural and unalienable right to the free exercise of religion according to the dictates of conscience, and that no particular religious sect or society ought to be favoured or established by law in preference to others." While North Carolina had previously disestablished the Anglican Church as its State church, it still prohibited non-Protestants from serving in office. This is an example of how the term "religion" was used synonymously at that time with Protestant Christianity.

Lastly, Rhode Island similarly weighed in, "That religion, or the duty which we owe to our Creator, and the manner of discharging it, can be directed only by reason and conviction, and not by force or violence, and therefore all men, have an equal, natural and unalienable right to the free exercise of religion, according to the dictates of conscience, and that no particular religious sect or society ought to be favoured, or established by law in preference to others."

What all of these proposed amendments were advocating is that religion (Christianity) is a cherished right, three of these ratifying resolutions refer to it as a "duty we owe to our creator." They all seem to imply that personal religion is a matter outside of the sphere of government, particularly the federal government. However, in practice, several of the States took an active role in religious matters.

Each State was unique in its own handling of religious issues. Where government had any role at all in religion, it was exclusively a State role, not a federal role, and that would remain true for the next 150 years. Several States at the time of the Constitution's ratification process maintained State supported Christian denominations, and Virginia had just disestablished its State church (Anglican) two years earlier.

In 1788 when Georgia ratified the new *U.S. Constitution,* the Anglican Church was the official State church of Georgia. Georgia's constitution was amended the following year to eliminate preference to any denomination. When New Hampshire ratified the Constitution in 1788, its official State church was the Congregational Church, which it disestablished in 1790. However, the New Hampshire Constitution required that any State legislator must be a member of the Protestant faith, and that remained State law until 1877.

Established by Quakers, Pennsylvania never had an official State church. However, as we have already seen, in 1787 when it ratified the new Constitution, before taking office, as provided in the Pennsylvania Constitution of 1776, State legislators were required to subscribe to this oath, "I do believe in one God, the creator and governor of the universe, the rewarder of the good and the punisher of the wicked. And I do acknowledge the Scriptures of the Old and New Testament to be given by Divine inspiration." That oath did not change with the ratification of the federal Constitution.

The official church of North Carolina was the Anglican Church until the North Carolina Constitution of 1776 disestablished the Anglican Church. Nonetheless, the North Carolina Constitution allowed only Protestant Christians to serve in office through 1835, and thereafter until 1876 only Christians (Protestants and Catholics) could serve in office. To this day the North Carolina Constitution prohibits from serving in office "any person who shall deny the being of Almighty God."

When South Carolina ratified the U.S. Constitution in 1788, their official State supported church was the Anglican Church. South Carolina disestablished the Anglican Church in 1790. When Connecticut ratified the U.S. Constitution in 1788, its State church was the Congregational Church, and that continued to be the case until 1818. The U.S. Constitution did not change that fact.

Similarly when Massachusetts ratified the U.S. Constitution in 1788, citizens were required to attend and to financially support their local parish church. According to the Massachusetts Constitution of 1780, the parish church had to be a Protestant church of a denomination in good standing with the State, and the denomination for each parish church was selected by the people of each individual town. These churches were for the most part Congregational, which came from the original Massachusetts Bay Puritans. Full freedom of religion was granted to the citizens of Massachusetts beginning in 1824, but the parish system of State support for local churches continued for another ten years after that.

An interesting article in the Salem [MA] Gazette, dated December 26, 1814, demonstrates how local governments, working in concert with the Massachusetts legislature, enforced Sabbath laws in the Massachusetts towns. Evidently the enforcement of Sabbath laws had become lax, and the Massachusetts legislature had issued a report to the towns urging them to enact local ordinances to enforce compliance with keeping the Sabbath holy. In response, Essex County called a convention of the towns of the county to which 43 delegates from 13 of the towns responded. The convention unanimously voted to take action against Sabbath violators, and to send a delegate to Concord in Middlesex County the following month to advise them of the Essex County actions and to encourage a similar response in that county. The convention had all the marks of a religious assembly with State backing. (See Appendix D)

The point of all of this is that the States all jealously guarded their sovereignty and authority over religious matters. When the Congress convened under the structure of the new U.S. Constitution in the Spring of 1789, one of the first tasks that U.S. Representative James Madison set his mind to do was condensing the State ratifying resolutions into a series of amendments to the Constitution. The House originally proposed seventeen amendments and referred them to the Senate. The Senate condensed those into twelve Amendments, and the House in turn, with a few minor edits, concurred with the Senate's version.

On September 25, 1789, Congress agreed on a set of 12 possible amendments to the Constitution and submitted them to the States for their consideration. The document submitted to the States contained a preamble, as did most similar documents of that day, which introduced the amendments and their purpose:

Congress of the United States
begun and held at the City of New-York, on
Wednesday the fourth of March, one thousand seven hundred and eighty nine.

> **THE** *Conventions of a number of the States, having at the time of their adopting the Constitution, expressed a desire, in order to prevent misconstruction or abuse of its powers, that further declaratory and restrictive clauses should be added: And as extending the ground of public confidence in the Government, will best ensure the beneficent ends of its institution.*

Congress was acknowledging that it must respond to the directives of the State ratification resolutions or it risked surviving no better than the Articles of Confederation. And what had the States demanded? Limitations. Limitations on the powers of the federal government. Assurances that their domestic sovereignty remained intact. As to the title "Bill of Rights" subsequently bestowed on the first ten amendments, the phrase "Bill of Rights" appears nowhere in the document, and it is clearly a misnomer. The first ten amendments are, as described in their own preamble, rather a Bill of "Restrictive Clauses" – limitations on federal power in deference to State power.

The title, "Bill of Rights," is also a misnomer in another sense. It implies that our Constitution contains a list of citizen rights which flow to us from the federal government. Nothing could be further from the truth. The States understood that rights come from God, and that it was their role and duty to recognize and protect God-given rights. In no sense did our founders believe that this was a list of rights. NO – it was a list of restrictions directed at the federal government – a "No Trespassing" sign as it were.

Although Madison originally opposed any such amendments, he recognized that not to address these State concerns was to risk the new federal government coming apart before it had a chance to succeed, and that the States would go their separate ways. Assuring the States that they retained their sovereignty and their religious prerogatives was part of that grand social compact that more clearly defined what the parties were agreeing to.

The third proposed amendment in the "Bill of Rights" document (later ratified as the First Amendment) incorporated several of the States' enumerated rights into one amendment. It dealt with freedoms of religion, speech, press, peaceable assembly, and petitions of redress of grievances – all to be State issues under the new government.

The two religion clauses can be summarized and paraphrased by one simple sentence. Religion is not a federal issue, period. This amendment says "Congress [specifically and exclusively the U.S. Congress] shall make no law respecting an establishment of religion, or prohibiting the free exercise thereof."

Now let's blend that with the language of the twelfth proposed amendment in the "Bill of Rights" document (eventually ratified as the Tenth Amendment): "The powers not delegated to the United States by the Constitution, nor prohibited by it to the States, are reserved to the States respectively or to the people."

This is the proverbial belt and suspenders assurance to the States. It not only says that the federal government must take a hands-off approach regarding religion because there is nothing in the Constitution which allows the federal government to involve itself in religious matters (Tenth Amendment), it also, in terms that cannot possibly be misconstrued by any reasonable person, specifically prohibited the federal government from being involved in religion at all (First Amendment) i.e. "Congress shall make no law..."

There is no wiggle room here. The First Amendment is not a statement of what the people may do or what the federal government may do with respect to these issues. No, rather the First Amendment is a clear statement of what the federal government may NOT do, relative to these several areas. "Congress shall make no law..." The federal government under the Constitution may not interfere in religion or any other of these specified liberties. And if Congress can make no law, then certainly the federal courts have no federal law with which to assert their own parochial interests.

When it came to religion, the U.S. Constitution itself changed absolutely nothing within the States, and the First and the Tenth Amendments were designed so that nothing in the States religious practices would or could ever be impacted by the federal government. Once implemented, the U.S. Constitution had no impact on the States' religious practices until the Constitution began to be misapplied by the federal courts in the mid-1900s.

Clearly the States, at the beginning, practiced both the establishment of religion as well as, one State in particular, Massachusetts, requiring attendance at particular churches. Virginia on the other hand took a hands-off approach to religious matters, but it did not bother or affect Virginia if Massachusetts took a more proactive role, and vise versa. That was their prerogative as sovereign States. While at the beginning some States had established State churches and one at least regulated to some degree the exercise of religion, the new U.S. Constitution didn't change any of that. Those were issues for the States to decide, and the States believed their citizens' rights were more secure with them than turning them over to a federal government.

Thus began this unique "balance of power" between the States and the federal government. The federal government was there to provide security, mostly of a military nature. It was there to provide a common diplomatic presence in the states across the ocean. It was there to assure fair trade between the disparate States with their individual economic strengths and weaknesses. And it was there to provide a court system to protect States from injustices from each other and to protect citizens from injustices from sources outside their own States. The States specifically, intentionally, and forcefully protected their individual sovereignty over their own domestic issues.

One of the great things about federalism, each individual State acting as an independent laboratory of democracy, is that States tend to gradually adopt what seems to be working in the other States, and so rather than drifting apart in their actions they tend to become more similar as they copy what is perceived as successful. By the mid-1800s, every State was pursuing generally the same course that Virginia had set in 1777 with Thomas Jefferson's first draft of *The Virginia Statute for Religious Freedom*. This statute did not make Virginia non-Christian nor did it make Virginia secular, nor did it make Virginia neutral with regard to religious practice. To the contrary, as we discussed in Chapter 4, the University of Virginia, while established as a non-sectarian college in 1819, was still a Christian institution from the beginning, as were most State colleges through the 1800s.

Throughout the late 1700s and the 1800s, the States made many changes regarding religious support and practices. However, it must be pointed out that all these changes were made by States exercising their own sovereign powers without any federal coercion. At that time the federal government knew its place. The States retained that exclusive power over religious issues right through the 1800s and well into the 1900s. Indeed, religious instruction in public schools continued right into the mid-1900s in many States.

In a short paragraph, the federal government was originally formed, just as the Declaration of Independence describes the purpose of forming any government, "... to secure these rights, governments are instituted among men, deriving their just powers from the consent of the governed." The federal government was a social compact, a voluntary alliance, formed by the consent of thirteen sovereign States. It was established to provide the added security which would ensure each State's ability to maintain its own individual Christian society, its individual governing philosophy, and that singular Christian world view upon which the States were all individually founded.

Why did the States demand that the federal government stay out of domestic issues, particularly, issues of religion? It was based upon their distrust of mankind. The whole notion of separation of powers is based upon the Biblical truth, "The heart is deceitful above all things, and desperately wicked: who can know it?" Jeremiah 17:9 Or, said another way, "who can comprehend the human heart and its propensity for evil?" Our founders believed all mankind were born in sin with tendencies to commit evil. By retaining the sovereign powers of the individual States, the States were trying to prevent an all-powerful federal government from emerging. They did not trust the eventual possibilities of nation-wide tyranny. In hindsight, they were absolutely right.

The 1994 edition of the American Heritage Dictionary defines the word *firewall* as "1. A fireproof wall used as a barrier to prevent the spread of fire." That is all. In the 1990s and before, the word was not used much in general conversation except perhaps by building contractors. However, if you look at a more recent dictionary you will see an added definition of *firewall*. The 2002 version of the American Heritage College Dictionary adds this second definition, "2. *Computer Science* Any of a number of security schemes that prevent unauthorized users from getting access to a network or that monitor transfers of information to and from the network."

Today we all know what a firewall is. That second definition, generally unknown in the 1990s, is the idea that we are most likely to think about when the word firewall is used today. All of our computers have firewalls – features that are designed to keep out intruders and unauthorized snoopers from our files. And as we have become accustomed to the concept of a firewall in our computers, the word has taken on a new proliferation of usage, many protective devices today now being described as a firewall of protection for this or that threat. The new federal government was widely regarded as a potential threat to State sovereignty, and the Tenth Amendment was devised as **the firewall** against federal intrusion and overreach.

Thus a federal system was created where the general government was granted certain specified but limited powers, mostly in war and foreign affairs. The States, at their insistence, through the Tenth Amendment, retained every other power enjoyed by a sovereign State. This critical separation of powers was designed to generally keep the federal government out of domestic issues, the States believing themselves fully capable of deciding such things for themselves, at least, as properly and efficiently as any federal government. Such rights and prerogatives were too critical and too precious to be entrusted to any other entity. And in so doing, the States were able to retain their unique Christian character for the first 175 years of the Republic.

Part III
The Corruption of the Original Ideal

"We have no government armed with power capable of contending with human passions unbridled by morality and religion. Avarice, ambition, revenge, or gallantry, would break the strongest cords of our Constitution as a whale goes through a net. Our Constitution was made only for a religious and moral people. It is wholly inadequate for the government of any other."
President John Adams - Letter to the Officers of the First Brigade of the Third Division of the Militia of Massachusetts (11 October 1798)

Adams understood that if America were made up of a substantial population holding a different world view from the original theistic beliefs of the founders, our system of government and the liberties contained therein would not last.

Chapter 10
Judicial Tyranny

In November, 1972, the people of Michigan went to the polls to elect their President, their representatives, and to express their will on whether abortion should be legal in Michigan. The people of Michigan voted overwhelmingly, by a 3-1 margin, not to allow abortions in Michigan other than to save the life of the mother. However, two months later, January, 1973, the U.S. Supreme Court issued the *Roe v. Wade* decision, effectively making abortion "legal" throughout the country, even in Michigan, despite the expressed conscience of the people of Michigan.

What happens when a country like ours, embracing a theistic world view, begins to abandon that world view where honesty and integrity are paramount? A number of things happen, all of them bad. One thing that happens as men shed their Christian based self-restraint is that more and more of our leaders give in to the temptation to expand their sphere of power, and as that power increases more unscrupulous leaders enlarge that sphere of power even more. This is what President Adams meant when he said, "We have no government armed with power capable of contending with human passions unbridled by morality and religion. Avarice, ambition, revenge, or gallantry, would break the strongest cords of our Constitution as a whale goes through a net." Nowhere is this more evident than in the federal courts.

Over the past sixty years America has experienced a systematic uprooting of our Christian heritage and our moral character. We can put blame in a number of areas: our pulpits, Hollywood, the media, and academia, but our federal judges have been largely responsible for this dramatic shift, or at least the speed at which it has taken place. While much of America's decline into various evils has had multiple causes, the one factor which "greased the skids," so to speak, was the changing of our laws through the judiciary – changes which could have never happened legislatively within our constitutional, federal system.

In Chapter 9 we discussed the Federalist nature of our country and the development of the Federalist system, and the *firewall*, which was the Tenth Amendment. We established the history of the ratification process of 1787-1790, as the States debated acceptance or rejection of the new U.S. Constitution. We established that the powers of the federal government were limited by the States through the amendments that followed that ratification process (the Bill of Restrictive Clauses – that is the Bill of Rights), and that the *States* had exclusive jurisdiction over the protections of the fundamental rights of citizens.

We established that among the first ten amendments to the Constitution, the Tenth Amendment, the *firewall*, was the one which a majority of the States specifically demanded during that ratification process. Once again, the Tenth Amendment is clear in its intent, "The powers not delegated to the United States by the Constitution, nor prohibited by it to the States, are reserved to the States respectively, or to the people." In other words, the powers of the federal government are *limited*, they are not to exceed those powers which are specifically laid out within the U.S. Constitution. Anything trespassing beyond those specified powers are an intrusion into State jurisdiction.

James Madison, writing in Federalist #45, argued that the liberties of the people are secured, not by the federal government, but by each individual State:

> *The powers delegated by the proposed Constitution to the Federal government, are few and defined. Those which are to remain in the State governments are numerous and indefinite. The former will be exercised principally on external objects, as war, peace, negotiation, and foreign commerce; with which last the power of taxation will, for the most part, be connected. <u>The powers reserved to the several States will extend to all the objects which, in the ordinary course of affairs, concern the lives, liberties, and properties of the people, and the internal order, improvement, and prosperity of the State.</u>* [Emphasis added]

But beyond the notion that domestic powers were to be retained by the States, of the three branches of the federal government, the judicial branch was regarded by the founders as being the least powerful and the least one that we needed to worry about in terms of our rights. Alexander Hamilton in Federalist #78 describes it thus:

> *Whoever attentively considers the different departments of power must perceive, that, in a government in which they are separated from each other, the judiciary, from the nature of its functions, will always be the least dangerous to the political rights of the Constitution; because it will be least in a capacity to annoy or injure them. The Executive not only dispenses the honors, but holds the sword of the community. The legislature not only commands the purse, but prescribes the rules by which the duties and rights of every citizen are to be regulated. The judiciary, on the contrary, has no influence over either the sword or the purse; no direction either of the strength or of the wealth of the society; and can take no active resolution whatever. It may truly be said to have neither force nor will, but merely judgment; and must ultimately depend upon the aid of the executive arm even for the efficacy of its judgments.*

So what happened? How did we get from the States' jealously guarded jurisdiction and powers over their own liberties and domestic issues, to the modern era where the federal government rules supreme over every State law and custom, and where the Christian character of the States has been under constant attack, all but snuffed out by an all-powerful judicial branch? We got here through the wholesale corruption of our federal judicial system.

As you might expect, none of this happened overnight. Actually it happened over a period of several key decades in the mid-1900s. The mid-1900s revealed just how easily and thoroughly the Constitution can be transformed without bothering with the constitutional amendment process. This chapter gets rather deep into the legal weeds, and I recognize there is a danger in this discussion of either boring you to death or of having your eyes glaze over and getting lost in the brush. Please bear with me because it is only in understanding what has happened in the courts that there is any hope in correcting it.

The Two Pillars of Judicial Activism

There are two basic pillars on which modern courts have built liberal, judicial activism. One of those pillars, *judicial review*, presumably goes back to the founding era and has no constitutional basis. The other pillar, a novel, purely philosophical view of the Constitution, suggests that the Constitution is a *living, breathing document* meant to change with the times. Neither of these two views are to be found in the Constitution itself.

Judicial Review:

In 1803, the U.S. Supreme Court issued the famous *Marbury v. Madison* decision. If liberals have a Magna Carta, this is it. According to liberals, *Marbury v. Madison* established the legal precedent of *judicial review*. According to President Thomas Jefferson, it did no such thing. *Judicial review* is simply the idea that it is the job of the U.S. Supreme Court to decide whether a law or an executive order is constitutional. According to liberal ideology, the federal courts have the power to declare any law or custom anywhere in the United States to be unconstitutional, even, perhaps especially, State laws.

The presidential election of 1800 was particularly nasty, pitting old friends against each other. President John Adams of the Federalist Party was being challenged by Thomas Jefferson and his Democratic Party. Jefferson, writer of the Declaration of Independence and former Governor of Virginia and ambassador to European princes, was a popular choice against the dour, stodgy Adams who embraced a more powerful role for the federal government. Jefferson believed in a far more democratic, limited form of government than the Federalists, with the States having the ultimate domestic powers.

The election was vicious and was not ultimately decided until February of 1801. Jefferson won. Adams and the lame duck legislature, mostly Federalists, rushed through the Judiciary Act of 1801 which created several new federal court positions, and Adams immediately packed these new positions with new Federalist Party appointees. In fact there were a total of 58 judicial positions created by the Judiciary Act of 1801. One of those new appointments went to William Marbury a wealthy, staunch Federalist from Maryland.

However, there was little time to actually get the commissions delivered to all of these new appointees prior to Jefferson taking office in March, 1801. A majority of the commissions were delivered. However, upon taking office, Jefferson ordered that the commissions, which had not already been delivered to these new appointees, be voided. William Marbury, who was one such appointee who had not received his commission, challenged Jefferson's action in the Supreme Court which was made up mostly of Federalists. Marbury sued to force James Madison, the new Secretary of State, to give him his commission, hence *Marbury v. Madison*.

The Federalist leaning Supreme Court didn't exactly rule with courage. They ruled that Madison's refusal to hand over the new commissions was illegal and correctable. However, they also ruled that a part of the Judicial Act of 1789 was unconstitutional, that part which allowed Marbury to file suit in the Supreme Court in the first place. This gave them a convenient out which enabled the Court to have its cake and eat it too. The decision ordered absolutely nothing, but at the same time they were able to give the new administration a verbal black eye without doing anything which might create a constitutional crisis or support the Democratic Party.

This decision, in contrast to the historic weight given to it by liberals, was nothing more than a partisan spat. It bears mentioning that Marbury never became a judge, and President Jefferson rightly pointed out that this decision and approach to the law was not backed by any constitutional authority. It was more a tantrum to demonstrate displeasure at the Jeffersonians for winning the election and for not facilitating President Adams' attempt to pack the courts with Federalists. It was the judicial equivalent of black robes taking to the streets.

The idea of judicial review was virtually non-existent after 1803 until *Dred Scott v. Sandford*, 1857, and we all know the repercussions which that decision had on the northern States. Some States simply declared the decision null and void, and resolved not to abide by it. Ultimately, it led to the great American Civil War. The intention of the Constitution is for judges to apply democratically passed laws to particular cases, not to question the laws themselves.

I am ambivalent concerning whether judicial review is ever warranted by the courts. While the Constitution gives the courts no such authority, the argument can be made, "Well, someone has got to do it!" and some laws are clearly unconstitutional. And clearly, Hamilton in *Federalist #78* seemed to assume that judicial review was an obvious power of the judiciary. Can we leave it to the legislature or the executive branches to voluntarily operate within the Constitution? Obviously not according to Hamilton.

Hamilton's view of judges, as expressed in *Federalist #78*, seems to be that because they are appointed for life, they will have no political motives, a presumption which has proven ridiculously false. Can we trust the Supreme Court to correct that overreach on the part of the legislative or executive branches? Definitely not. The courts have demonstrated that they cannot be trusted to refrain from rewriting the Constitution for their own philosophical or political purposes, as we shall see later in this chapter. I would suggest a review which is closer and more subject to the people – perhaps a majority of the States themselves – as the better place for review of constitutionality.

While we may argue whether *judicial review* is constitutional, we all must agree that the courts used it sparingly, if not judiciously, the first 150 years of the republic. Today the wholesale use of *judicial review* is often the first resort rather than the last; the federal courts declaring just as soon as a law is passed or as soon as virtually anything happens that they do not like, that it is unconstitutional. This presumed authority to be the ultimate arbiter of what is or is not constitutional has become the ultimate tool against the States and the other branches of government. Nowhere is this type of judicial power or judicial review contemplated or even hinted at in the U.S. Constitution.

However, despite the absence of any clear constitutional authority for such a level of court power, liberals have made *Marbury v. Madison* the cause celebre of American judicial education. Any school history book will now devote a large section to explaining to students, through *Marbury v. Madison*, how the courts always have the last word over the other branches of government.

As I mentioned in a previous chapter, even our government is involved in this liberal propaganda. On my last visit to the National Archives in Washington, D.C., I observed a new display in the rotunda right next to the founding documents. This new display was evidently added to perpetuate this extra-constitutional theory. In a glass casement right next to our founding documents was a special display honoring this one obscure court case, most worshipped by liberals, *Marbury v. Madison*. Liberals do not dare let us forget that the Supreme Court always has the last word. And supposedly, in the view of the powers at the National Archives, the foundation for that legal tradition is as important to the Republic as the Declaration of Independence.

The "Living Constitution":

Over the past 75 years the second pillar upon which judicial activism rests was developed as a governing philosophy among liberals. That view is that the Constitution is a *living, breathing document,* its meaning changeable with the times. Or in other words, the Constitution may have meant one thing a hundred years ago, but today we have progressed and society has progressed and become more modern and complex, so that the Constitution must be allowed to shift with the times – its meaning to change with the society. Exactly, who decides *how* the Constitution has changed since one hundred years ago or even ten years ago? Federal judges, of course. Not the States, not legislators who are elected and accountable.

Of all the new ideas and doctrines of judges over the past 100 years, this idea that the Constitution is a *living, breathing* document is the most pernicious. It is the refuge for those who do not believe in our Constitution in the first place. This tragic theory is the ultimate in Constitutional rejection. It is the polar opposite of original intent, or "originalism." Like the date stamp on a gallon of milk, the meaning of the Constitution lasts no longer than the generation that drafted it. After that limited timeframe the Constitution becomes whatever we want it to be.

The *Living Constitution* idea is the ultimate resort for those who do not like the clear principles contained in the U.S. Constitution. If they did like the original Constitution there would be no need for demanding something different. President Barack Hussein Obama, a self-styled "constitutional scholar" spoke frequently about how the Constitution was mainly a restriction on what the federal government could/should do, and although he didn't like that, he was right about the intended restrictive nature of the Constitution when it comes to government powers. He did not like those limits, preferring instead more latitude to expand government powers. This *Living Constitution* notion gives judges the ability to ignore constitutional limits and the latitude to concoct new rights or governmental powers which, they claim, prior generations had no need for.

The choice of the words "living" and "breathing" has almost spiritual overtones – even evoking a reverential response, much as the Bible, the Word of God, declares of itself that it is "alive and powerful." However, unlike sacred Scripture, this *living, breathing* doctrine is the ultimate repudiation of the U.S. Constitution. It renders its historic meaning void and imparts to it no meaning or any meaning, whatever the mood of the courts.

This would be true of Supreme Court Justice Ruth Bader Ginsberg who evidently does not much like the U.S. Constitution as written. Asked her opinion when Egypt was writing a new constitution and was looking for a pattern to follow, her response was that she certainly would not view the U.S. Constitution as a good template for a modern constitution. She urged Egypt to look elsewhere.

Conveniently for her, Justice Ginsberg can use her *living, breathing document* philosophy to make the Constitution say whatever she wants it to say, all its deficiencies notwithstanding. If the Constitution means nothing for sure then it means nothing at all, and that is exactly as liberals like it. America has always been characterized as "A nation of laws and not men" when describing where judicial authority lies. Embracing the idea of a "living Constitution" allows liberal elitists to rule as a nation of men, and not laws.

During the ratification hearing on Supreme Court nominee Neal Gorsuch, this contrast could not have been clearer. Sen. Patrick Leahy (D-Vt.), the ultimate liberal voice, described the traditional view that the Constitution actually means what it says as a judicial philosophy "outside the mainstream" and perhaps even dangerous.

> Judge Gorsuch appears to have a comprehensive originalist philosophy. It's the approach taken by jurists such as Justice Scalia, Justice Thomas, or former Judge Bork. While it has gained some popularity within conservative circles, originalism, I believe, remains outside the mainstream of modern constitutional jurisprudence. It's been twenty-five years since an originalist has been nominated to the Supreme Court. Given

> *what we've seen from Justice Scalia and Justice Thomas, and Judge Gorsuch's own record, I worry that it goes beyond being a philosophy and becomes an agenda.*

Liberal Senator Dianne Feinstein added her voice in an attempt to stop the advancement of this judge that actually believes in the Constitution.

> *Judge Gorsuch has also stated that he believes judges should look to the original public meaning of the Constitution when they decide what a provision of the Constitution means. This is personal, but I find this originalist judicial philosophy to be really troubling. In essence, it means that judges and courts should evaluate our constitutional rights and privileges as they were understood in 1789. However, to do so would not only ignore the intent of the Framers, that the Constitution would be a framework on which to build, but it severely limits the genius of what our Constitution upholds.*
>
> *I firmly believe the American Constitution is a living document intended to evolve as our country evolves. In 1789, the population of the United States was under four million. Today, we're 325 million and growing. At the time of our founding, African-Americans were enslaved. It was not so long after women had been burned at the stake for witchcraft, and the idea of an automobile, let alone the internet, was unfathomable.*
>
> *In fact, if we were to dogmatically adhere to originalist interpretations, then we would still have segregated schools, and bans on interracial marriage. Women wouldn't be entitled to equal protection under the law, and government discrimination against LGBT Americans would be permitted. So I am concerned when I hear that Judge Gorsuch is an originalist and a strict constructionist.* [I think it goes without saying that none of the bogeymen she alludes to are required by an originalist view of the Constitution.]

These two Senators could not be more wrong, and it would take pages to debunk the numerous factual errors contained in these two statements. Apparently, factual errors are not a concern to relativists when arguing for unlimited liberal power. And never mind that the original Constitution has been amended 27 times to allow it to change as the people believe it needs to be changed. These senators understand that their liberal agenda has no chance of advancing through the democratic process, and that advancing abortion, secularism, and homosexuality can simply be done by just five like-minded judges, whereas amending the Constitution to allow for this liberal agenda requires the agreement of thirty-eight states and would be politically impossible.

In my view and in the view of Abraham Lincoln (as we shall discuss) and of the founders, the meaning of the Constitution *as originally intended* does not ever change from its original words and intent unless amended. If we truly had a *living, breathing* Constitution, then there would be no real reason for the amendment process found in Article V of the U.S. Constitution. For our protection the amendment process is, and was intended to be, a difficult challenge, the rationale being that the entire nation, not just a noisy few, must agree on a proposed change before that change is implemented.

Two New Legal Doctrines – The Sky is the Limit

Even with *judicial review* and the *living, breathing document* philosophy, words still have specific meanings, and those meanings have their limits. For example, you can view the phrase "a brown cow" in its literal form, and you can give it a fairly wide range of possible meanings. A cow, for instance, certainly means at least cattle. However, giving it a broader application, it might represent any number of species including buffalo, elk, moose or even an elephant. Also within the word brown could be included a great variety of shades from almost black to very light tints. But there is no way you could make the phrase "a brown cow" to apply to horses or swine, and you certainly could not make those words to mean "a flying unicorn" unless you were able to write in some very broad rules of interpretation which would allow for that sort of mischief. Words have meaning.

From the 1920s through the 1940s liberal, federal judges did just that. They began to flirt with two new legal theories which would give them broad latitude for interpreting the Constitution in ways that the founders could never have imagined. These two legal doctrines are *incorporation* and *substantive due process*. I will explain both in detail later in the chapter. <u>First, though, it must be understood that both of these novel judicial doctrines are drawn from an overly broad reading of the Fourteenth Amendment to the U.S. Constitution</u>, originally ratified by the States in 1868. Therefore it is necessary that we first understand the historical context and intended scope of the Fourteenth Amendment.

Early Supreme Court decisions of the late 1800s – early 1900s saw no conflict between the Fourteenth and Tenth Amendments. The court applied the Fourteenth Amendment strictly and narrowly as it was originally intended by the States. This strict application continued for at least 60 years following the ratification of the Fourteenth Amendment – two entire generations.

However, beginning in the 1920s and extending through the 1940s the Supreme Court, in complete defiance of the Tenth Amendment, began to develop the self-serving legal doctrine that the Fourteenth Amendment in 1868, interpreted broadly, gave the federal courts virtually unlimited power over the States.

At least two of the greatest liberal legal minds of the early 1900s were able to see the terminus of this road. In *Baldwin v. Missouri*, 1930, Justice Oliver Wendell Holmes wrote a dissenting opinion against a decision in which the Supreme Court overturned the application of a Missouri State law which provided for inheritance taxes on assets held in Missouri by persons residing outside of Missouri. The Court struck down the Missouri law, replacing the clear reading of the law with their own preferences. Justice Holmes wrote, with Justice Louis Brandeis concurring:

> *I have not yet adequately expressed the more than anxiety that I feel at the ever increasing scope given to the Fourteenth Amendment in cutting down what I believe to be the constitutional rights of the States. As the decisions now stand, I see hardly any limit but the sky to the invalidating of those rights if they happen to strike a majority of this Court as for any reason undesirable. I cannot believe that the Amendment was intended to give us* carte blanche *to embody our economic or moral beliefs in its prohibitions. Yet I can think of no narrower reason that seems to me to justify the present and the earlier*

> decisions to which I have referred. Of course, the words "due process of law," if taken in their literal meaning, have no application to this case, and, while it is too late to deny that they have been given a much more extended and artificial signification, still we ought to remember the great caution shown by the Constitution in limiting the power of the States, and should be slow to construe the clause in the Fourteenth Amendment as committing to the Court, with no guide but the Court's own discretion, the validity of whatever laws the States may pass.

We will later explain how federal judges justified that expansive interpretation of the Fourteenth Amendment through these two novel legal theories, but before we do, a brief history of the Thirteenth, Fourteenth, and Fifteenth Amendments is in order here.

The Thirteenth (1865), Fourteenth (1868), and Fifteenth (1870) Amendments were passed in the immediate aftermath of the Civil War to deal with slavery issues. The Thirteenth Amendment specifically abolished slavery; the Fourteenth Amendment guaranteed that persons of color, including former slaves, were U.S. Citizens and equal under the law with white people – that they enjoyed the same rights within a State as every other U.S. Citizen within that State; the Fifteenth Amendment guaranteed the right to vote to all persons regardless of race.

The applicable text in the Fourteenth Amendment reads as follows:

> Section 1. All persons born or naturalized in the United States, and subject to the jurisdiction thereof, are citizens of the United States and of the State wherein they reside. No State shall make or enforce any law which shall abridge the privileges or immunities of citizens of the United States; nor shall any State deprive any person of life, liberty, or property, without due process of law; nor deny to any person within its jurisdiction the equal protection of the laws."

These three amendments were not originally adopted by the States to change the jurisdictions of State and federal government, as the Supreme

Court promptly affirmed shortly after passage. They were not adopted by the States to give the federal government any new, general authority over State laws or local customs or to solve presumed inadequacies of federal powers. They were designed rather to eradicate slavery and to guarantee that all people, regardless of race, were treated under State laws like everyone else was treated.

The Fourteenth Amendment established, first, that former slaves and their children were now American citizens and citizens of their respective States. It changed State laws only to the extent that State laws did not recognize citizenship of former slaves or sought to treat them differently from other citizens. The obvious intent was to simply make existing laws equal in their application to all citizens within the States, regardless of their race, color, or their prior servitude. The purpose of the Fourteenth Amendment was *never* to give the courts new powers or jurisdiction over long-existing State laws.

At this point it would be good to understand what the law actually is or is not. Does the Fourteenth Amendment mean what it was originally intended to mean, or does it mean whatever we can get it to mean by taking broad language out of its historical context and torturing that language until it says what we want it to say? Can a brown cow become a horse, or indeed, a flying unicorn? Clearly, the Supreme Court, from the 1870s through the first two decades of the twentieth century, believed the Fourteenth Amendment meant something far different than the federal courts declare it to mean today – generations after it was adopted.

Abraham Lincoln in one sentence described what the law means – what *any* law means, dispelling any notions of a *living, breathing* Constitution in his time. In terms of the law, Lincoln was a brilliant scholar. He had a unique talent for boiling things down to their clear substance. In his first inaugural address, Lincoln sought to reassure the southern States that he would abide by the law – that it was not his intention to change the clear meaning of the Constitution. He said:

> *... There is much controversy about the delivering up of fugitives from service or labor. The clause I now read is as plainly written in the Constitution as any other of its provisions:*

> "No person held to service or labor in one State, under the laws thereof, escaping into another, shall in consequence of any law or regulation therein be discharged from such service or labor, but shall be delivered up on claim of the party to whom such service or labor may be due."
>
> It is scarcely questioned that this provision was intended by those who made it for the reclaiming of what we call fugitive slaves; and **the intention of the lawgiver is the law**. . . [emphasis added]

With that succinct eight-word statement, "the intention of the lawgiver is the law," Lincoln was telling the South that he understood what the Constitution originally intended and that he was willing to abide by it even though he did not agree with it. The language was clear and, more importantly, the original intent of the law was clear. Lincoln explained what the law is and what it is not. Lincoln clearly was an originalist.

If there had ever been a time in the history of the United States where it might have been considered laudable to deviate from the original intent of a law, to apply a more modern view of the law for the betterment of society, this would certainly have qualified. However, Lincoln understood that the law is not whatever you can make it become. The law is not a *living, breathing* entity. It does not evolve over time. The law is what the lawgiver intended the law to be at the time it was written – nothing more. This is true of any law, regulation, rule, or constitution, and it retains its original meaning until it is lawfully changed.

This "original intent" approach in interpreting laws and amendments was embraced by virtually all of our founding fathers. In 1823 Thomas Jefferson wrote to Supreme Court Justice William Johnson, who he had originally nominated to sit on the court, "On every question of construction, carry ourselves back to the time when the Constitution was adopted, recollect the spirit manifested in the debates, and instead of trying what meaning may be squeezed out of the text, or invented against it, conform to the probable one in which it was passed."

In 1833 Justice Joseph Story in his Commentaries on the Constitution of the United States wrote, "The first and fundamental rule in the interpretation of all instruments [documents] is to construe them according to the sense of the terms and the intention of the parties."

So what do Lincoln's words mean? If you are on a city council and you pass an ordinance, you become the lawgiver of that ordinance and your intention in passing that ordinance is in fact the law. It is hoped that the language of the ordinance would clearly communicate what the intention of the city council is and is not, but often laws and ordinances are worded clumsily so that the full intention of the lawgiver is not obvious without doing a bit of research. The same is true for statutes at the State and federal levels. When a State legislature enacts a law, they become the lawgiver and hopefully the language of that law clearly explains the full intention of the legislature or lawgiver.

Unfortunately, as we saw in Chapter 2 in examining the Alien Contract Labor Law of 1885, it does not always work that efficiently. In any event the lawgiver is the entity(s) which is empowered by law to enact the law in the first place. If it is a city council ordinance, the city council is the lawgiver. If it is a State law, the lawgiver is the State legislature. If it is a federal law the Congress is the lawgiver. But what about a constitutional amendment?

With respect to the Fourteenth Amendment, two questions first must be asked and answered. First, who is the lawgiver? Second, what did the lawgiver intend? The answers to both questions are pretty clear – not difficult to comprehend.

First, who is the "lawgiver" of the Fourteenth Amendment? Article V of the U.S. Constitution provides for amending the Constitution two different ways. One way is for the Congress to recommend to the States specific amendments. The second way is provided as a means for the States themselves, apart from Congress, to initiate the amendment process. Under this clause, if 2/3 of the State legislatures submit a request to Congress for a convention of the States, Congress "shall call a convention for proposing amendments..."

All twenty-seven amendments to the U.S. Constitution thus far have been initiated by Congress itself, but that limited role does not make Congress the lawgiver. The second mode of amending the Constitution has never been done (though in my opinion it needs to be done – neither Congress nor judges are ever going to relinquish their own powers).

However, in either mode of proposing amendments described in Article V, proposed amendments are then referred to all of the States. That ends the role of Congress. If the States do nothing, then the proposed amendment dies.

There are those who argue that an amendment is based on the intent of Congress. And certainly the intent of Congress in the amendment process should not be ignored. But Congress has no power in the amendment process beyond suggesting. Amendments become law only if ratified by ¾ of the States, either by vote of the legislatures or by special conventions within the individual States. Ultimately in amending the Constitution, the States themselves are the lawgivers, not the Congress.

If the Constitution were ever amended through the second method of proposing an amendment, a Constitutional Convention of the States, that amendment would have no congressional fingerprints on it whatsoever – it would be entirely a product of the States. In that event, there would certainly be no way to attribute "lawgiver" status to Congress as it wouldn't even have a power of suggestion as it does in the first mode of proposing amendments. If that were to happen there would not be two types of constitutional amendments, one in which Congress was the lawgiver and one in which the States were. In either mode, *the States are the lawgivers* because the States alone, decide what will or will not be included in the Constitution, and *the intention of the lawgiver is the law.*

So when the States ratified the Fourteenth Amendment, what did they intend? That is the critical question. No other question of meaning is relevant. Did the States intend that the Fourteenth Amendment would effectively repeal the Tenth Amendment, as it is currently interpreted (though never admitted)? Dream on. Today a small handful of States might actually trade their Tenth Amendment sovereignty for liberal judicial activism, but certainly no State in 1868 would have done so and allow that critical *firewall* to be breached (See Chapter 9). No State would have forfeited all of its retained powers to the courts.

In considering what the intention of the States was in ratifying the Fourteenth Amendment, it is easier to arrive at the correct answer by considering what the intention of the lawgiver *clearly was not.* There is a clear Supreme Court precedent for applying law in a manner that recognizes the intention of the lawgiver, and in this precedent we arrive at the intention of the lawgiver by recognizing what that intention was *not*. As we discussed in Chapter 2, the Supreme Court in 1892 used exactly this same logic in rendering an opinion in the *Church of the Holy Trinity* case.

Recall from Chapter 2 that the Church of the Holy Trinity in Manhattan, New York City, had been charged with illegally importing foreign labor because they hired a pastor from England. This violated the clear textual language of the Alien Contract Labor Law of 1885. The broad language of the Alien Contract Labor Law, taken at face value, clearly covered all imported labor:

> *Be it enacted by the Senate and House of Representatives of the United States of America in Congress assembled, that from and after the passage of this act it shall be unlawful for any person, company, partnership, or corporation, in any manner whatsoever, to prepay the transportation, or in any way assist or encourage the importation or migration, of any alien or aliens, any foreigner or foreigners, into the United States, its territories, or the District of Columbia under contract or agreement, parol or special, express or implied, made previous to the importation or migration of such alien or aliens, foreigner or foreigners, to perform labor or service of any kind in the United States, its territories, or the District of Columbia.*

That language is extremely broad and all-inclusive. The Church of the Holy Trinity was charged with violating this law which prohibited all imported foreign labor. If the Court had not understood the intent of Congress, they could (perhaps should) have applied the law to every citizen alike, including ministers of the gospel, because that is what the words in the law seem to say. However, the Court concluded unanimously that such an application was clearly not "*the intention of the lawgiver.*" They asked the rhetorical question,

> *Suppose, in the Congress that passed this act, some member had offered a bill which in terms declared that if any Roman Catholic church in this country should contract with Cardinal Manning to come to this country and enter into its service as*

pastor and priest, or any Episcopal church should enter into a like contract with Canon Farrar, or any Baptist church should make similar arrangements with Rev. Mr. Spurgeon, or any Jewish synagogue with some eminent rabbi, such contract should be adjudged unlawful and void, and the church making it be subject to prosecution and punishment. Can it be believed that it would have received a minute of approving thought or a single vote? Yet it is contended that such was, in effect, the meaning of this statute.

So I would ask a parallel question concerning the Fourteenth Amendment. Suppose the Congress of the United States proposed a new constitutional amendment to the States which repealed the Tenth Amendment and gave the United States Supreme Court unlimited power to repeal or strike down any existing or proposed State law. "Can it be believed that it would have received a minute of approving thought," or that a single State would have ratified it? That is the necessary test in determining what the law is, or at least what the law is not – indeed what the Fourteenth Amendment is not.

In ratifying the Fourteenth Amendment did the States intend that they would forfeit the protections of the Tenth Amendment and all of their exclusive prerogatives in domestic issues to the federal courts? Not a chance. The Supreme Court, until the 1920s at least, recognized that fact. Yet this is how modern federal courts routinely interpret the Fourteenth Amendment today. Today's application of the Fourteenth Amendment by the federal courts is clearly NOT what the States intended, nor would any State have ratified the amendment if they believed it ever would or could be so construed.

The Incorporation Doctrine:

As mentioned earlier, the federal courts have used two novel legal theories since the 1920s to expand the Fourteenth Amendment into the blank check that it has become today. These two legal doctrines are *incorporation* and *substantive due process*. The *incorporation doctrine*, supposedly coming from the due process clause of the Fourteenth Amendment, suggests that the limitations on the federal government contained in the first eight amendments of the Constitution are incorporated by the Fourteenth Amendment to apply to the States as well.

Justice Hugo Black, for instance, in his dissenting opinion in *Adamson v. California* (1947), argued that the Fourteenth Amendment should be construed broadly. To defend that position he argued that it was the intent of Rep. John Bingham, the legislator which drafted the Fourteenth Amendment, that it be interpreted broadly – that the first eight Amendments to the U.S. Constitution be *incorporated* into *State* law. Hence the word *incorporation*. Setting aside for a moment the obvious problem, that Justice Black, 79 years after the Fourteenth Amendment was ratified, understood what was intended better than the Supreme Courts that were contemporary with the Fourteenth Amendment. Let's examine the merits of Black's claim.

In the amendment process under Article V of the U.S. Constitution, if the intent of the States differs from the intent of the legislators who promoted the amendment in the first place, which reading of the law is the proper reading, or said another way, what is the law? The simple answer to that question is, *the intention of the lawgiver (the States) is the law*. It doesn't really matter what the bill drafter intended. It doesn't even matter what the whole Congress intended. Congress can only suggest. It only matters what the States – the lawgiver in this case – intended, and the Fourteenth Amendment means today only what the States intended when it was ratified.

Black argued in 1947 that Bingham's intention back in 1868 was that the Fourteenth Amendment would *incorporate* the first eight amendments of the Constitution to the States. Or, in other words, the words "Congress shall make no law" should be expanded to read "Congress [nor any State] shall make no law."

Under the recent view of the Fourteenth Amendment, the Tenth Amendment is unofficially repealed. Although activist judges continue to give lip service to the Tenth Amendment – they simply never let the Tenth Amendment interfere with their desired application of the Fourteenth Amendment as federal courts in the late 1800s did.

We can see that *incorporation* was not the original intent of the States or the Congress by simply looking at a single instance of congressional history. In 1875, the U.S. Speaker of the House, James G. Blaine, introduced a proposed amendment to the U.S. Constitution which would have *incorporated* the First Amendment religious protections to the States, and which read as follows:

> No State shall make any law respecting an establishment of religion, or prohibiting the free exercise thereof; and no money raised by taxation in any State for the support of public schools, or derived from any public fund therefor; nor any public lands devoted thereto, shall ever be under the control of any religious sect; nor shall any money so raised or lands so devoted be divided between religious sects or denominations.

The proposed Blaine amendment would have taken the language of the First Amendment which contained prohibitions directed exclusively at the U.S. Congress and would have applied those same prohibitions to the State governments. In addition, the amendment would have prohibited any subsidization of anything religious using State funds. However, while it passed the House by a wide margin, the Blaine Amendment did not get the necessary 2/3 votes in the Senate to submit the amendment to the States for ratification, and so the Blaine Amendment died.

The failed Blaine Amendment is historically significant. The founders had made it clear that issues of religion were reserved to the States and off limits to the federal government. We discussed in Chapter 9 that several of the States had State designated/supported religious denominations during the establishment of the federal government, and that these practices did not change in some of the States until well into the 1800s.

The Blaine Amendment was an explicit attempt to now move First Amendment religious issues from State jurisdiction into federal government jurisdiction. Recognizing this fact, Congress would have supported the Blaine Amendment had they had enough Senators who believed that such constitutional limitations on the federal government should also apply to State governments. Whether the States would ever have ratified such a suggestion is debatable.

Bear in mind that senators at that time were not elected by the public, but rather, they were appointed by their individual State legislatures, presumably to protect the parochial interests of the States that sent them to Washington. Under the former process for electing senators, senators were far more concerned with protecting the interests of their particular State governments and State sovereignty than in playing to the voters. (This benefit which had long protected federalism was forfeited with the enactment of the Seventeenth Amendment in 1913, which provided for election of senators by popular vote.)

Why is this discussion of the failed Blaine Amendment significant? The intent clearly of the States in ratifying the Fourteenth Amendment, and even the intent of Congress, was NOT to change any jurisdictional balance between the States and the federal government. If there was an *incorporation doctrine* intent within the Fourteenth Amendment, Congress had clearly missed it in trying to move the Blaine Amendment. Under a modern interpretation of the Fourteenth Amendment, the Blaine Amendment in 1875 had already been constitutional law for seven years. There would have been no need for it.

Perhaps more importantly, the U.S. Supreme Court had missed it as well as Congress. This issue was put to the test in a number of Supreme Court cases beginning in the 1870s and extending into the early 1900s (See The *Slaughter-House Cases* [1873)] and *Presser v. Illinois* [1886] as examples where the idea of incorporation was rejected.) In each case, the Supreme Court upheld a narrow view of the Fourteenth Amendment, relying on a broad interpretation of the Tenth Amendment instead. Nowhere is this early interpretation of the Fourteenth Amendment more clearly articulated than in *The United States v. Cruikshank* (1876). In *Cruikshank* the Supreme Court made it clear that nothing had changed with respect to the jurisdictional Tenth Amendment boundary between federal and State with the passing of the Fourteenth Amendment.

The 1876 *Cruikshank* case came about when there was an appeal to the U.S. Supreme Court following a massacre of black Republicans in Louisiana by white Democrats after a disputed State election in 1872. In April 1873, both the white Democrats and the black Republicans claimed victory in the preceding elections. The ensuing riots resulted in over 100 black men being killed, mostly by execution style, after the blacks had been apprehended by the white mob.

In the aftermath of the Fourteenth Amendment, the U.S. Congress had passed a law called The Enforcement Act of 1870 which made it a crime for two or more persons to deprive any person of their constitutional rights. This law was passed to give the federal government a tool to use against the

Ku Klux Klan and other vigilante groups that sprung up in the South during Reconstruction.

Under this federal law several members of the white mob were charged with violating the black Republicans' rights of assembly and their rights to bear arms, among other specified violations. The case made its way to the U.S. Supreme Court, and in 1876 the Court ruled **unanimously** that the charges in question were not federal issues but rather State issues, to be adjudicated by, and only by, the State of Louisiana. The Court ordered all federal charges dropped.

The rationale of the Court in *Cruikshank* is clear, and it represents what the Court at that time, as well as what the States which ratified the Fourteenth Amendment, believed to be the purpose and the limits of the Fourteenth Amendment. The *Cruikshank* opinion was consistent with the opinion of the courts and the States throughout the 87 years that led up to this decision, from the founding of the new government in 1789, to the decision in 1876.

The Court in *The United States v. Cruikshank*, 1876, began by describing the balance of powers between the federal government and the State governments.

> *The first amendment to the Constitution prohibits Congress from abridging "the right of the people to assemble and to petition the government for a redress of grievances." This, like the other amendments proposed and adopted at the same time, was not intended to limit the powers of the State governments in respect to their own citizens, but to operate upon the National Government alone.* Barron v. The City of Baltimore, 7 Pet. 250; Lessee of Livingston v. Moore, *id.*, 551; Fox v. Ohio, 5 How. 434; Smith v. Maryland, 18 *id.* 76; Withers v. Buckley, 20 *id.* 90; Pervear v. The Commonwealth, 5 Wall. 479; Twitchell v. The Commonwealth, 7 *id.* 321; Edwards v. Elliott, 21 *id.* 557. *It is now too late to question the correctness of this construction.* <u>As was said by the late Chief Justice, in Twitchell v. The Commonwealth, 7 Wall. 325, "the scope and application of these amendments are no longer subjects of discussion here."</u> [Emphasis added] *They left the authority of*

> the States just where they found it, and added nothing to the already existing powers of the United States. The particular amendment now under consideration assumes the existence of the right of the people to assemble for lawful purposes, and protects it against encroachment by Congress. The right was not created by the amendment; neither was its continuance guaranteed, except as against congressional interference. <u>For their protection in its enjoyment, therefore, the people must look to the States. The power for that purpose was originally placed there, and it has never been surrendered to the United States.</u> [Emphasis added]

This is a monumental observation and application on the part of the Supreme Court. As Madison said in *Federalist #45*, domestic issues are State issues, not federal issues. The Fourteenth Amendment did not change that fact. The Supreme Court then went on to explain that the federal government "can neither grant nor secure to its citizens any right or privilege not expressly or by implication placed under its jurisdiction." The *Cruikshank* opinion continues:

> The people of the United States resident within any State are subject to two governments -- one State and the other National -- but there need be no conflict between the two. The powers which one possesses the other does not. They are established for different purposes, and have separate jurisdictions. Together, they make one whole, and furnish the people of the United States with a complete government, ample for the protection of all their rights at home and abroad...
>
> The Government of the United States is one of delegated powers alone. Its authority is defined and limited by the Constitution. All powers not granted to it by that instrument are reserved to the States or the people. No rights can be acquired under the Constitution or laws of the United States, except such as the Government of the United States has the authority to grant or secure. All that cannot be so granted or secured are left under the protection of the States.

It is interesting to observe here that the Court declared that in passing the Fourteenth Amendment, nothing had changed with respect to the meaning and scope of the Tenth Amendment.

With respect to the Fourteenth Amendment, the Court ruled that the amendment only gave the federal government jurisdiction concerning the official acts of States, not the acts of individual citizens. If a State passed a law which systematically singled out a particular group of citizens for unjust treatment, the federal government through the courts could step in and force the State to correct that law. However, if individual citizens were guilty of violating a person's rights, well that was exclusively a State issue, as *Cruikshank* goes on to say:

> *The Fourteenth Amendment prohibits a State from denying to any person within its jurisdiction the equal protection of the laws; but this provision does not, any more than the one which precedes it, and which we have just considered, add anything to the rights which one citizen has under the Constitution against another. The equality of the rights of citizens is a principle of republicanism. Every republican government is in duty bound to protect all its citizens in the enjoyment of this principle, if within its power.* <u>*That duty was originally assumed by the States, and it still remains there. The only obligation resting upon the United States is to see that the States do not deny the right.*</u> *[Emphasis added] This the amendment guarantees, but no more. The power of the national government is limited to the enforcement of this guaranty.*

Both the U.S. Congress, in 1875, through the failed Blaine Amendment, and the U.S. Supreme Court, through numerous opinions, made it crystal clear that both institutions, Congress and the Supreme Court, understood that the Fourteenth Amendment had changed nothing by way of federal jurisdiction over established State laws and customs, and had changed nothing with respect to the Tenth Amendment.

By the mid-1900s, the Supreme Court had changed its tune. It began to declare, under their novel *incorporation doctrine,* that the Fourteenth Amendment, by design, had incorporated the Bill of Rights specifically into the laws of each State, and that administering the Bill of Rights as they saw fit was now within the ultimate jurisdiction of the federal courts rather than the States themselves. Or at least part of the Bill of Rights – at first they applied this principle selectively. It is always nice to be able to decide on the fly which parts of the law you want to apply and which parts you don't, and the courts have applied parts of the Bill of Rights arbitrarily and have just as arbitrarily declined to so apply other parts of the Bill of Rights to the States.

One of the problems with dealing with a pernicious legal doctrine such as the *incorporation doctrine* is that on the surface it sounds so good. Should the rights listed in the Bill of Rights apply to the States? And our knee-jerk response without giving it much thought is, of course they should. We all value our God-given rights, and we all believe that we should be free to exercise them without government interference, whether that interference be State or federal in its origin. That is why the *incorporation doctrine* is difficult to contend with – it sounds so right if you don't think about it too deeply.

Think of it this way: The *incorporation doctrine* is not about rights, but rather it is all about who gets to decide those rights. The *incorporation doctrine* does not enhance a person's rights in any respect. By concocting such a doctrine and then applying it, the federal courts have used this pretext to declare unto themselves vast powers which were never intended to be theirs.

As we have quoted James Madison several times, liberties and domestic issues are *State* issues by design, not federal issues. The *incorporation doctrine* was devised by liberal federal judges, and is nothing more than a power grab on the part of the federal courts. It is the insertion of itself into areas that, according to the first ten amendments, are explicitly off limits to the federal government.

It was an activist judge in an activist court, generations after the Fourteenth Amendment was ratified, that decreed that the religion clauses of the First Amendment were now and henceforth would forever be within the jurisdiction of the federal courts. In 1947 in the Supreme Court case *Everson v. Board of Education*, Justice Hugo Black wrote the infamous, historically bankrupt opinion which totally misapplied a private letter written by President Thomas Jefferson to the Danbury Baptists as though it were a founding document.

(U.S. Supreme Court Chief Justice William Rehnquist would later describe Black's opinion as bad law based upon bad history. See Rehnquist's dissent in the case *Wallace v. Jaffree* (1985). It is available online in numerous places. In this dissent Rehnquist explains in great detail, and with much original source support, a proper historical understanding of the First Amendment's religion clauses.)

Justice Black's opinion in *Everson v. Board of Education* claimed that Jefferson's letter described the First Amendment as having erected a "wall of separation between Church and State." Never mind that Jefferson was in France when the Constitution was drafted and when the Bill of Rights amendments were composed. This out-of-context, private letter from Jefferson was neither a founding document nor a legal document, but it was the best Black could come up with. Weak on proof, it nonetheless provided the pretext for the court to do what it wanted to do anyway.

Thomas Jefferson's true attitude toward federal vs. State jurisdictions in matters of religion is better understood from his second inaugural address. "In matters of religion, I have considered that its free exercise is placed by the constitution independent of the powers of the general [Federal] government... but have left them, as the constitution found them, under the direction and discipline of State or church authorities acknowledged by the several religious societies." In other words, Jefferson rightly understood that religion is subject to State or ecclesiastical jurisdictions, but not federal jurisdiction.

The question in the *Everson* case was a State law which allowed parochial school children to use the tax-supported school transportation system of the local public school district. The charge was that using public school buses to transport children to a religious school was an illegal subsidy for religious instruction and, therefore, a violation of the First Amendment establishment clause. Up to that time such a question was none of the federal government's business but rather a State issue.

Justice Hugo Black decreed that this case did not quite rise to the level of a violation of the First Amendment (thus he avoided any public backlash), but that there was indeed, based on Jefferson's letter, a "wall of separation" between Church and State, and that wall applied to the States as well as the federal government. It applied to the States because, in the opinion of Black, the Fourteenth Amendment was passed to *incorporate* First Amendment limitations into all State laws. Because this was a majority opinion of the Supreme Court, the *incorporation doctrine* became "the law of the land." The legal precedent had been set and the foundation was now laid to attack religion at the State level. (Chief Justice William Rehnquist would later comment in his dissent in *Wallace v. Jaffree* with this acerbic reminder concerning *Everson* being used as precedent concerning religious clause issues. It bears repeating here, "... stare decisis may bind courts as to matters of law, but it cannot bind them as to matters of history.")

Certainly there would have been no rationale for proposing the Blaine Amendment in 1875 if that were already the law. Once introduced, Congress did not argue that the Blaine Amendment was redundant – that it was not needed because the Fourteenth Amendment had already seen to that. Rather, in 1875 opponents argued that the First Amendment did not and should not apply to the States, nor was it ever intended to.

The *incorporation doctrine* of the mid-1900s was contrary to established Supreme Court precedent clearly articulated in *United States v. Cruikshank 1876*, in which the Court made it clear that the Bill of Rights was a limitation on the federal government alone, but not on the States. In making that ruling, the Supreme Court cited numerous Supreme Court precedents from the beginning of the Republic to prove that the Tenth Amendment created a clear line between federal and State jurisdiction.

Since the watershed *Everson* case in 1947, the *incorporation doctrine* has been used as a pretext to give the U.S. Supreme Court ultimate jurisdiction over every aspect of State and local law, particularly on "separation of Church and State" issues. Though never originally intended to be, every State law or local custom is now under federal jurisdiction, simply because federal judges have declared for themselves that power. It is this precedent which was used to force the Bible out of public schools (*Abington School District v. Schempp*, 1963) and to outlaw prayer in public schools (*Engel v. Vitale*, 1962).

Substantive Due Process:

Within that same timeframe – early to mid-1900s – the federal courts began to apply another new judicial doctrine known as *substantive due process*, also drawn from the Fourteenth Amendment's due process clause. When we read the due process clause of the Fourteenth Amendment ("nor shall any State deprive any person of life, liberty, or property, without due process of law") understanding the post-Civil War context, we have no problem understanding what the States are saying. They wanted former slaves to receive the same treatment as former slave masters under the law. They wanted to make sure that no former slave was subjected to loss of life or liberty or property except as provided by a required process of written laws, general and equally applicable to all citizens.

Substantive due process is the idea that due process of law requires that the law is a just law in the first place, otherwise a procedural due process is not relevant. And who gets to decide whether a law is just? Not the Congress, nor the States, but the Supreme Court, of course. Because the Constitution says so? No, because the court says so.

Substantive due process gives judges the power to make up new rights which fit their own set of values, regardless of what the written law prescribes. For instance, the *Obergefell v. Hodges* (2015) case which discovered a new right to homosexual marriage in all of the States was largely a *substantive due process* case, as was *Roe v. Wade* (1973), in which judges made up new rights to privacy and abortion, and in *Lawrence v. Texas* (2003) in which the Supreme Court discovered new and unlimited rights of homosexual expression. In each of these instances, liberal judges used *substantive due process* to replace standing laws, some of which were centuries old, with their own particular set of personal values and morals (or lack thereof).

Just what is the theory behind *substantive due process*? It is easy to understand by simply inserting a single word into the due process clause, so that it reads, "nor shall any State deprive any person of life, liberty, or property, without due process of *proper* law." Or, to say it another way, due process of written law is invalid if applied to laws which are themselves improper. The U.S. Constitution gives the federal courts the power to apply law as it is. *Substantive due process*, however, confers to the federal courts the power to apply law as it isn't, but in their view, should be.

The laws which grab the attention of liberals and their relativistic allies on the federal bench, and for which this wonderful sounding idea of *substantive due process* is designed, are moral laws which go directly to the conscience of the people. These are laws which prohibit things which are inherently evil as described in the Bible – laws which penalize abortion or sexual perversion, things which relativists demand the whole nation embrace as "rights."

Never mind that in a republican form of government as laid out in our U.S. Constitution, it is never the job of the judiciary to decide what the law should be or which version of morality should be honored. It is their job to decide how to apply the laws which exist to specific cases, no less and no more. It is the people and the people's elected representatives who determine what is proper, what is right, what is wrong, and what is law. That is not the job of judges, and for that reason, if for no other reason, *substantive due process* is a bogus theory. It gives the courts the sole discretion in determining what is proper for society. It was an early abuse of *substantive due process* which drew the strong dissenting protest in 1930 from Supreme Court Justices Holmes and Brandeis, cited earlier.

That was the view of Justice Clarence Thomas in his dissent in the *Obergefell* case. Thomas, who believes substantive due process is a bogus proposition in the first place, writes powerfully on the subject:

> *The majority's decision today will require States to issue marriage licenses to same-sex couples and to recognize same-sex marriages entered in other States largely based on a constitutional provision guaranteeing "due process" before a person is deprived of his "life, liberty, or property." I have elsewhere explained the dangerous fiction of treating the Due Process Clause as a font of substantive rights. McDonald v. Chicago, 561 U. S. 742, 811–812 (2010) (THOMAS, J., concurring in part and concurring in judgment). It distorts the constitutional text, which guarantees only whatever "process" is "due" before a person is deprived of life, liberty, and property. U. S. Const., Amdt. 14, §1. Worse, it invites judges to do exactly what the majority has done here— "'roa[m] at large in the constitutional field' guided only by their personal views" as to the "fundamental rights" protected by that document...*
>
> *By straying from the text of the Constitution, substantive due process exalts judges at the expense of the People from whom they derive their authority. Petitioners argue that by enshrining the traditional definition of marriage in their State*

> *Constitutions through voter-approved amendments, the States have put the issue "beyond the reach of the normal democratic process." Brief for Petitioners in No. 14–562, p. 54. But the result petitioners seek is far less democratic. They ask nine judges on this Court to enshrine their definition of marriage in the Federal Constitution and thus put it beyond the reach of the normal democratic process for the entire Nation. That a "bare majority" of this Court, ante, at 25, is able to grant this wish, wiping out with a stroke of the keyboard the results of the political process in over 30 States, based on a provision that guarantees only "due process" is but further evidence of the danger of substantive due process.*

The federal courts have become virtual dictators concerning social issues. Building on the *Everson* case, the liberal Warren Court of the 1960s used the *incorporation doctrine* to decree that the Bible and prayer could no longer be a part of a State's public education. Education and religion, two things which were always the exclusive domain of the States, were stripped away from the States and decreed by federal judges to be within their exclusive jurisdiction. In the same way, the *incorporation doctrine* and *substantive due process* would form the legal rationale for later landmark cases beginning with *Roe v. Wade* (1973), *Lawrence v. Texas* (2003), and *Obergefell v. Hodges* (2015).

In the wake of *Everson v. Board of Education* (1947), the phrase "separation of Church and State" came into common usage. Most people are not aware that this phrase was rarely a part of the national conversation before the 1960s. With that societal shift, a systematic, court-mandated secularizing of government institutions at all levels was implemented. From the exclusively Christian heritage of our founders we have come a full 180 degrees, to an overtly secularist government system, beginning with our children's schools, enforced almost entirely by federal courts and openly hostile to Christianity and to Biblical Creation. States are no longer sovereign but rather are administrative functionaries on behalf of federal rulers, federal judges in particular.

In recent years federal judges with an atheistic/materialistic world view, acting on political ideology, routinely overturned the actions of State governments and overruled ballot initiatives supported by a super majority of citizens with regard to homosexual marriage and LGBT related issues. They used the Fourteenth Amendment as their excuse. Many of these laws which were overturned by federal judge(s) were State constitutional articles which have been decided by large majorities of the entire State's voting population.

Call to mind from Chapter 9 the fundamental founding truth expressed by the New York ratifying resolution of 1788, "That all Power is originally vested in and consequently derived from the People, and that Government is instituted by them for their common Interest Protection and Security." Call to mind the language of the Tenth Amendment, "The powers not delegated to the United States by the Constitution, nor prohibited by it to the States, are reserved to the States respectively, or to the people." Today, all powers of government are vested ultimately in the federal courts, not the States, or the people.

Kennedy, in writing the *Obergefell* opinion was so arrogant as to proclaim that Supreme Court judges now know better than our founders and better than the States that gave us the Bill of Rights and the Fourteenth Amendment, what they really mean, a meaning far different than originally intended. He even goes so far as to imply that the founders intended its meaning to be so radically changed by future courts.

> *The nature of injustice is that we may not always see it in our own times. The generations that wrote and ratified the Bill of Rights and the Fourteenth Amendment did not presume to know the extent of freedom in all of its dimensions, and so they entrusted to future generations a charter protecting the right of all persons to enjoy liberty as we learn its meaning. When new insight reveals discord between the Constitution's central protections and a received legal stricture, a claim to liberty must be addressed.*

(We can thank our lucky stars those restrictive founders who believed in Biblical marriage, Sabbath observance, marital faithfulness, and protection of the lives of our children were at least smart enough to give us a *living, breathing document* that could later be reshaped according to our own modern conceits. What absolutely rationalizing nonsense! Moreover, what unspeakable evil!)

As we saw in Chapter 9, the first ten amendments to the Constitution were originally adopted in response to the debates of the State ratifying conventions in 1788 to list specific areas in which the federal government was prevented by the Constitution from trespassing – powers the States reserved for themselves as a condition of entering into this social compact. These amendments, particularly the Tenth, represented specifically retained powers by and for the States or the people and a firewall against federal government intrusion. This was a condition of ratification by several of the States.

The supreme irony is this: Today the U.S. Supreme Court, employing the *incorporation doctrine* and *substantive due process*, has unconstitutionally declared unto itself exclusive powers to ultimately rule in all of those areas which were originally and *specifically* off limits to the federal government in the first place. In so doing, the federal government has succeeded in rendering the Tenth Amendment meaningless, eradicating the State sovereignty that the States so carefully guarded back in 1788 when this social compact was negotiated.

Here I would insert a practical point. One might argue, "Well, what if an individual State doesn't properly recognize religious freedom or perhaps some other God-given right? Certainly States like California or New York come to mind with such questions. What if a State decided to confiscate all of its citizens' firearms? Isn't it better if the federal government guarantees those rights by laws and positive action?"

I suppose the smart alec response is, "How's that working for you?" Realistically, I would answer in this way: True, a State could become tyrannical and could infringe on citizens' rights. If a single State were to do that, only a relatively small portion of the overall U.S. population would be affected. Ultimately, people could move from a tyrannical State, to a State where they have more freedom. Citizens from other States would be able to observe the mistakes that such a State might make and avoid making the same mistakes. Having experienced an exodus of its population such tyranny at the State level would hopefully be corrected.

However, when the federal government infringes on the people's rights, that affects all 330 million people. To where can you flee if the tyranny is nation-wide? Furthermore, bad laws, bad decisions, and bad judges are far more easily remedied at the State level than at the federal level. I would much rather my rights were secured by a State government than by the federal courts. True, today religious liberty is under attack in many of the more liberal States. People, as a result, are moving from those States. I can easily foresee a time, soon, when our religious liberty is abolished in the whole United States. Where do we go then?

The founders would agree. Did the founders seek to make the federal government the guardian of our rights – *any* of our rights? No, they did not. They believed the best guardians of rights were the States themselves, and they regarded the federal government as a threat to those rights. To remedy these threats they insisted on amendments that took the federal government entirely out of the picture with regard to rights, and especially the rights of conscience. The Fourteenth Amendment as intended changed none of that.

The above-mentioned, novel, legal theories of the early-to-mid-1900s represent naked and brazen usurped power on the part of the federal courts, unconstitutionally federalizing all State and local laws by judicial fiat. It happened gradually and case-by-case so that while it was happening few, other than perhaps Justices Holmes and Brandeis, saw the implications for the future. In retrospect, it is clear to see how effectively it produced the desired result – that a small handful of rulers of a particular world view could work their will to fundamentally alter society in ways that would never have been permitted under any democratic process.

Today it is common for a single federal judge to overturn the will of the people of an entire State, or a Presidential order executing clear, existing immigration law. This can go by no other name than *judicial tyranny*. This tyranny will continue, and will become increasingly malignant unless, and until, it is stopped. Our liberty depends on it.

I recognize that it sounds as though I have a low opinion of all federal judges, and I also recognize that I have perhaps painted with an overly broad brush in describing federal judges. I freely admit that I have great contempt for what the federal courts have become and what they have historically done, but not of all individual judges.

I recognize that there are many good federal judges who fight valiantly for a proper understanding of the U.S. Constitution. Some of those judges are heroes of mine and they are indispensable in setting right what has been lost. However, I cannot stress enough how damaging the federal courts as a whole have been to our culture and our laws – of making unspeakable evil which was long illegal the norm in modern America.

I also recognize that many federal judges are mere products of the academic values inculcated during their educational experience. An attorney friend of mine brought up this salient point to me one day, recounting his educational experience in law school. He noted that in his classes on constitutional law the students were not once asked to read any part of the U.S. Constitution. They were instead simply lectured on all the great precedent-setting court cases which shaped modern legal doctrines. Since his days in law school, that attorney has asked several other attorneys if their experiences were similar, and most have agreed that little or no time was spent in actually getting to know the U.S. Constitution.

Chapter 11
The Great Swamp – A Comfortable Aristocracy

One of my hobbies over the past several years has been to research my family's genealogy. During that research I came across the memoirs of a distant uncle by the name of Nehemiah Cleveland Bradstreet written in 1907. N.C. Bradstreet had a remarkable life span, born in 1821 and died in 1910. He was the mayor of Rochester, New York, during the Civil War, and during his political career he had the privilege of meeting Presidents John Quincy Adams, Martin Van Buren and Abraham Lincoln.

In his memoirs N. C. Bradstreet recalled one of his first memories as a five-year-old child, as his father at the dinner table announced to the family news of the deaths on the same day, July 4, 1826, of former presidents Thomas Jefferson and John Adams. He recalled the shocking sensation this news created around the table. His professional life took him through the era of the development of canal and rail travel, and he lived to see the invention of the automobile and the airplane. His life uniquely linked the founding fathers and the American frontier with modern America.

N.C. Bradstreet recounts his years in the New York legislature. A few years after the end of the Civil War, Democratic leaders around Rochester persuaded Bradstreet to run for a seat in the New York Assembly. He was successful and as a legislator was appointed to a powerful position, Chairman of the Committee on Canals, which oversaw some of the main thoroughfares of commerce.

He served two one-year terms in the Assembly, and then retired from the legislature. He remarked that two terms were plenty, he had done his duty and he returned home to the farm. His tenure in State politics was more the rule than the exception at that time. Most politicians in America viewed government service as a duty, not a career. To most, serving in a State legislature was a financial burden – something that had to be done by someone – it was rarely seen as a special lifestyle or financial benefit. It was a public service they were willing to do, but not eager to do.

That is rarely the case today. Today, at the federal level and in many States, especially those with a full-time legislature, politics is viewed first and foremost as a career. Having served six years in the Michigan House of Representatives, I can vouch for that fact. Even with term limits, legislators remain in office as long as they possibly can. Once there, eventually most of their actions are focused on staying there or moving up to the next level.

My "class" of legislators, elected in 1998, was the first class after Michigan's term limits law of 1992 went into effect. Almost every one of us 63 freshmen lawmakers were there because of term limits – our predecessors having been required by law to move on. Yet at the end of our allotted six years, there was a movement within my class to get rid of the term limit law. They had had a taste, and they didn't want to let go.

Not long ago I was watching a fascinating vote developing in the U.S. House of Representatives on repealing Obamacare. The House had several times passed repeal bills during the tenure of President Barack Obama, but they never made it out of the Senate, as House members knew they wouldn't. However, now with a Republican President Donald Trump, House members were agonizing over a vote that they had had no problem with back when they knew it could never actually become law.

As I watched this drama develop, Fox News commentator Martha MacCallum commented, "These people need to go back home and get re-elected. That's the number one thing on their minds." It didn't appear to me that her comment was meant as a criticism, but rather an explanation why there were so many who had run on a promise to repeal Obamacare who would vote "no" when it came right down to doing it when it really counted. Sadly, I believe what she said was an accurate assessment concerning many of them, perhaps even most.

During my political life I have personally observed many in the Michigan legislature who it seemed were initially running for all of the right reasons, but after serving for a year or so were getting caught up in the career aspect of the job. Where do I go from here? How do I enhance my career opportunities? My observation is that this problem is multiplied in the federal legislature where there are no term limits.

Careerism is one of the biggest problems in Congress. Originally Congressmen were paid $6 per diem. That was it. Now I know $6 went a lot farther back then than it does now. However, most Congressmen did the job as a duty, not as a career. Their primary occupation was back home waiting for them. Other than a brief two-year span (1815-1816 when the $1,500 salary amounted to about $20,000 in 2017 dollars), the per diem system was used until 1855 when an annual salary of $3,000 was paid to federal legislators. $3,000 in 1855 dollars amounted to just under $80,000 in 2017 dollars, not a bad income but nothing exceptional. Since that time Congress has been paid an annual salary.

That annual salary grew steadily in inflation adjusted terms for the next 114 years until it reached a peak of over $278,000 in inflation adjusted dollars ($42,000) in 1969. Since 1969 the inflation-adjusted salary for legislators has varied from a low of about $167,000 in 1986, to a high of $225,000 in 1993, with the current rate at $174,000 (higher – up to $223,500 – for members of house and senate leadership). This places legislators currently in the top 3% of wage earners in the United States.

However, that isn't the whole story. Legislators have provided generously for themselves in terms of benefits, retirement, expense accounts, and tax advantages. The result of this additional largess is that Congressmen earn the equivalent of a salary about 1½ times their actual annual salary, which for all practical purposes places them in the top 1-2% of wage earners.

According to the U.S. Census Bureau, the average income for a person with a PhD degree is just under $94,000 in 2017 dollars. The average income for a person with a professional degree (medical doctors, dentists, pharmacists, etc.) is just over $109,000. This is average individual income – certainly many in those categories earn much more than that, and there are those who earn less. A Congressman needs no education to far exceed these levels of income for professional occupations.

Add to this level of congressional income the special lifestyle of being a Congressman or Senator. While Congress has a notoriously low approval rating, individual legislators are generally regarded highly by their own constituents. They attend political functions and are featured at special banquets, receiving general adulation and being introduced as exceptional public servants and honored by special awards. Eventually most legislators begin to believe they are special and indispensable.

Legislators rarely have to buy their own meals and they receive numerous special benefits in the form of world travel, gifts, and entertainment, often funded by the bottomless expense account of lobbyists. It is the medieval aristocracy in modern terms. So, why would a legislator ever want to risk all that? Most would never risk that: the money, the adulation, the power, and the perks.

I recall hosting a Congressman for a convention down in Florida in the mid-1990s when I was the Executive Director of a national trade association. I will not mention his name, but I will describe him. He had a reputation as a rising star in the Republican Party, and as a committed Christian. I had not scheduled him because he was a Christian, but rather, because he was promoting legislation which would help our association. However, because of his reputation as a Christian I did want to get to know him personally, so I took advantage of the situation and spent as much time with him as I could. I appointed myself to pick him up at the airport (about a 30 minute drive from the hotel) and to return him there after his speech.

What I discovered was a young man who appeared to me to be obsessed with the possibilities of power. I detected something wasn't quite right, so I asked him about his reputation as a Christian and his walk with the Lord. He sort of hung his head and said, "I know I'm not walking close with the Lord as I once did. I really need to get back to that." Not wanting to pry I didn't press it beyond that, but later I read that he had left his wife and then later lost a bid to move up the political ladder. The job had destroyed his spiritual and family life. I have not heard of him since.

It should be understood that this lifestyle and all the perks come from Congress itself. They pass the laws which provide so generously for themselves, or put another way, they help themselves to the treasury and to the rules. "But we must pay enough," the argument from Congress goes, "or we will be made up only of the rich and the incompetent."

Let's evaluate that thought for just a moment. Many members in Congress would find it difficult to find a job in the private sector which paid them near what their income package in Congress pays. However, if Congress was paid just a per diem stipend, the average Congressman would have to be someone successful enough to be able to afford to serve. My guess is that the motivations and competence levels would improve remarkably in an environment comparable to that of the early Congresses. They also would not be dependent on the job for their personal wealth and security.

I would argue that overpaying Congress and promoting outside largess and benefits from interest groups lead to even greater self-interest and fewer true statesmen. It also results in a Congress so risk-averse as to not get anything meaningful done which does not amount to the purchase of a new block of voters. That purchase is inevitably made in public dollars the treasury does not have.

Many voting blocks are people who believe in a particular policy objective. Two of the most powerful voting blocks are pro-life voters and gun owners. These voters support candidates who believe as they do on a particular issue. There are lesser, but just as effective, voting blocks of philosophical voters such as libertarians and environmentalists. If you can stack enough blocks to exceed 50% of the voters in your district you get to come back.

However, the most potent voting blocks, as liberals have discovered, are those who have become dependent on government subsidies. Government welfare, food stamps, and social security benefits are groups which, once benefitted, are fearful of losing what government provides. Liberals have discovered that all they need do is promise ever increasing amounts of government help in order to "set the hook" on a particular block of voters.

This is also why liberals are so determined to import from other countries low-skilled individuals who will ultimately become dependent on government. Liberal legislators are constantly trying to create all sorts of amnesty schemes for illegal aliens (those who are not already illegally registered to vote) because they recognize this voting block as a means for their perpetual existence.

This is simple human nature, divorced from the moral and ethical restraints that true Christianity would impose. Congress has access to the treasury for its own advancement. Understanding unrestrained human nature, it is no wonder that Congress gets paid in the top 3% of wage earners, why their voting blocks are supported by all manner of public dollars, and why America is for all practical purposes financially bankrupt.

Was this aristocracy the intention of our founding fathers? Of course not! The founding balance of power was unique in its design. By design the legislative branch was to be the most powerful of the three branches. The legislative branch devised all the laws and had power over all spending. The House of Representatives held all of the power of the purse, and it had to give assent to every law devised in either chamber of Congress. The judicial branch by design was to be the least powerful. Its only constitutional function was to apply existing laws to particular cases. As we quoted in the previous chapter from Federalist #78 (Alexander Hamilton):

> *The Executive not only dispenses the honors, but holds the sword of the community. The legislature not only commands the purse, but prescribes the rules by which the duties and rights of every citizen are to be regulated. The judiciary, on the contrary, has no influence over either the sword or the purse; no direction either of the strength or of the wealth of the society; and can take no active resolution whatever. It may truly be said to have neither force nor will, but merely judgment; and must ultimately depend upon the aid of the executive arm even for the efficacy of its judgments.*

In parallel with that design, the legislative branch was of the three branches the most accountable to the people. Originally, the House of Representatives was the only federal office which was directly elected by the people, and for that they gained the moniker "The People's House." They were required to stand for election every two years.

In contrast, under the original Constitution, the Senate was appointed by the individual States, and the President was elected by a group of independent "electors" which made up the Electoral College. So, while the Senate and the President were indirectly accountable to the people, the House could be changed in very short order.

By that same design the judicial branch, being the least powerful, was the least accountable. The terms of the federal judges were indefinite – they could serve as long as they lived if they desired. The only way to get rid of a federal judge contrary to their wishes was by impeachment.

Today, both the House and the Senate are directly elected by the people. And since Congress has attained such an unanticipated level of income and prominence, the key to staying in that exalted position is by avoiding risk.

And how do you avoid risk? The main mechanism for avoiding risk is to delegate as many controversial decisions as possible to the other branches of government. Today Congress routinely defers tough decisions to executive branch departments and to the judicial branch. In this way they can wash their hands of unpopular actions and point their fingers at others.

In the same way that Congress over the past 75-80 years has helped itself to a lavish lifestyle, the federal courts have helped themselves to unlimited social power. There is little to deter Congress from going too far financially since they have unlimited access to the treasury, and there is little to deter the courts from going too far in the law because they serve for life and have declared for themselves the unrestrained oversight of the law.

In Chapter 10 we described the role of the "out of control" federal courts in moving America away from Christianity and morality. Whose fault is this? Certainly many sins of commission can be laid squarely at the feet of liberal judges and their influencers. That is human nature – to grasp for more power. Recognizing that human tendency, our Founders placed in the Constitution checks and balances between the branches, and each branch is limited by the other branches in some way.

None of this judicial overreach could have happened had Congress lived up to its responsibilities under the Constitution. True, the sins of commission are sins of the judges. However, there are countless sins of omission which need to be laid at the feet of Congress, and these sins extend back for nearly a century.

In our checks and balances system, understand that the Supreme Court has one, and only one, constitutional limit to its powers, and that is Congress. Federal judges serve for life, but it was never the design by framers of the Constitution that judges would have the last word on all issues or that they would be completely unaccountable. It is Congress' job to assure that does not happen. The Constitution states in Article III, concerning the powers of the federal courts,

> *In all Cases affecting Ambassadors, other public Ministers and Consuls, and those in which a State shall be Party, the supreme Court shall have original Jurisdiction. In all the other Cases before mentioned, the supreme Court shall have appellate Jurisdiction, both as to Law and Fact, <u>with such</u>*

Exceptions, and under such Regulations as the Congress shall make. [Emphasis added]

Notice that Congress, not the courts, was intended to have a free hand with respect to the Court's appellate powers. There are no constitutional limits on Congress applying exceptions and regulations to the courts. Throughout the Federalist Papers there is only one mention of this Article III congressional power. In Federalist #81, Hamilton makes note of this congressional power without elaborating as to the scope of congressional power in this area or what it might mean. He simply mentions that the judicial branch has certain specified powers, and then he adds "with such Exceptions, and under such Regulations as the Congress shall make."

Because so little is written about this congressional power I have asked various attorneys what this might mean, and a colleague of mine even asked a former Chief Justice of the Michigan Supreme Court what this might mean. In each case there was no clear answer of just how or how much Congress may control the federal courts. It is such an ignored power that no one is quite sure what to do with it. Absent any other explanation, we must take the framers at their words – this is an area where Congress has a free hand.

Clearly this clause is in the Constitution to provide a check on the powers of the federal courts. Otherwise it would not be there. Through these "exceptions and regulations," Congress could at any time tell the courts to, "Knock it off!" or "Don't go there!" However, that would require statesmanship and political courage (not to mention a working knowledge of the Constitution), something that a comfort-oriented institution such as Congress generally finds not to be in its interest. Most legislators would rather not stir up controversy of this type, not to mention the scathing rebuke that would surely come from the liberal mainstream media.

Unfortunately, Congress has only in rare instances placed restrictions on the runaway federal courts. Limiting the federal judiciary poses a risk to Congress, and Congressmen know they would have too much to lose to risk it. They know that if they were to attempt to rein in the courts' social agenda the media would be all over their cases, and maintaining positive press is one of the keys to staying in power. Realistically, since nearly a century has gone by with no congressional restraint on the courts, it is likely now that the courts would simply declare any congressional oversight unconstitutional, thus creating a constitutional crisis.

Congress has a long history of avoiding tough decisions which would be unpopular with the liberal media and could lose them votes back home. Potentially damaging political decisions are delegated to unelected bureaucrats in the executive branch. That way Congress does not suffer any political consequences for unpopular decisions – they can simply explain that the bureaucracy made that bad decision. The expansive presence of the federal bureaucracy is for the most part a direct result of a risk-averse Congress ducking responsibility for tough decisions.

Let's use the Environmental Protection Agency as an example. The EPA has run amok with stolen powers that go way beyond their statutory authority. Congress has passed some generally worded statutes such as the Clean Air Act (1963) and the Clean Water Act (1972) which give certain authority to the EPA to make "administrative rules" which, incidentally, have the force of law. On its face, this is an abrogation of Congress' legislative powers. When the EPA decides to make a rule outside the limits of their statutory authority, rarely does Congress step in to remedy the situation. Instead, unconstitutional decisions by the EPA are litigated in the federal courts, where many of those decisions are upheld by liberal judges.

Another problem in Congress is the ever-present question of what the responsibility of a legislator actually is. This centuries-old debate pits those who view representatives as mere delegates versus those who see representatives as trustees. My experience is that "representing the views of the folks back home" is often used as a cop-out to avoid a tough vote. So, what is the difference?

In the delegate model, the representative seeks to find what the majority of people he represents thinks. He is more a pollster than anything else. If the people in his district are pro-life, then he votes pro-life, regardless of his personal views. If they are pro-abortion, then he votes pro-abortion. He simply seeks to vote the opinions of his constituency. Thus, he can argue that he is properly representing the views of his constituents.

In the trustee model, the representative is elected to investigate issues, after which he uses his own informed judgment in voting. If he takes the time to research the implications of a particular view, then it should be assumed that he has better information to make a judgment than his aggregate constituency. After due diligence, he casts his vote for what he believes to be the best course of action for his State or nation, even if it is contrary to the will of his own constituents. Edmund Burke argued strenuously for the trustee model, "... your representative owes you, not his industry only, but his judgment; and he betrays, instead of serving you, if he sacrifices it to your opinion."

Anyone who watched Jay Leno's segment of the Tonight Show which he called *Jaywalking*, or who has watched Jesse Watters' *Watters World* on the Fox News channel understands that there are a lot of uninformed Americans, particularly young Americans, those who can name the last American Idol or Sole-Survivor, but can't tell you who their senator is, nor can name the Vice President (a recent poll revealed that 13% of Americans had never heard of Vice President Mike Pence). These are people who Rush Limbaugh refers to as "low-information voters" whose opinions are shaped mainly by their liberal-leaning educational experience or by Hollywood opinion shapers. They can't name the three branches of government, but they want you to vote a certain way because that is what the herd wants.

A representative sensitive to the herd's opinion will likely have a long and prosperous career. The delegate model requires no political courage, and it can even lead to great quantities of pork for the politician inclined to enrich his own district at the expense of the whole. A representative at the State or federal level *should* be there to vote for the moral and financial betterment of his State or country, even if such votes are contrary to the opinions or interests of his own district. In contrast, representative government inclined toward the delegate model will end up morally and financially bankrupt.

Here again, I realize my cynicism has induced me to paint everyone in Congress with the broad brush of opportunism and greed. I know that is not the case, but I believe it is true of far too many legislators to a greater or lesser extent, and certainly the temptation is present with all of them. At the same time I acknowledge that there are many good legislators who are statesmen, who practice a trustee form of legislating and have good judgment and high integrity. It has been my privilege to know several such legislators.

However, there are far too few true statesmen in the legislature who will cast a vote that they are convinced is right if it endangers their career and perks. It is difficult to remove oneself from lucrative income, notoriety, power, and lifestyle knowing that it probably could not be otherwise duplicated. It is human nature to tenaciously grasp those things and hold on, sacrificing so much of value to keep it.

Another danger to a legislator's career is caucus discipline. Legislators routinely have a number of advantages supplied by the caucus leadership if they are willing to go along with the leadership's wishes. Among these advantages are campaign assistance, both in manpower and financial assistance. Another advantage comes through the committee assignment process. A legislator who rocks the boat within the caucus will likely not get any good committee assignments, leaving him to look powerless and ineffective back home.

Also available to the "team" player is a host of caucus services. Caucus services will constantly turn out professionally written press releases which make the most incompetent members look thoughtful and statesmanlike. Cross the leadership and you can say good-by to all such perks that are designed to prolong your career.

In an April, 2017, op-ed piece, George Will commented on the influence and value possessed by a relatively new group of committed conservative legislators in the U.S. House, known as the Freedom Caucus. These are individuals who are committed to the trustee model of legislating. Most of these Representatives have had successful, good income careers in the private sector and are not dependent on the U.S. Congress for their lifestyle. They are committed to doing what is best for the country, not for their own careers.

George Will, commenting on the independence of the caucus, quotes the caucus's chairman Rep. Mark Meadows for an explanation of why this group is so effective, "The HFC's [House Freedom Caucus] 30 members, and six others informally affiliated, are barely 8 percent of the House, but their cohesion is a force multiplier. The cohesion comes, Meadows says, from its members being 'here for a purpose.' And, he adds dryly, from the fact that, for many, 'This is not the best job they've ever had.' Among the never more than 537 people who are in Washington because they won elections, none are more threatening to tranquility than the few who are not desperate to be here. They do not respond to the usual incentives for maintaining discipline."

Is there a solution? Yes, there is a spiritual solution. With a spiritual, Biblical revival comes greater integrity in the people and their leaders, and we are doomed if that does not happen. As we will discuss in the final chapter, America has no future without a spiritual revival and a new Great Awakening. America's political leadership needs to be people who are influenced by the moral principles of such an awakening.

However, there two practical fixes as well which could improve things. I may be one of a very small handful of former legislators who believe in term limits, but I do firmly believe in them. It is my personal observation that serving in the legislature, even the State legislature, changes a person, and usually not for the better. I believe the best legislators are the ones that have been in office a short amount of time and have no ambition to make a career out of it. Their decisions are based on their judgment, not their career.

The longer one serves in the legislature the more likely he is to be influenced by bureaucrats and special interests and to change from the altruistic first-termer and start voting with his personal preservation and perks in mind. He becomes a pragmatist rather than an idealist. He becomes convinced by his longer-serving "friends" that needed reform is politically unrealistic "at this time." The best, indeed likely the only, chance there is to enact the tough medicine our country needs in our budget and our policies is for a majority of Congress to be made up of citizens who don't realize such reforms are "unrealistic" and who do not view the job as a career nor have a passion for staying there indefinitely.

When a new legislator comes into office, his perspective is that of one of the governed. His recent experience makes him sympathetic to those suffering the problems caused by government's excesses. He is concerned about the national debt and the exorbitant annual deficits. He goes into the job with a desire to make things better, particularly for his own children and grandchildren. And he will vote accordingly for the first few years perhaps. The longer he stays, the tendency is to experience a subtle change in his perspective from the governed to the governing. If he stays a long time, he *becomes* the government and its defender.

Finally, I believe that legislators in the U.S. House and Senate are overpaid. Perhaps with term limits this would be less a problem since term limits eliminate most of the career motivations. Without term limits, however, congressional pay should be reduced, perhaps substantially.

The salaries and benefits cannot be at such a high level that members are terrified of the necessary risks of the job, the main risk of course being tossed out of office. It cannot be a job which members will do anything to avoid losing. If an unpopular but principled vote cost the statesman his office, it would not represent an unbearable sacrifice, the likes of which today's Congressmen do all in their power to avoid.

Coupled with term-limits, I believe such changes would result in a far greater number of citizen-statesmen who, like distant uncle Nehemiah Cleveland Bradstreet, did their duty for a few years and then returned home to live according to the rules and budgets that they had a part in writing.

Part IV
True Exceptionalism

What is American exceptionalism? Is it legitimate? What are the modern views of exceptionalism? What is the cause of American exceptionalism? Is it possible to understand what made America such an exceptional nation?

Chapter 12
Opposing Views of American Exceptionalism

American exceptionalism has recently become the subject of renewed interest, particularly in reaction to the viewpoint that former President Barack Obama once expressed, that American exceptionalism is nothing special, no more special than the exceptionalism that those from other countries embrace in contemplating their own native lands. President Obama's view has divided the country on the subject, and many Americans are now being exposed to the idea of American Exceptionalism for the first time in their lives.

While I take issue with President Obama, I am grateful for the discussion that has followed his comments. The simple, obvious truth is that America's founding was different, its people seemed to have a different type of commitment, and the result was exceptional among nations. It is that different type of commitment of America's founding generations that I have tried to explain in the preceding chapters.

That is not to say that America is or ever was perfect. It is to say, however, that America succeeded beyond the success of any other society in the history of the world. The obvious question, then, is, "What caused that success, and was that cause a good thing or a bad thing?"

In this chapter I would like to consider generally two competing ideas about American exceptionalism. Each of these two views will be represented by a noted author who explains his particular viewpoint in a recently published work on that subject. The first viewpoint we will consider is that there is really nothing exceptional at all about America – that each feature which contributed to America's exceptional rise was borrowed from elsewhere, mostly Europe, and America simply had the advantage of room and resources. Indeed, any other country given the same set of circumstances and a willingness to trample on the property and rights of native inhabitants and black slaves could have similarly succeeded.

The second viewpoint is that America is different, and that American exceptionalism is the natural product of that difference. Assumed in this view is that America, although not perfect, is pretty good morally speaking, and has no need to hang its collective head over its past. This natural "cause and effect" theory suggests that if any other nation were to copy America's approach to economics, work ethic and morality, and most of all, system of government, they too could be exceptional.

Two recently written books illustrate these two approaches to America's success. The first book we will look at is a book entitled *The Myth of American Exceptionalism* by Godfrey Hodgson (2009). Hodgson, a Britain who lived much of his life in the United States, is a journalist, prolific writer, and historian. Hodgson's view of America is simply that she borrowed all of her exceptional traits from Europe or elsewhere – nothing really that novel here in America that couldn't have been duplicated by a European power given the same advantages, space, and willingness to similarly take advantage of lesser peoples and countries. This European perspective is the view often embraced by academia in America as well as many liberal political leaders.

In his desire to set straight the wrong-headed mythology embraced by simple American patriots, Hodgson wrote *A Great and Godly Adventure: The Pilgrims and the Myth of the First Thanksgiving*. Other books by Hodgson include *More Equal than Others: America from Nixon to the New Century* (2006), a diatribe against conservative trends in America, and biographies of Daniel Patrick Moynihan (2000) and Martin Luther King (2010). In the preface to *The Myth of American Exceptionalism*, Hodgson gives an honest evaluation of his bias by declaring, "... my sympathies have generally been with Democrats and liberals."

The second book we will look at was published by the American Enterprise Institute for Public Policy Research (AEI). Titled *American Exceptionalism, An Experiment in History* (2013), it was written by best-selling conservative author Charles A. Murray, author of such works as *Losing Ground* (1984) and the *Bell Curve* (1994). This short booklet (just 50 pages) summarizes several characteristics, particularly those developed during the first three centuries of America's existence, that were uniquely predominant in American life and culture. It also notes the decline of some of these attributes over recent decades and the resulting, relative decline of America herself. This is the view held by many patriotic conservative Americans who view our country as exceptional.

I do not know much about Charles Murray. He writes from a conservative perspective on most subjects. His *American Exceptionalism* booklet does not suggest anything about his religious views, and on those I have no knowledge. Suffice it to say, Murray treats the subject of American exceptionalism as a completely natural, cause and effect phenomenon. I would not suggest that there is anything wrong, or inaccurate, or poorly reasoned in Murray's work. I would only submit that there is something missing, as I will try to explain in the following chapter.

But first, let's take a look at both of these perspectives and try to consider what is accurate or inaccurate about both. It might surprise you to learn that I believe both Hodgson and Murray are generally accurate and that both books are largely true. However, neither one really gets to the root cause of American exceptionalism. My own view, which I will explain in the next chapter, is that American exceptionalism is real, not entirely unique, and that it has a far different, less complex cause than most people ascribe to it.

First, let's look at *Myth of American Exceptionalism* by Godfrey Hodgson, published by Yale University Press, (2009). *The Myth of American Exceptionalism* is written to cast doubt on the whole idea of exceptionalism. Hodgson's historical research is somewhat impressive, his conclusions generally accurate. His perspective, though, is haughty and dismissive, and generally represents a typical leftist diatribe against all things American.

His book begins with an effort to dismiss the "myths" of the "city on a hill," along with much of America's founding history, and it ends in a prolonged attack against President George W. Bush, and particularly, his invasion of Iraq. In the middle portion, however, are some worthwhile thoughts which are generally true, perhaps even obvious. America didn't invent everything.

From the very first chapter, Hodgson, like Barack Obama, assures us that all peoples of the world believe their own nations to be exceptional. In subsequent chapters Hodgson sets out to list all of the things he can think of where America's outstanding characteristics are borrowed from elsewhere, almost always Europe. The thesis of Hodgson's book is simple (and very

European): *all of America's greatness was plagiarized from somewhere else,* not altogether dissimilar from Barack Obama saying, "You didn't build that."

Among his most obvious points is that America is big. It has a lot of land. The insinuation is that if Europeans had all that land to distribute to its people, Europe would have developed to be just as rich and successful as America was.

Hodgson even goes on to describe the concept and benefits of land ownership in the early Plymouth Colony. This is the account of William Bradford in explaining what happened in the first two years of the settlement. In the original settlement all land and food was held in common. People were expected to do their share in exchange for food enough to get by. Bradford discovered that there were those who observed that they would get no greater share if they worked harder, nor no lesser share if they worked little or not at all. This led to scarcity and hunger.

Hodgson describes the episode generally but fails to mention that this change to personal ownership of the land brought about a harvest of plenty whereas before, with the same acreage they were barely able to survive under a communal system.

In contrast, many European countries historically practiced forms of land ownership, but in the final analysis, land was held at the pleasure of the monarchy. Under the old feudal system the king could grant, the king could revoke. He could give large tracts of land to assure loyalty on the part of powerful lords. As the feudal system dissolved, land was still theoretically owned by the monarch, but ownership rights could be purchased, sold, or inherited. However, there were relatively few land owners in Europe as most lands were owned by wealthy aristocrats and most of the poor were merely tenants.

> *Their circumstances, as Europeans possessed of unused and unexploited resources of land and minerals on a scale that had not been freely available in Europe ... changed the character of American society ... in eighteenth-century America a continent lay open to be exploited ...*

In America, as the country developed and expanded westward after the revolution, land ownership was within reach of most citizens. The State governments and the federal government made land available to just about anyone who would work it at prices that could be afforded by virtually anyone, and oftentimes for free. Indeed, from the beginning of the colonies right through the Civil War, a majority of the population of America were farmers, providing for their own needs and yielding enough excess agricultural output to provide a comfortable living. So, while Hodgson's observation that land played a major part in the success of America, it does not explain why on other continents where there is much agricultural potential, no such prosperity developed.

Hodgson points out that American education is also one of the chief reasons for American success, and I would certainly agree with that. From the beginning of the colonies, education was emphasized, as we pointed out in Chapter 3. And yes, as Hodgson points out, much of the educational technique was copied from European educational norms.

> *Yet until long past the middle of the nineteenth century, American education was essentially derived from European models . . . Even Noah Webster . . . relied heavily on English models . . .*

It is recognized that some of the educational techniques in early America drew from English models, even English textbooks. It is also recognized that educational techniques copied heavily from European techniques. However, it must be pointed out, as discussed in Chapter 3, that beginning in the late 1700s the thrust of America's educational system and its textbooks was uniquely American, uniquely religious, and uniquely Protestant. Certainly what is taught is more critical to a society than the design of the building or the mechanics of teaching.

Hodgson also discusses America's unique republican form of government as a possible cause of exceptionalism, but attributes even that to events and thinking in Europe.

> *. . . Without the French fleet, the American army would not have won the decisive victory at Yorktown, where almost as many French as American soldiers fought on the winning side.*
> *. . . It was also an event whose root causes went back deep*

> *into the political and intellectual history of Europe. The political ideas of Benjamin Franklin, Tom Paine, James Madison, and Thomas Jefferson were hardly American ideas ... their ideas were not original. They had literally been to school to the Common Law of England. They were the intellectual heirs of the "commonwealthmen" and radical Whigs who had kept alive the principles of the English Revolution. They were also the children of the English, Scots, and French Enlightenment...*

So, in Hodgson's view, all American successes have their origin in Europe or are explainable by our vast size and resources. But even those advantages would not be enough to create America's greatness if America had been ravaged by two world wars as Europe was. No, according to Hodgson, America was not ruined by the wars – indeed America was the one nation that *benefitted* from them.

However, Hodgson does believe that America is exceptional in many negative ways. He spends quite a bit of his time criticizing America from his distinctly left-wing perspective. Here is Hodgson's view of where America is truly exceptional.

> *Understandably, perhaps, it was foreigners, and especially Europeans, who were the first to point out that the United States is exceptional in some less attractive ways ... Although American incomes do remain comparatively high, especially when measured in ways that exclude services that are free or subsidized elsewhere, the distribution of income and wealth in the United States is now exceptional for its extreme and growing inequality.*
>
> *... The American political system, once so widely admired, puzzles many foreigners, and indeed many Americans too, in its rejection of assumptions that are generally shared elsewhere—for example, in respect to global warming,*

So, in Hodgson's view, America is now exceptional only in ways that are detrimental to itself and the rest of the world. He joins the choir of liberals who routinely attack America for being mean to criminals and not being progressive enough, not socialistic enough, or gullible enough to embrace global warming (or perhaps, by the time you read this, global cooling again).

Charles Murray presents the polar opposite of Hodgson's views in his book, *American Exceptionalism,* published in 2013 by AEI Press (American Enterprise Institute), Washington D.C. In his introduction, Murray points out the obvious about American exceptionalism, that it is a simple fact of history.

> *American exceptionalism is a concept that was shared by observers throughout the Western world, not just Americans…*
>
> *American exceptionalism is a fact of America's past, not something that you can choose whether to "believe in" any more than you can choose whether to "believe in" the battle of Gettysburg.*

He continues his introduction by pointing out that exceptionalism should not be assumed to be the permanent state of the United States of America. The key question is whether the qualities that made America exceptional are still in operation to the quality and degree that they were there in the first hundred years of our history. Beginning in Chapter 2, Murray begins to describe what he believes to be the ingredients that made America exceptional.

First was the unique physical setting of the North American continent which was in a sense exclusionary toward weak immigrants. The treacherous ocean crossing, the less than ideal agricultural setting along the coast (thin, rocky soil), the heavy forests, and the hard labor needed to clear and farm the same, and perhaps most of all, the scarcity and unavailability of tools, goods, or services. These difficulties at the beginning of American settlement weeded out all but the most hardy, courageous, and self-sufficient of immigrants.

Later this very hostile setting would become an advantage as it provided for unlimited expansion of land for settling by anyone willing to work hard. Further, it enjoyed a large oceanic buffer from the constant wars and conflicts which characterized seventeenth and eighteenth century Europe, thus freeing early America from the huge expense of maintaining a large military establishment.

Murray goes on to point out that America developed an exceptional ideology. Americans believed in rights for all, not just a privileged few. They distrusted government in general, opting rather to provide for their own needs, reaping for themselves the benefits of their own labor. They developed an economic system where promotion was based on individual merit, not the status of one's birth.

Putting the above two attributes together, Americans developed certain personal traits which formed the basis for a prosperous society. Americans were industrious. They possessed a dynamic work ethic and self-reliance. Because the society was largely classless, nearly all Americans who had to work for a living eventually identified themselves as "middle class" so far as social status was concerned. This was true whether an individual was well-to-do or whether just scraping by. Nearly all working Americans viewed themselves as "middle class" and as such, enjoyed an economy where nearly everyone was a peer. There was general disdain for aristocracy or hereditary titles.

Murray points out that Americans were very religious, and that they put great importance in maintaining a religious society. While I disagree with his characterization of the Founders (and I will address the individual founders' beliefs in the following chapter) his point in the last sentence of the quote is well taken.

> *Ironically, given the importance they placed on religion, few of the Founders were themselves traditionally devout. They were men of the Enlightenment and its skepticism. Some, like Jefferson, were explicitly deists; others, like Washington, attended church but were vague about their belief in the details of Christian doctrine. But they emphatically agreed that religion was essential to the success of the American experiment.*

Murray suggests that another positive American trait springing from all of the above is a community spirit. Americans viewed each other as equals and were good neighbors. They helped each other when in need. They were quick to volunteer for charitable causes. They were generous with their resources to those who were in need.

But beyond those individual, general traits, Murray also develops the idea that America gave birth to a unique form of government, a democratic republic. People chose their own leaders. And that government was intentionally limited to allow the least infringement possible on the liberties of the people. Americans enjoyed the most freedom of any people – freedom to pursue their own success and to enjoy the fruits of their labors in a free enterprise economy.

Murray points out the obvious evils in which Americans are often criticized, namely slavery and treatment of Indians. We address the slavery issue in some depth elsewhere. Suffice it to say, our American ancestors were guilty of grievous sins visited on African slaves, and there is no justification for that. So Murray's comments in that regard are a just criticism.

With regard to our treatment of Indians, however, that issue is less cut-and-dried, and this might be a good place to address that. There seems to be an overwhelming desire on the part of those who openly despise America's founding to view indigenous peoples as all living peaceably in harmony with nature until the white man came and massacred them mercilessly. Nothing could be further from the truth. American Indians were human. They, like Europeans, were engaged in constant intertribal warfare. Displacement of tribes from one region to another through warfare was commonplace long before Europeans arrived.

Two fascinating books were published on this subject in 2007 by the University of Arizona Press, edited by Richard J. Chacon and Ruben G. Mendoza. These books were the by-product of a presentation at the American Anthropological Association symposium in Chicago in 2003. The books are titled *North American Indigenous Warfare and Ritual Violence* and *Latin American Indigenous Warfare and Ritual Violence*. Both volumes are filled with ample archeological and osteological evidence of frequent warfare and displacement among Indian tribes in centuries leading up to European contact, enough to disabuse any honest researcher of the inane "noble savage" ideas popular among academics.

First contact with Europeans did decimate many Indian tribes with diseases that they did not have immunity from, leaving most of the eastern coast sparsely populated by the time English settlements began to arrive. At the time Europeans did not understand the nature of these diseases any better than the Indians, and this devastation visited on indigenous tribes was certainly not intentional.

The few indigenous peoples who were originally impacted by English settlers were treated with friendship, and in most cases English settlers attempted to purchase territories to settle in from the Indians. For those who would accuse our predecessors of injustices toward the Indians, understand that the culture of most of these tribes was a warring culture, and there are two sides to that story. No doubt there were gross injustices on both sides.

Murray points out that many of America's positive traits were derided in many European countries. Our strong work ethic has always been derided – Americans live to work whereas Europeans work to live – to smell the roses, so to speak. To many European critics Americans are "equal," but there are huge disparities of income which go uncorrected. Americans' religiosity is outdated and superstitious. Murray quotes the typical European critic, "Intelligent people gave up the superstitions of religion long ago. Europe, which is effectively a secular continent except for Muslim immigrants, is more advanced than America in this regard. The continuing vitality of religion in America is a force for reactionary policies, not a force for good."

Murray asks the question, is the United States still exceptional?

> *The short answer is that America is still exceptional to some degree, but a lot less than it used to be…*
>
> *As the American welfare state has expanded, the risks of immigrating to the United States and starting from scratch that once were such an effective mechanism for selecting people with unusual determination have been eroded.…*
>
> *The common understanding of the limited role of government that united the Founders, including Hamilton, are now held only by a small minority of Americans, who are considered to be on the fringe of American politics.… it cannot be argued that the Founders' views of the proper scope of the Federal government bear any resemblance to the platforms of either the Democratic or the Republican Parties.*

Those exceptional traits found in early Americans have diminished as well, according to Murray. There is a far lower percentage of working age men employed full time. Many Americans do not know their neighbors nor get involved in their lives in any positive way. Religiosity is in decline.

In 1965 70% of Americans described their religion as "very important" to their lives and actions. By 1978 that number had dipped to just 52%. Those describing themselves as having "no religion" rose from 8% in 1990 to 18% in 2010.

> *In terms of governing agendas, the distinctions between America's and Europe's politics have blurred. Republican presidents from Dwight Eisenhower through George W. Bush, with the single exception of Ronald Reagan, governed in ways that are similar to those of Europe's center-right leaders.*

Murray concludes by expressing concerns over the future of America, pointing out that "factions" – today we would generally refer to them as "special interests" – are bringing down America's exceptionalism just as the founders predicted they would.

> *America still has exceptional aspects, but we are no longer the unique outlier that amused, amazed, and bemused the rest of the world from its founding through the first half of the twentieth century...*
>
> *As James Madison explained in Federalist 10, human beings pursue power and, in its pursuit, form factions... "who are united and actuated by some common impulse of passion, or of interest, adverse to the rights of other citizens, or to the permanent and aggregate interests of the community."... The power that only a government can legitimately wield ... is such a potent force for advancing one's own interests that some people will do almost anything to achieve that power... "If men were angels," Madison wrote in one of the most famous passages from The Federalist, "no government would be necessary...."*

We see from the writings of these two men, Hodgson and Murray, the two representative views of American Exceptionalism today. But, as we shall see in the following chapter, both men are right and both also wrong.

Chapter 13
Divine Providence, The Missing Ingredient

I want to try to help you understand what "American Exceptionalism" and greatness is all about. It does not mean that we Americans are better than anyone else. It does not mean that there is something uniquely different about us as human beings compared to other people in the world. It does not mean that we as a country have never faced problems of our own.

American Exceptionalism and greatness means that America is special because it is different from all other countries in history. It is a land built on true freedom and individual liberty and it defends both around the world. The role of the United States is to encourage individuals to be the best that they can be, to try to improve their lives, reach their goals, and make their dreams come true... [Rush Limbaugh in the preface to *Rush Revere and the Brave Pilgrims*, 2013.]

In the first book of Rush Limbaugh's popular *Rush Revere* children's series, he explains his reason for writing the book. It is so that future generations will know and understand the uniqueness of America, and will come to appreciate the reasons for that incredible success. From Rush's perspective American exceptionalism is mostly about our founders' love of liberty and the type of government they devised to secure liberty for all Americans.

There was clearly an unprecedented greatness in America – an effect which had a cause. This whole book is about understanding that cause. I trust as I have taken you chapter by chapter through two Supreme Court cases, our early education system, our founding philosophy and our unique system of government that you have seen a common thread.

Beginning in Chapter 1 we examined the history of early America. We established that the American States were founded by Christians with an exclusively Christian point of view. We discovered that all of our early educational institutions and efforts were exclusively Christian; that our early K-12 education right up through the late 1800s and even into the 1900s was exclusively Christian; that our early colleges and universities were founded mainly by Christian sects for the purpose of training ministers of the gospel, and that even our early State colleges were exclusively Christian in their founding and curricula, extending throughout the 1800s.

All of this was done intentionally, or as the Northwest Ordinance of August, 1789 pointed out, "Religion, morality and knowledge [are] necessary to good government and the happiness of mankind." The 1844 case, *Vidal v. Girard's Executors* that we looked at in Chapter 1 demonstrates that our educational system was intentionally Christian and indeed mandated to be so.

We noted in Chapter 2 that our Supreme Court judges understood the unique Christian character of our States and nation, and that as late as 1892, with the *Church of the Holy Trinity* case, the Supreme Court declared that this is a Christian nation, and that Christianity has a privileged place in America, which could not be said of any other religion. We have heard the exclusively Christian declarations of our founders, and we have read the wisdom of those Christian philosophers that our founders believed and trusted, men like John Locke, Montesquieu, and especially Sir William Blackstone whom our founders embraced in establishing our system of laws and jurisprudence.

That is all history, undeniable by any knowledgeable historian, even the secularist who would try to convince you otherwise. But what does that have to do with American exceptionalism? Does Christianity always produce prosperity? There have been dozens of "Christian" nations throughout history, and few have experienced unique success to the degree that America has. What made America different?

Our founding fathers believed in Divine Providence, that Providence rules. Providence was not just a cliché in our founding documents. It represented the belief system of the founders. No one can read our founding documents, our Declaration of Independence, or George Washington's Farewell Address without seeing that. The words "Providence" or "Divine Providence" are scattered throughout our founding documents for all generations to see. However, seeing it is one thing – understanding it is something very different.

The word Providence, or often Divine Providence, which was used by many of our founders in their writings and in our founding documents, has a specific meaning which was understood the same by all of our founders. Providence is an outcome directed by the hand of the all-powerful God of the Bible, whereby He controls natural forces (Matt. 8:27) and human decisions (Prov. 21:1) to work His will, either in support of, or in opposition to, human desires and plans. This is often done in response to the prayers of His people, or to the actions, good or evil, of people on earth. ("What manner of man is this, that even the winds and the sea obey him?" Matt 8:27 and "The king's heart is in the hand of the LORD, as the rivers of water: he turneth it whithersoever he will." Proverbs 21:1)

In the previous chapter we looked at two perspectives on American exceptionalism by Godfrey Hodgson and Charles Murray, both tasked with analyzing and explaining American exceptionalism. Both are guilty of a common misconception. That misconception is simply this – America's obvious success had a *natural* cause that secular research and observation can discover and understand. It argues that exceptionalism in general is an effect, and coming to understand its natural cause will allow us to prolong this success in America or to duplicate this success elsewhere. This is the evolutionary theory of exceptionalism – held to strict Darwinist standards. Whatever is observable must have a natural cause.

Where Hodgson and Murray both missed the mark is their view that the exceptionalism of nations is from natural causes. The whole point of this book is that American exceptionalism had a *spiritual* cause, not a natural cause. It was all about Divine Providence. What I have tried to accomplish in this book is to paint a picture of American history with special emphasis on the spirituality and accompanying belief system of our founders and what they tried to put into practice. Our history of settlement, and eventually of government, is a particularly Biblical Christian history about the exceptional blessing of God.

Like the Creation/Evolution debate, if you limit the debate on exceptionalism or on origins to natural, observable causes you are rigging the rules so that only one side can possibly win the debate. If those are the rules, then evolutionists win the argument every time because the rules prohibit us from considering the God of Creation as a possible cause. While winning the debate in favor of evolution might be gratifying to the atheist, it proves nothing. It is only sophistry. It seeks to suppress the truth of what really happened or how we really got here.

There is a cause that resulted in the earth, the planets, and the life we see all around us. However, it is not a natural cause but rather a supernatural cause. "In the beginning God created . . ." That is truth. In spite of all the fancy natural theories, the *truth* is that God did it all by Himself. Truth is all that really matters. After all, isn't truth what we are really looking for in considering the cause of American exceptionalism?

So, in considering American exceptionalism, let's explore this bedrock *truth* which pertains to and is binding on all nations at all times: *"Righteousness exalts a nation, but sin is a reproach to any people."* Proverbs 14:34. How is that for a simple cause and effect statement? If you seek Biblical righteousness, God exalts your nation. If you allow sin to dominate, your nation will be brought low. Pretty simple, isn't it? If you thought I was going to reveal some new, magic political formula for diverting America's decline, or some new insight that would explain our exceptionalism as a natural by-product of doing this or that, I offer instead this old idea, written 3,000 years ago. Righteousness builds – sin tears down. Divine Providence rules.

How is this for a related truth? *Our founders believed that.* However, they believed much more than just that. They believed that God gives us life, that He gives us our rights, and that He is our governor and judge – the one who prescribes what is right and what is wrong – that these truths and obligations are not man-made but are spelled out in God's Word, the Bible. This is what President George Washington meant when he said in his farewell address:

> *Of all the dispositions and habits which lead to political prosperity, religion and morality are indispensable supports. . . . And let us with caution indulge the supposition that morality can be maintained without* [Christianity – see Introduction]. *Whatever may be conceded to the influence of refined education on minds of peculiar structure, reason and experience both*

forbid us to expect that national morality can prevail in exclusion of [Christian] *principle.*

Washington went on to conclude with this rhetorical question, "Can it be that Providence has not connected the permanent felicity of a nation with its virtue?" In other words, it is unthinkable that our nation's state of morality will not be rewarded or punished by the God who sees all. Whatever our resources, whatever our circumstances, Divine Providence rules. George Washington believed that.

Or how about this from the old "deist" himself, Benjamin Franklin. Following is part of a speech delivered by Franklin at the Constitutional Convention in the summer of 1787 in support of a motion to begin every session on their knees in prayer before God. This motion was made at a time of crisis, when the Convention was at a stalemate and facing imminent failure. (If you understand the meaning of the term "deist" as it is defined today you will recognize from this speech that this is certainly no deist speaking.)

> *... In this situation of this Assembly, groping as it were in the dark to find political truth, and scarce able to distinguish it when presented to us, how has it happened, Sir, that we have not hitherto once thought of humbly applying to the Father of Lights to illuminate our understandings? In the beginning of the contest with Great Britain, when we were sensible of danger we had daily prayer in this room for the Divine protection. Our prayers, Sir, were heard, and they were graciously answered. All of us who were engaged in the struggle must have observed frequent instances of a superintending Providence in our favor.*
>
> *To that kind Providence we owe this happy opportunity of consulting in peace on the means of establishing our future national felicity. And have we now forgotten that powerful friend? Or do we imagine that we no longer need His assistance? I have lived, Sir, a long time, and the longer I live, the more convincing proofs I see of this truth - that God governs in the affairs of men. And if a sparrow cannot fall to the ground without his notice, is it probable that an empire can rise without*

> his aid? We have been assured, Sir, in the Sacred Writings, that "except the Lord build the House they labor in vain that build it." I firmly believe this; and I also believe that without His concurring aid we shall succeed in this political building no better, than the builders of Babel: We shall be divided by our little partial local interests; our projects will be confounded, and we ourselves shall become a reproach and bye word down to future ages...

Franklin's motion, while rejected at the time, ultimately established the precedent of beginning every session of the U.S. House and Senate with prayer, a revered custom which continues to this day. It was also soon followed by a cooperative spirit at that Convention which broke through the logjam with the Great Compromise between the large States and the small States, a compromise which became such a successful part of our nation's political structure.

Consider, if you will, Franklin's statement, "I have lived, Sir, a long time, and the longer I live, the more convincing proofs I see of this truth - that God governs in the affairs of men. And if a sparrow cannot fall to the ground without his notice, is it probable that an empire can rise without his aid? We have been assured, Sir, in the Sacred Writings, that 'except the Lord build the House they labor in vain that build it.' **I firmly believe this** ..." [Emphasis mine]. Ben Franklin was simply saying that Divine Providence rules.

Imagine that for just a moment – one of the three founders most accused of atheism, skepticism or deism by secularists says "I firmly believe that God governs in the affairs of men, and I firmly believe that except the Lord build the house, they labor in vain that build it, and if we do not seek God's assistance we will fail just as the builders of Babel failed."

Most modern historians love to assert that Franklin was a skeptic and deist. They assert the same of Thomas Jefferson and George Washington. They do this because these three men were in today's mind the most influential in the founding processes. They then try to extend that portrayal of skepticism and unbelief to all of the founders, suggesting that these were generally secular men just like modern academics, desiring to rid government from the last vestiges of Puritanism, establishing a secular government with strict *separation of Church and State*.

So how about this from the another similarly portrayed founding father, Thomas Jefferson. "And can the liberties of a nation be thought secure when we have removed their only firm basis, a conviction in the minds of the people that these liberties are of the gift of God? That they are not to be violated but with his wrath? Indeed I tremble for my country when I reflect that God is just: that his justice cannot sleep for ever..." (*Notes on the State of Virginia*, 1781-1782)

Jefferson was referring here specifically to the national sin of slavery, and he was pondering the future of America in relation to God's justice. He feared that this sin of slavery would be severely judged by God, impacting the whole of the people. He was saying that our future well-being is dependent upon our righteousness before God. Or in other words, as Washington and Franklin proclaimed, so also Jefferson proclaimed, *"Righteousness exalts a nation, but sin is a reproach to any people. Divine Providence rules."*

And as the United States Supreme Court in 1892 explained (see Chapter 2), after a thorough investigation of our founding circumstances and documents, the country as it existed more than one hundred years after our independence was still the same Christian society:

> *...And in the famous case of @ 43 U. S. 198, this Court, while sustaining the will of Mr. Girard, with its provision for the creation of a college into which no minister should be permitted to enter, observed: "It is also said, and truly, that the Christian religion is a part of the common law of Pennsylvania."*
>
> *If we pass beyond these matters to a view of American life, as expressed by its laws, its business, its customs, and its society, we find everywhere a clear recognition of the same truth. Among other matters, note the following: the form of oath universally prevailing, concluding with an appeal to the Almighty; the custom of opening sessions of all deliberative bodies and most conventions with prayer; the prefatory words of all wills, "In the name of God, amen;" the laws respecting the observance of the Sabbath, with the general cessation of all secular business, and the closing of courts, legislatures, and other similar public assemblies on that day; the churches and church organizations which abound in every city, town, and hamlet; the multitude of*

charitable organizations existing everywhere under Christian auspices; the gigantic missionary associations, with general support, and aiming to establish Christian missions in every quarter of the globe. These, and many other matters which might be noticed, add a volume of unofficial declarations to the mass of organic utterances that this is a Christian nation.

And so it was – by design. The founders designed it that way, seeking God's blessing. As we have already demonstrated, they established a system of laws and of education which advanced Christianity and righteousness, believing that *"Righteousness exalts a nation, but sin is a reproach to any people."* Can you read that famous 1892 Supreme Court case and, in honesty, come to any other conclusion?

I believe it is easy to establish from our history what our founders believed – they believed that God would either reward them or judge them for their national righteousness or lack thereof. We heard from Washington, Franklin, and Jefferson about their view of God and His Providence. Those are the three that are routinely questioned as to their beliefs. None of the other founders are so questioned other than Thomas Paine, because almost all of the other founders left a legacy in their personal lives and writings demonstrating faith in God, His Word, and Providential rule.

It is easy to establish from the history of our country that Christianity was embraced and generally practiced from our founding years through at least the early 1900s by generally everyone. It was inculcated into our early educational system because it was believed that future generations needed to understand the key to their own success and prosperity. This unique characteristic was not lost on Alexis de Tocqueville in the mid-1800s when he wrote, "The Americans combine the notions of Christianity and of liberty so intimately in their minds, that it is impossible to make them conceive the one without the other," as we quoted back in the Introduction.

I realize that anyone with a minimum of research will be able to show me specific examples of American behavior and even official policies through the years that were not Christian or God-honoring. Even the personal lives of some of our founders were not all they should have been. However, we knew right and wrong from the Bible, and America was generally agreed on what was right and what was wrong. America has never been all it should have been before God. We have embraced and, indeed, paid for grievous sins through our history.

One of my favorite places in Washington DC is the Lincoln Memorial. I have gone there many times just for reflection and inspiration. It is inspiring in its architecture and in its spacious design, but most inspiring are the words which are engraved in its stone walls. On its south wall is carved the full text of the Gettysburg Address. On its north wall is carved the full text of Lincoln's Second Inaugural Address. This is a shrine dedicated to a man who believed, as our founders believed, particularly Jefferson, that "Righteousness exalts a nation, but sin *is* a reproach to *any* people." While Jefferson spelled out his concerns about God's justice and wrath in faith, not yet seeing the culmination of his prophesy, Lincoln spoke of that great struggle from his own history which directly embodied Jefferson's greatest fears.

Lincoln's Second Inaugural Address was delivered just a few weeks before the Civil War ended. When that great speech was delivered it seemed apparent that this great war, a national calamity in which over 600,000 American soldiers were killed, and almost no family was left untouched, was nearing a conclusion. In that context, read Lincoln's greatest speech with the fears of Thomas Jefferson ringing in your ears, "... Indeed I tremble for my country when I reflect that God is just: that his justice cannot sleep for ever..."

> *Fellow-Countrymen:*
>
> *AT this second appearing to take the oath of the Presidential office there is less occasion for an extended address than there was at the first. Then a statement somewhat in detail of a course to be pursued seemed fitting and proper. Now, at the expiration of four years, during which public declarations have been constantly called forth on every point and phase of the great contest which still absorbs the attention and engrosses the energies of the nation, little that is new could be presented. The progress of our arms, upon which all else chiefly depends, is as well known to the public as to myself, and it is, I trust, reasonably satisfactory and encouraging to all. With high hope for the future, no prediction in regard to it is ventured.*

>On the occasion corresponding to this four years ago all thoughts were anxiously directed to an impending civil war. All dreaded it, all sought to avert it. While the inaugural address was being delivered from this place, devoted altogether to saving the Union without war, insurgent agents were in the city seeking to destroy it without war—seeking to dissolve the Union and divide effects by negotiation. Both parties deprecated war, but one of them would make war rather than let the nation survive, and the other would accept war rather than let it perish, and the war came.
>
>One-eighth of the whole population were colored slaves, not distributed generally over the Union, but localized in the southern part of it. These slaves constituted a peculiar and powerful interest. All knew that this interest was somehow the cause of the war. To strengthen, perpetuate, and extend this interest was the object for which the insurgents would rend the Union even by war, while the Government claimed no right to do more than to restrict the territorial enlargement of it. Neither party expected for the war the magnitude or the duration which it has already attained. Neither anticipated that the cause of the conflict might cease with or even before the conflict itself should cease. Each looked for an easier triumph, and a result less fundamental and astounding. Both read the same Bible and pray to the same God, and each invokes His aid against the other. It may seem strange that any men should dare to ask a just God's assistance in wringing their bread from the sweat of other men's faces, but let us judge not, that we be not judged. The prayers of both could not be answered. That of neither has been answered fully.
>
>The Almighty has His own purposes. "Woe unto the world because of offenses; for it must needs be that offenses come, but woe to that man by whom the offense cometh." [Matthew 18:7] If we shall suppose that American slavery is one of those offenses which, in the providence of God, must needs come, but which, having continued through His appointed time, He now wills to remove, and that He gives to both North and South this terrible war as the woe due to those by whom the offense

came, shall we discern therein any departure from those divine attributes which the believers in a living God always ascribe to Him? Fondly do we hope, fervently do we pray, that this mighty scourge of war may speedily pass away. Yet, if God wills that it continue until all the wealth piled by the bondsman's two hundred and fifty years of unrequited toil shall be sunk, and until every drop of blood drawn with the lash shall be paid by another drawn with the sword, as was said three thousand years ago, so still it must be said "the judgments of the Lord are true and righteous altogether."

With malice toward none, with charity for all, with firmness in the right as God gives us to see the right, let us strive on to finish the work we are in, to bind up the nation's wounds, to care for him who shall have borne the battle and for his widow and his orphan, to do all which may achieve and cherish a just and lasting peace among ourselves and with all nations.

The thrust of Lincoln's Second Inaugural Address is clear, and it is the answer to Thomas Jefferson's speculated fears. Lincoln suggested something that no American President would dare suggest today, that a national calamity was the judgment of God against a specific national sin. He gave no other accounting for the American Civil War other than that this terrible war was God's judgment on the nation for the sin of slavery. And clearly he was right.

While Jefferson worried, "Indeed I tremble for my country when I reflect that God is just: that his justice cannot sleep for ever," Lincoln explained the great war as the fulfillment of Jefferson's prophesy,

> *He [God] gives to both North and South this terrible war as the woe due to those by whom the offense came... if God wills that it continue until all the wealth piled by the bondsman's two hundred and fifty years of unrequited toil shall be sunk, and until every drop of blood drawn with the lash shall be paid by another drawn with the sword, as was said three thousand years ago, so still it must be said "the judgments of the Lord are true and righteous altogether."*

This is how our founders thought, and how our national leaders used to think, right into the early-1900s.

But was their belief really true? Or was it just religious superstition that we of a more educated, enlightened society have now outgrown? Those of us who believe that the Bible is the Word of God and that it is completely true from cover to cover will answer a firm "YES, it IS true" to that question. Spiritual rot has severe consequences to a nation. To many in our nation it will not be true until we reach a time of terror in our country so powerful that it drives the nation to its knees, back to God and His righteousness. To many skeptics and atheists it will never be true until they personally stand before God in judgment.

It must also be emphasized that America's exceptional rise to power was in no way a reflection of America's inherent ingenuity or superiority. It is that suspicion in the hearts of too many Americans, patriotic Americans, even Christian Americans – that arrogance, that we are greater because we are somehow better that translates into a giant chip on the shoulder to the rest of the world. While some resentment from other countries is simply envy, it has to be said that some resentment is deserved from our own attitudes and condescension toward other countries. That arrogance is the opposite of faith in God and His Providence and humble gratitude for all His blessings.

Our heartfelt attitude must be to acknowledge in true humility that to whatever extent America is great, it is completely by the blessing of God, bathed in the prayers of its founders, and to whatever extent it remains great, it will be by the grace of God. Throughout our history, *we have been Exceptionally Blessed*. We are neither better nor stronger nor smarter than citizens of any other country. Our mission is still the same as it was in 1620, "for the Glory of God, and advancements of the Christian faith..."

But what about all those exceptional traits that we discussed in the previous chapter? Weren't those the real cause of our exceptionalism? The type of freedom we embraced? The community spirit? Free enterprise? That Puritan work ethic? Equality of opportunity? Equality under the law? Weren't these the things that caused us to become great?

If you get nothing else out of this book, you need to understand this one important fact. All of the above American traits are Bible principles. Bible principles were embraced on purpose by our founders who were students of the Bible, not necessarily because they thought these things would make of them an empire, but because they believed the practical application of Biblical principles was right, and that it would lead to God's blessing. They feared the stern warning, that not to apply Bible principles would lead to God's judgment on the nation. They believed that the Bible is the "users manual" for all human life created in God's image, written by the Creator, to be understood and literally put into practice by His creation. And so, they did their best to do just that.

The very liberty we enjoy is a Bible principle. Community spirit – helping your neighbor, giving to the poor are all Bible principles. Our free enterprise economic system is based on Bible principle. The right to enjoy the fruits of your own labor is a Bible principle. Hard work is a Bible principle. Equality before man is an extension of natural law (see Chapter 6), the principle of equality before God, and the creation principle that our founders embraced, that "all men are created equal" and all are "endowed by their creator" with the same rights – Bible principles one and all. *"There is neither Jew nor Greek, there is neither bond nor free, there is neither male nor female: for ye are all one in Christ Jesus."* Galatians 2:28

In America, given a blank slate for the first time in history, Christian men were free to practice Biblical precepts without interference and to incorporate those into their laws. No, they didn't practice it consistently, and slavery was ever before them as a mockery to what they held sacred, and for which they were destined to pay an awful price. However, they believed the Bible, and they endeavored to incorporate it into every aspect of their lives. So, when Charles Murray in his book *American Exceptionalism* lists the traits that described early Americans, he fails to mention that these traits were all Bible principles that early Americans embraced, not because they would lead to exceptionalism per se, but because they were right.

It is probably good to point out that America was not the first or the only Christian nation. That is an important point, that is, that the history of Western civilization is predominately the story of applied natural law and Christianity to varying degrees. However, Christianity in other countries has had to contend with governments and traditions which are not based on pure Biblical Christianity. The monarchies and the "divine right of kings" philosophies of Europe were neither Biblical nor Christian, even though they characterized themselves as "Christian States."

The blank slate that represented the early independent American

States allowed for an opportunity to design from scratch a government, laws, and customs which were as Biblical as our founders could conceive, with a uniquely Puritan perspective. For the most part it was the practical application of the principles of Reformation Protestantism, the greatest principle being the authority of the Word of God over everything else. It was the complete authority of the Bible that distinguished Reformation Christianity from the older forms of "Christianity" and monarchy that ruled in Europe.

America's founders were unique in this sense, that they allowed their faith in the Bible to shape their thoughts, their actions, and their government. They were true, practicing Christians. The bottom line, and the thesis of this entire book, is simply this, <u>America became exceptional, not because of what we did, but because of what we were</u>. As a result, Divine Providence smiled on that undertaking.

In contrasting the medieval "Christian" nations of Europe with American republicanism, there is an interesting parallel with church polity. For those of you who have never studied church structure, there are three types of church government. Episcopal governance, coming from the Greek word for "overseer," is a top-down form of hierarchy, such as characterizes the Roman Catholic and the Anglican churches. Presbyterian governance, coming from the Greek word for "elder," utilizes more of a representative form of governance in which multiple mature men are selected to oversee church operations. This is the type of government which is employed by Presbyterian and Reformed churches. Congregational governance is simple democracy, meaning a church run pretty much by popular vote. This is generally the governance in Congregational and most Baptist churches.

Before King James I became king of England he was already king of Scotland. In feuding with the Scottish Presbyterians who believed in a divided leadership, James argued for strong bishop rule in the Scottish church, based primarily on his Roman Catholic sympathies which tended to be self-serving. He was famous for declaring to the Presbyterians, "No bishop, no king!" In other words, James believed in the Episcopal form of church governance, and that extended into his ideas about civil government. He believed that if the church were to engage in divided power, this would threaten the powers of the monarchy as well. Indeed, most of Europe was dominated by various hierarchal forms of church governance, mostly Roman Catholic.

In contrast, because 98% of Americans in the late 1700s were Protestant, they applied the principles of the Protestant Reformation to civil government. They leaned more toward either Presbyterian or Congregational forms of church polity. They saw no Biblical basis for any dictatorial form of church government, and that, along with painful personal experience with European monarchs, shaped their thinking in structuring the civil government. Most of the sympathies for our current democratic republican form of government came from the founders' belief that the Bible prescribed this type of structure.

There is somewhat of a parallel with America in more recent Europe. England in the 1700s and 1800s began to separate from the Anglo-Catholic practice of the Church of England toward more evangelical forms of Christianity in which the authority of the Bible was recognized and practiced, while at the same time the power of monarchy was giving way to more Parliamentary power and more religious freedom. During that period England experienced numerous revivals and a greatly expanded missionary effort to spread Christianity around the world. England was exceptionally blessed, and even though a small island nation, "The sun never set on the British Empire."

The same can be said of our neighbor to the North, Canada. While not as populous or as powerful as the United States, the people of Canada experienced a similar exceptionalism and for the same reasons. Their general practice and government were based on a Biblical foundation, and the result was the blessing of God in much the same way that the blessing of God elevated the States to the South.

Through the years American legislators, and those in several other English-speaking countries, drawing from Sir William Blackstone's lead, wrote moral laws with the Bible in mind. Blasphemy of God and Jesus Christ was against the civil law, and in many places still is (see Chapter 2). Taking God's name in vain was against the law. Engaging in commerce on Sundays was against the law. Adultery was against the law, a felony in most States. Homosexuality was against the law, a felony in every State until 1962. Pornography was against the law. (As we have seen, most of these moral laws have since been struck down unconstitutionally by our U.S. Supreme Court.)

In Chapter 9 we mentioned the Essex County, Massachusetts convention in December, 1814, which brought 13 of the towns together to address the problem of many in the county not properly observing the Sabbath. They had convened because the General Court (Massachusetts State legislature) had passed a resolution that instructed the towns to act on this important issue. Why would a State legislature encourage the local governments to enact ordinances which enforced Sabbath observance? Because the Word of God instructed them to "Remember the Sabbath, to keep it holy." (See Appendix D)

And why were homosexuality, adultery, profanity, and blasphemy against the law? Because our forefathers believed that these things were wrong, a violation of both natural law and the Bible. They believed that the God who gave us our rights, and defined those rights, expected society to recognize this fact – that His blessings or chastening would be upon them depending on their righteousness. Freedom at that time was not a disconnected abstract to be practiced unrestrained by libertine perverts. Freedom was understood as the liberty to do what is right and good, for self, family, or community, with no one preventing it. Freedom was the birthright of Americans to be free from immorality and its corrosive influences on persons and on society in general.

Our forefathers found all of these moral principles in the Bible. They believed that the eyes of God were upon them, and that *"Righteous exalts a nation, but sin is a reproach to any people."* They believed in the absolute morality of the Bible – that many things are inherently evil. As a practical matter, they had faith that the application of Bible truth would produce a positive result for society. Indeed, it produced an exceptional blessing.

They took oaths – oaths of honesty, oaths of office – with an appeal to God. They believed that God would hold them personally accountable for the fulfillment of these oaths. As George Washington asked, and quoted in our introduction, where is there any incentive to following through on an oath without the fear of God? It is so fundamental.

While both Godfrey Hodgson and Charles Murray were mostly right in their accounting of American history and the traits that made America unique – even the origins of those traits – they both missed the most important ingredient. That ingredient was the special blessing of God. Hodgson alludes to it in a mocking way:

> *President Bush [43] has struck the pure exceptionalist vein again and again in his speeches. More than most, he has added his own religious color to the exceptionalist rhetoric, never more clearly than in his speech accepting the Republican nomination at the 2004 convention: "Like generations before us," he cried in his peroration, "we have a calling from beyond the stars to stand for freedom. This is the everlasting dream of America, and tonight, in this place, that dream is renewed. Now we go forward, grateful for our freedom, faithful to our cause, and confident in the future of the greatest nation on earth."*
>
> *A calling from beyond the stars! The phrase recalls the quip of the Victorian radical member of Parliament, Henry Labouchere, about another evangelical Christian in politics, the prime minister, William Gladstone. He didn't mind the prime minister's having the fifth ace up his sleeve, Labouchere said, he just objected to his saying that the Almighty had put it there.*

Hodgson's mockery notwithstanding, our founders clearly believed in God and His Word. They were students of the Bible, and they sought to live out the principles of God's Word in their everyday lives. And as we have seen throughout Part I of this book, they infused our culture and our laws with those Bible principles. They believed God would bless them for that, and righteousness did indeed exalt that nation. God blessed them exceptionally, just as He promised. Drawing from the beliefs of "generations before us," President Bush's comment was a subtle recognition of that historical fact.

But is this distinction important, that America's greatness was the blessing of God as opposed to our physical or political attributes? This distinction is not only important, it is critical to understanding our way forward. If we believe our problems can be remedied simply by physical or political actions, then we will continue to slide into the oblivion of once-great empires. It is only in understanding that our exceptionalism is the blessing of Divine Providence that we have the key to saving America.

There is yet another Providential reason besides righteousness which promoted America to greatness. Genesis 12:1-3 describes God's calling of Abraham, and His covenant with Abraham.

> Now the LORD had said unto Abram, Get thee out of thy country, and from thy kindred, and from thy father's house, unto a land that I will shew thee:
> And I will make of thee a great nation, and I will bless thee, and make thy name great; and thou shalt be a blessing:
> And I will bless them that bless thee, and curse him that curseth thee: and in thee shall all families of the earth be blessed.

Later in Genesis 17:7-8, God expands on that covenant, promising Abraham's descendants the land of Canaan as an everlasting inheritance and his covenant with the nation of Israel to be an everlasting covenant. Although we see Israel today in a general state of unbelief concerning their Messiah, Jesus Christ, the apostle Paul writes in Romans 11 that the nation of Israel will all one day turn to their Messiah in faith, believing. So, we see from these passages that God has a special plan for the Jewish people and the nation of Israel.

But go back to the Genesis passage quoted above and notice how the "seed of Abraham" impacts other nations. God said, "And I will bless them that bless thee, and curse him that curseth thee: and in thee shall all families of the earth be blessed." In addition to righteousness, God in His Providence blesses nations based on how they treat His special people, Israel and the Jewish people. America, through the years has been blessed by God because generally we embraced Biblical righteousness, and because America has always been a refuge for the Jewish people and has always been a friend of the nation of Israel.

Throughout the centuries for over 2,500 years, the world in general has had a hatred for the Jewish people and has persecuted the Jews mercilessly. This did not start with Hitler. It goes back at least as far as Haman in the book of Esther, several hundred years before Christ. Throughout history, from Haman to Hitler, the Jews have been pushed out of one country after another, and have suffered persecution in almost every other country. Yet, in the Providence of God, the Jewish people over that 2,500 years always miraculously maintained their special identity until 1948, when, for the first time in two and a half millennia, the Jewish people had their own home and government.

Hatred of the Jewish people is as universal as it is illogical, apart from the Bible explanation. There is no explaining the degree to which other nations will go to single out and persecute Jews. In 1967 all the surrounding nations decided to simultaneously attack Israel and drive them out of their homeland back into the sea once and for all. And in just six days, in response to that scheme, Israel expanded their territory three times over. Providence rules.

During our entire history, from the beginning right up to the recent stand in favor of Israel and against the other nations of the world at the United Nations, America has stood with Israel. And just as God promised, "I will bless them that bless thee," God has blessed America. God has blessed America for its righteousness and God has blessed America as a friend of His chosen people. Indeed we are *exceptionally blessed*.

There is yet one aspect to Providence that I haven't touched on, that is the nature of Providence itself. While most of God's dealings with nations are cause-and-effect, based on a nation's obedience or disobedience to God and His Word, some of God's dealings with nations are simply Providential. God sometimes exalts nations simply for His own reasons, usually as a tool to bring down a nation which defies Him.

Jeremiah, the Old Testament prophet wrote of the great empire, Babylon, *"Thou art my battle axe and weapons of war: for with thee will I break in pieces the nations, and with thee will I destroy kingdoms."* (Jer. 51:20) Babylon certainly had done nothing deserving of the assistance of Divine Providence. It was a pagan, immoral society, and its rule was relatively brief. But it was God's tool in God's time to punish ungodly nations and to discipline His chosen nation Israel.

> *Who hath directed the Spirit of the LORD, or being his counsellor hath taught him? With whom took he counsel, and who instructed him, and taught him in the path of judgment, and taught him knowledge, and shewed to him the way of understanding? Behold, the nations are as a drop of a bucket, and are counted as the small dust of the balance: behold, he taketh up the isles as a very little thing. And Lebanon is not*

sufficient to burn, nor the beasts thereof sufficient for a burnt offering. All nations before him are as nothing; and they are counted to him less than nothing, and vanity.

Have ye not known? have ye not heard? hath it not been told you from the beginning? have ye not understood from the foundations of the earth? It is he that sitteth upon the circle of the earth, and the inhabitants thereof are as grasshoppers; that stretcheth out the heavens as a curtain, and spreadeth them out as a tent to dwell in: That bringeth the princes to nothing; he maketh the judges of the earth as vanity. Yea, they shall not be planted; yea, they shall not be sown: yea, their stock shall not take root in the earth: and he shall also blow upon them, and they shall wither, and the whirlwind shall take them away as stubble.

Seek ye the LORD while he may be found, call ye upon him while he is near: Let the wicked forsake his way, and the unrighteous man his thoughts: and let him return unto the LORD, and he will have mercy upon him; and to our God, for he will abundantly pardon. For my thoughts are not your thoughts, neither are your ways my ways, saith the LORD. For as the heavens are higher than the earth, so are my ways higher than your ways, and my thoughts than your thoughts.

(Isaiah 40:13-17, 21-24; 55:6-9)

God's thoughts are far above our thoughts. He does what He wills concerning nations even though we might not understand it or even agree with it. What He wills and does is always good and right.

On September 13, 2001, as a member of Michigan's House of Representatives I was asked by House Speaker, Rick Johnson, to offer a special prayer for the country at the beginning of a House Republican Caucus retreat. The country had just been stunned by the terrorist attacks on the World Trade towers in New York City two days before. There was now a mixture of shock, confusion, and anger in the hearts of most Americans.

The request to offer a prayer was, I think, a last-minute impulse on the part of Speaker Johnson in view of the tragic events two days earlier, and I didn't really have any time to think in advance about what I would pray. I was accustomed to praying in public, and had often offered the invocation at party functions and at the beginning of House sessions, so I was comfortable in saying I would be happy to do so.

As the retreat was called to order, Speaker Johnson asked me to step forward, and I recall beginning my prayer with a statement saturated in righteous indignation, "Our dear Heavenly Father, You tell us over and over in Your Word that one of the things you most hate is the shedding of innocent blood..." and immediately as I began to pray for God's righteous judgment to be meted out on all of those who had committed this terrible atrocity, I was struck by the thought of the millions upon millions of unborn babies that our nation had slaughtered over the past three decades. As the thought of justice permeated my thinking, it was with great difficulty that I finished that prayer with all the right thoughts for the victims, the first responders, the bereaved, and the nation, every word sticking in my throat. I had long believed that "sin is a reproach to any people." Now I was beginning to understand America's national sins in a new way.

God allowed slavery to exist for more than a hundred years before violently bringing it to a close, because He is a merciful God, slow to anger, preferring repentance over judgment. Under God's law Providence and righteousness are inseparable elements. Righteousness or its opposite will always reap a Providential response. Ultimately, God's Providence is engaged for better or worse based on a nation's righteousness even though He delays judgment in most cases to give opportunity for righteousness to prevail. However, in the absence of righteousness, God's judgment is certain.

Now, in a new way, America is beginning to experience the fruits of that inseparable Providence/righteousness connection. On September 11, 2001, we lost nearly 3,000 Americans, and have lost over 4,000 since in wars relating to that event, not to mention the billions of $$ in associated costs. For many years we experienced this blessed truth, that righteousness exalts a nation. Now we are once again beginning to experience the second part of that equation, that sin is a reproach to any people, Americans included. This is just an early warning, and our sins since 9/11 have not diminished; to the contrary they have multiplied to include perversions that could hardly be imagined even in 2001. There is yet a massive debt to repay with little hint of general repentance. And there appears to be no Abraham Lincoln in sight who rightly understands this.

1 And it shall come to pass, if thou shalt hearken diligently unto the voice of the LORD thy God, to observe and to do all his commandments which I command thee this day, that the LORD thy God will set thee on high above all nations of the earth:

2 And all these blessings shall come on thee, and overtake thee, if thou shalt hearken unto the voice of the LORD thy God.

3 Blessed shalt thou be in the city, and blessed shalt thou be in the field.

4 Blessed shall be the fruit of thy body, and the fruit of thy ground, and the fruit of thy cattle, the increase of thy kine, and the flocks of thy sheep.

5 Blessed shall be thy basket and thy store...

12 The LORD shall open unto thee his good treasure, the heaven to give the rain unto thy land in his season, and to bless all the work of thine hand: and thou shalt lend unto many nations, and thou shalt not borrow...

15 But it shall come to pass, if thou wilt not hearken unto the voice of the LORD thy God, to observe to do all his commandments and his statutes which I command thee this day; that all these curses shall come upon thee, and overtake thee:

16 Cursed shalt thou be in the city, and cursed shalt thou be in the field.

17 Cursed shall be thy basket and thy store.

18 Cursed shall be the fruit of thy body, and the fruit of thy land, the increase of thy kine, and the flocks of thy sheep...

20 The LORD shall send upon thee cursing, vexation, and rebuke, in all that thou settest thine hand unto for to do, until thou be destroyed, and until thou perish quickly; because of the wickedness of thy doings, whereby thou hast forsaken me.
Deut. 28:1-5, 12, 15-18, 20

Part V
America on the Brink

Where does America stand today from God's perspective? Can America be restored to its former greatness? Can a nation which forgets God avoid God's judgment? What will it take for America to once again enjoy the blessings of God?

Chapter 14
Understanding Where We Are Headed

For You, O God, have heard my vows; You have given me the heritage of those who fear Your name. Psalm 61:5

In Psalm 61 David, king of Israel, is praising God for His power and His protection. Israel is beginning to become a great nation under David's leadership, and as he looks back at that national progress he cries out to God in thanksgiving, "You have given me the heritage of those who fear Your name."

David could look back a few years to the godly prophet Samuel who had anointed him to become king. He could look further back at great and godly leaders like Joshua and Gideon. He could look back at Moses who had given the children of Jacob their national identity and had, through God's leading and power, delivered them from the slavery of Egypt. What a great and God-blessed heritage! God had brought the children of Israel from a nation of slaves to a world power.

David's own son Solomon, who brought Israel to the zenith of its power, looking back on that same heritage, would observe, "Righteousness exalts a nation, but sin is a reproach to any people." Proverbs 14:34. Solomon could see not only the blessing of God for a nation's obedience, but also he could see in the history of Israel those instances where the chastening hand of God brought a rebellious nation to its knees when it wandered away from God.

Truly we here in America today can say with David, *"You have given me the heritage of those who fear Your name,"* and I trust that in reading the foregoing chapters you have seen ample evidence that our founders and forefathers feared God in a unique and special way among nations. The crux of the matter for America today is the realization that our nation's righteousness, or lack thereof, will determine our future course and destiny. If America repents of its many sins and comes back to its early faith in God, God will prosper and bless our country, for the promise of God is certain, *Righteousness exalts a nation.*

The original idea for this book came from a daily radio program, "Freedom's Foundation," which Pastor Rusty Chatfield and I have been doing since 2006. Over the years we covered most of the themes in this book with a desire to educate our corner of the world about our Christian heritage.

That radio program was the impetus for a Power Point presentation on the same topics which I and State Representative Lee Chatfield have presented in numerous churches throughout the State of Michigan. One of the key slides in that presentation shows a woman reclining in a small boat, oblivious to the world around her. She is relaxed and reading a book, paying no attention to her surroundings. The slide is entitled "Drift" and it introduces the concept of moving downstream with the culture until we have unwittingly lost our original principles.

This river upon which we are adrift starts out as a calm, slow stream whose relentless decline is barely noticeable. However, downstream the river begins to pick up speed, and the calm waters become faster moving. It would still be quite easy to row the boat back up to where we began, but as the river drops down and picks up speed, a return back to the starting point becomes increasingly difficult. At last the quickening pace of the stream turns into a rapids from which it would be impossible to reverse course.

This is the form that "drift" takes in a culture, whether an individual or an institution or a nation. As we mentioned in the chapter on America's colleges, Harvard University started out as a Bible college for the expressed purpose of training ministers of the gospel of Jesus Christ. As we traced in Chapter 4, today Harvard is the enemy of all that is called Christian. Harvard drifted from strict orthodoxy to unbelief, not suddenly, but over a span of almost two hundred years. In like manner, most Bible colleges which were established in the early to mid-1900s have drifted far from their original positions, and some have become completely non-Christian.

The drift can be seen in many of our national trends and features. I will use one example of this which is obvious when you think about it. Many, if not most, of America's leaders right up through the early 1900s were devout

Christians. We have reviewed many of the sentiments of our founders in preceding chapters. We have discussed the second inaugural address by Abraham Lincoln, who dared to conclude with that great speech what few modern presidents would dare pronounce today, that the Civil War was God's judgment on a nation for the national sin of slavery.

During World War I most soldiers who served in battle in Europe were issued Bibles, New Testaments actually, when they entered the service. The Bibles that they were issued contained a preface either by President Woodrow Wilson or by General John Pershing, and some of the Bibles contained both. Below are the prefaces to Bibles issued to American Soldiers in World War I:

> *The Bible is the Word of Life. I beg that you will read it and find this out for yourselves, -read, not little snatches here and there, but long passages that will really be the road to the heart of it. You will find it full of real men and women not only, but also of the things you have wondered about and been troubled about all your life, as men have been always; and the more you read the more it will become plain to you what things are worth while and what are not, what things make men happy,-loyalty, right dealing, speaking the truth, readiness to give everything for what they think their duty, and, most of all, the wish that they may have the approval of the Christ, who gave everything for them, -and the things that are guaranteed to make men unhappy,-selfishness, cowardice, greed, and everything that is low and mean. When you have read the Bible you will know it is the Word of God, because you will have found in it the key to your own heart, your own happiness, and your own duty.*
>
> *Woodrow Wilson*

> *To the American Soldier aroused against a nation waging war in violation of all Christian principles. Our people are fighting in the cause of Liberty. Hardships will be your lot, but trust in God will give you comfort; temptation will befall you, but the teachings of our Savior will give you strength. Let your valor as*

a soldier and your conduct as a man be an inspiration to your comrades and an honor to your country."

Pershing, Comdg.

During World War II American soldiers were again issued similar Bibles upon entrance to the service. World War II era Bibles contained a preface by President Franklin Roosevelt. While it is a generally good statement about the inspirational nature of the Bible, it contains nothing of the heart of Wilson's Word of God or of Pershing's personal reference to "our Savior." The spiritual drift was perceptible. The Bible still had a place of honor, but it was no longer God's book – just an inspiring book.

> *As Commander-in-Chief, I take pleasure in commending the reading of the Bible to all who serve in the armed forces of the United States. Throughout the centuries men of many faiths and diverse origins have found in the Sacred Book words of wisdom, counsel and inspiration. It is a fountain of strength and now, as always, an aid in attaining the highest aspirations of the human soul.*
>
> *Franklin D. Roosevelt*

Since World War II there have been no similar promotion of Bibles to our soldiers. Many soldiers since that time have received Bibles from Gideons International. This is a wonderful ministry, and the Gideons get as many Bibles to our servicemen as they can through various local efforts, but that does not involve all, or even most, of those serving in the armed forces. My own personal experience in serving in the Army in the early 1970s was that I was never issued or offered a Bible as a serviceman. And in many places where American servicemen are stationed, particularly Muslim nations, they are urged to leave their personal Bibles at home. We have indeed come a long way.

It is on this theme, the idea of "drift," that I would like to focus for the remainder of the chapter. In doing so, I want to consider the Apostle Paul's warning to the church of Rome as he describes what a society looks like that at one time honored God, but later drifted from their faith in Him. If you can read the second half of the first chapter of Romans and not see

America in every verse, then you are not paying attention to what is going on around you.

In May of 2007 Pastor John MacArthur, in observance of the National Day of Prayer, preached a sermon at the Woodman Valley Chapel in Colorado Springs, Colorado, which was to some controversial, and to all very sobering. The message was titled *A Nation Abandoned by God*. The thesis of his message was that individuals and nations can reach a point in their lives where, because of consistent neglect, disobedience, or abandonment of God's Word, God gives them up to go their own way without His protective grace.

Much of what I write in the remainder of this chapter either comes directly from that sermon, or it is influenced by the principles that MacArthur outlined in that notable message. Rev. MacArthur has preached that sermon a number of times since, and it is generally available online. I encourage you to search it out and listen for yourself. It is a powerful message that every Christian needs to hear.

Perhaps the saddest verse in the Bible is found in the book of Judges (16:20) concerning Samson, "And he wist not that the Lord was departed from him," or in more common English, "He didn't realize that the Lord had left him." Samson had told Delilah the secret of his strength, and while he slept, she had his long hair cut. When he woke up under attack by the Philistines, he assumed he would simply take care of business as he always had, with God's strength. However, he didn't realize that the Lord had left him. He didn't feel any different, but he was very different. He had lost the blessing of God.

Has God abandoned America? That is a startling question. We claim that our motto is "In God We Trust." That was certainly true for much of our early years. It is fearful to contemplate that we may have already been abandoned by the God who raised us up to such exceptional heights. Yet Romans 1 seems to lay out such a scenario for nations which turn their backs on God. It is a sad thing indeed when a nation which once knew God's blessing and goodness is abandoned by God.

You will notice, beginning in Romans 1:18, a series of at least five distinct sins, possibly more, that a once Godly society experiences once they begin to move away from God in their thinking, and in each stage God removes Himself from them increasingly further until He cannot be found at all. Each of these sins is a sin that generally characterizes the society, either in the form of a large majority actually committing this sin or else a general acceptance, even an affirmation among the society toward those who do commit each of these sins. Each represents a further, downward step away from God and His righteous demands. In America, each one of these five sins represents a time period which distinctly corresponds with that particular sin.

America has not abandoned God just in the last few years. It is rather a long process, and throughout that process God waits patiently for America to return to Him. As that process hardens over decades of time the likelihood of America returning to God gets more and more remote, barring a cataclysmic event which drives the whole nation to its knees.

Step #1 of National Decline – Questioning God and His Word – Romans 1:18-20

It all starts with the questioning of God's Word. *"For the wrath of God is revealed from heaven against all ungodliness and unrighteousness of men, who hold* [literally withhold, or suppress] *the truth in unrighteousness"* Romans 1:18.

If you recall nothing else from the first chapters of this book, you certainly could not miss the truth that America's colonies and early States were by design constructed according to God's word. Blackstone regarded Scripture as the highest law of the land, as did most of America's founders. The founders required (See Chapter 1; *Northwest Ordinance*) the teaching of Scripture in the public schools through at least the first hundred years of the republic, and in many places, including most of rural America, far into the 1900s.

The first of five national sins from Romans 1 which take a society away from God's blessing is the sin of restraining the truth of God's Word, questioning it, replacing it with manmade philosophies. It is no more profound than the original temptation, beginning with Satan's challenge to Eve, "Hath God said?" Did God really do that? Did God really say that? Does God really expect that? Would God really enforce that? Notice the subtle questioning of God's work of creation which introduces this downward progression in a society that begins to turn away from God.

Throughout most of our history, God's Word was revered by most of the society. America's founders questioned little what was written, and they tried to pattern society after God's righteousness. As we saw in earlier chapters, it was illegal to blaspheme God. It was generally illegal to engage in commerce on Sundays. Profanity was illegal. Adultery was illegal. Homosexuality was illegal. Children were taught these moral absolutes in our nation's public schools. The textbooks of our early public schools assumed the truth of the Bible and of God's creative work.

In this passage we are considering, Paul goes on to explain that there is no logical reason to question God. First, God places within each human being a fundamental knowledge of Himself and of right and wrong. *("That was the true Light, which lighteth every man that cometh into the world."* John 1:9) Further, with this inner knowledge, all we have to do is look around us to see unmistakable evidence of God's power and supremacy. *"Because that which may be known of God is manifest in them; for God hath shewed it unto them. For the invisible things of Him from the creation of the world are clearly seen, being understood by the things that are made, even His eternal power and Godhead; so that they are without excuse."* (Romans 1:19-20) The beauty and complexity of God's creation are irrefutable proof of God's existence and His power, so that there is no excuse for questioning God.

Men have always questioned God's Word, but from the beginning of American colonies through the 1800s and even into the 1900s, those who questioned God's Word were a small, but growing minority. Even Darwin's theory of evolution was rejected well into the 1900s, the Scopes Monkey Trial in 1925 being an example of where the American heart was at the time. In that trial, John Scopes was convicted of teaching evolution in a public school in Tennessee, contrary to a law known as the Butler Act. Scopes appealed to the Tennessee Supreme Court in 1926, claiming that the Butler Act was unconstitutional, and lost again. Americans, especially rural Americans, believed the Bible.

But as academia began to question creation and God's existence, and as that unbelief began to trickle down into seminaries and into the pulpit, the mind of the nation in general began to question God. By the late 1940s most high schools were teaching evolution, and a whole generation of skeptics was born. Thus, the slide away from God and His truth was well under way.

Step #2 of National Decline – Proud & Rebellious Hearts – Romans 1:21-23

Once you have questioned God, God brings you to a point of decision. What will you do with those doubts? In this passage Paul describes the response toward these doubts in a nation that, though blessed by God, decides to turn its back on God.

> *Because that, when they knew God, they glorified him not as God, neither were thankful; but became vain in their imaginations, and their foolish heart was darkened. Professing themselves to be wise, they became fools, and changed the glory of the uncorruptible God into an image made like to corruptible man, and to birds, and four-footed beasts, and creeping things.*

These reactions start out as pride and unthankfulness – assuming for themselves the credit for what God had done. When God gave us victory at the close of World War II, we came out of that experience as an emerging super power. We had won. Our power and smarts had been demonstrated on the world stage on the seas of the Pacific and the battlefields of Europe. We were Americans, the strong, the brave, the victorious. While the conclusion of previous wars had driven Americans to their knees in churches for thanksgiving and praise to God for the victories, World War II was a celebration of American power. WE did it! We set about to rebuilding our economy in the 1950s, and WE did it. We set about to rebuilding war-torn Europe and Japan, and WE did it.

And while we were at it, we began to reject God's account of man's origin and purpose. We began instead to totally embrace evolution as a society. We embraced the ascendency of mankind and his ingenuity and powers as supreme. In our public schools we replaced worship of God with worship of man, otherwise known as secular humanism.

Verse 25 explains this ultimate rejection of God's truth, *"Who changed the truth of God into a lie, and worshipped and served the creature more than the Creator, who is blessed forever. Amen."* By the 1960s, by order of the U.S. Supreme Court, we had officially thrown God out of our schools, we had thrown the Bible out of our schools. And those decisions were met with hardly a whimper of opposition.

We all seemed to agree that the schools of America were no place to teach Christianity. Let all children believe as they like – it is not a government issue, we all agreed. Fairness demands that we must treat every religion as equal and of equal value, we all agreed. If we allow Christians to offer prayers in schools, we also must allow Muslims, Buddhists, and atheists the same honor, just to be fair.

The rejection of God's truth in America was now a consensus view. While Americans still attended church, they allowed their children to be taught a completely naturistic, godless view of the world around them, in the process unraveling every value that even the children of Godly parents learned at home and at church. Instead of being taught that they were a special creation of God in His own image, children were taught that no such creation really happened and that they were all just animals. Our rebellion against God's supremacy was complete and nearly unanimous.

Step #3 of National Decline – A Sexual Revolution – Romans 1:24-25

Beginning in the 1960s, with the Supreme Court ruling that the Bible and prayer must be eradicated from all public schools, children were taught that they are accidents of nature – that they are mere animals. In the aftermath of that growing trend in the schools, it should have come as no surprise that a growing percentage would actually believe what had been drilled into their heads, that they are nothing more than animals. And they would, no surprise, begin to act like animals in terms of sexual promiscuity and violence.

These children of the World War II heroes were confronted with a new stage of temptation, and they embraced it fully. Without the Biblical morality and accountability to their Creator that earlier generations of Americans had been taught, children of the 60s and 70s underwent a celebration of sexual immorality, just as Paul predicted. *"Wherefore God also gave them up to uncleanness through the lusts of their own hearts, to dishonor their own bodies between themselves, who changed the truth of God into a lie, and worshipped* and served the creature more than the Creator, who is blessed forever. Amen." (Romans 1:24-25)

In this passage God begins to withdraw from a society that turns its back on Him. "God gave them up . . ." He literally gives them over to their own unrestrained sexual lusts. Without any Biblical restraint, and often without any real knowledge of Biblical morality in the first place, these people who had embraced the creation rather than the creator were allowed to sink into complete sexual immorality.

This was the era of Woodstock, the burning of the bra. No longer would a young couple wait until marriage. No longer would a man settle for just one sex partner in life. Divorce skyrocketed. Communes spread throughout the country, where "free love" was practiced. Campuses across the country welcomed co-ed dorms. Hollywood and the media poured fuel on the fire by sexualizing everything. At the local drugstore pornography which had been illegal just a decade earlier exploded into no-holds-barred excess. What had been available only in illegal stag movies a few years before was now readily available in the local theater.

By the mid-1970s, what you had to go outside of your home to get was now available in your own living room. Do you remember Charlie's Angels and "jiggle vision?" Then cable TV and HBO? Then the Playboy channel and multiple pornographic options, right in your own living room. As God pulled back, Americans were left to the consequences of their excesses: STDs, no-fault divorce, broken homes, and skyrocketing suicide rates.

Step #4 of National Decline – A Homosexual Revolution – Romans 1:26-27

> For this cause God gave them up unto vile affections: for even their women did change the natural use into that which is against nature: And likewise also the men, leaving the natural use of the woman, burned in their lust one toward another; men with men working that which is unseemly, and receiving in themselves that recompence of their error which was meet.

Not much needs to be said on this fourth downward step. Anyone with a TV or who reads the news knows that we have been washed downstream at an ever-increasing, alarming rate over the last 30 years by a flood of homosexual propaganda and numerous supportive court decisions.

Of course homosexuality has always been with us. From the earliest colonial settlement in America through the mid-1950s it was universally recognized that homosexuality was a moral issue. It was understood that homosexuality was a sin against God and against natural law (see Chapter 6), and that it would weaken the moral fabric of the society as well as gain the disapproval of a Holy God.

Homosexuality, often classified as sodomy, was clearly labeled in the Bible as an "abomination" (Leviticus 18:22) and as a "vile affection" (Romans 1:26, 27). It was clear from I Timothy 1:10 and I Cor. 6:9, 10 that no person who regularly practiced a homosexual lifestyle could be called a true Christian, although the apostle Paul makes it clear that such practices were forgivable by God, as was any other sin, as long as there was a turning away from such sin, "... and such were some of you, but ye are washed..." (I Cor 6:11). All states until 1962 had laws against homosexuality, a felony in every state and the District of Columbia. Many states classified homosexuality as a "crime against nature."

The sodomy law of Michigan, struck down in 2003 by the U. S. Supreme Court is still on the books. It reads:

> **750.158 Crime against nature or sodomy; penalty.**
> Sec. 158.
> Any person who shall commit the abominable and detestable crime against nature either with mankind or with any animal shall be guilty of a felony, punishable by imprisonment in the state prison not more than 15 years, or if such person was at the time of the said offense a sexually delinquent person, may be punishable by imprisonment in the state prison for an indeterminate term, the minimum of which shall be 1 day and the maximum of which shall be life.

In 1952 the American Psychiatric Association classified homosexuality as a mental disorder rather than as a moral issue. In 1962, after the publication of the *Model Penal Code* by the American Law Institute, Illinois acted on the Code's recommendation to decriminalize homosexual acts, becoming the first State to do so. In 1973 the American Psychiatric Association reclassified homosexuality as simply an alternative, normal sexual practice, thus removing any psychological stigma from their previous characterization.

Through the late 1900s laws against homosexuality remained on the books in most States. In the wake of the sexual revolution of the 1960s most people began to take a "live, and let live" attitude toward any sexual acts between consenting adults. As a result, by the last two decades of the 20th century such laws were rarely enforced, though State laws against homosexual activities were upheld by the U.S. Supreme Court in *Bowers v. Hardwick* (1986).

Through the 1980s and beyond, homosexuals became organized and effective in an effort to decriminalize and "normalize" their lifestyle. It was a campaign for "tolerance." After all, this is how we are, they argued. We were born this way, and we have no more power to change our sexual proclivities than to change our skin color, the campaign declared. It is a civil rights issue, they declared. In 2003 the U.S. Supreme Court took up the case *Lawrence v. Texas* in which two Texas men were charged with violating Texas's law against homosexual sodomy. In this landmark case, not dissimilar to the reckless overreach of *Roe v. Wade*, the court overturned *Bowers v. Hardwick,* ordering that all State laws against homosexual activity were unconstitutional.

In the meantime, in 1993 a statute limiting marriage to opposite sex couples was struck down as unconstitutional by the Hawaii Supreme Court. Many other States were challenging the traditional definition of marriage at the same time, and this prompted the U.S. Congress to pass the Defense of Marriage Act (DOMA) in 1996 by an overwhelming margin (House 348-57; Senate 85-14, both veto-proof margins), and signed into law by President William Jefferson Clinton. This act declared that for federal purposes, especially tax and inheritance, the only union recognized as "marriage" by the U.S. Government was a union of one man and one woman.

The Defense of Marriage Act had a short life as the radical gay agenda was gaining support in State after State. In 2013, in *United States v. Windsor*, Section 3 of DOMA, the definition of marriage, was struck down by the U.S. Supreme Court. In 2015 in *Obergefell v. Hodges,* the court then struck down all State laws which prohibit homosexuals from marrying each other. Now, rather than seeking tolerance, homosexuals routinely target Christians who provide wedding related services (flowers, photography, wedding cakes) to serve their weddings or be sued. Evidently tolerance is a one-way street in the campaign for normalizing this deviant behavior.

Hollywood has been at the forefront of this vile campaign. I use the word "vile" intentionally because that is the word God uses in Romans 1:26 to describe the hearts of those who give themselves to homosexual activity. Hollywood had been making movies now for several decades glamorizing homosexuals or creating sympathetic AIDS victims, all for the sake of promoting this destructive behavior. In 1998 NBC introduced the popular comedy sit-com *Will & Grace* to American viewers. It ran for eight years, went through a suspension of several years, and has just recently been reinstated in the NBC lineup for 2017.

The whole purpose of *Will and Grace* has been to portray homosexuals as just normal, lovable, funny people. The main character, Will Truman is a handsome hunk of a man who is highly educated and a successful corporate lawyer. He is homosexual. His best friend Jack is a fickle, funny, flamboyant homosexual whose erratic life and multiple jobs take on a hilarious contrast to the competent, professional Will. Will is the stable one, a rock to ground his sometimes unstable roommate, Grace Adler, who is a non-homosexual interior designer.

This radical gay agenda is well organized and attacks every aspect of our lives. The effort to normalize homosexuality has been ongoing in public schools for decades. Efforts to incorporate homosexual children's literature in public school libraries have created a battle ground in public schools all over the country since the publication of *Heather Has Two Mommies* (1989) and *Daddy's Roommate* (1991). Homosexuals have been busy trying to incorporate their perversion in sex education curricula.

The most recent phenomena has been the introduction of "gender identity" which assumes that biological gender is actually meaningless in a person. The words of Jesus Christ are not particularly profound but rather a pointing out of the obvious, "And he answered and said unto them, 'Have ye not read, that he which made them at the beginning made them male and female?'" (Matthew 19:4) Jesus here is specifically talking about marriage, and what it takes to qualify as a marriage in God's eyes, but He is also saying that within God's creation and purpose for mankind there are but two genders.

Radical homosexuals are currently on a mission to replace the male-female genders of God's created order with an endless continuum of genders, only two of which are deemed invalid, those being biological male and female. Those who view themselves consistent with their biological gender are derided by many homosexuals as "cisgender" and are now somehow the odd ones.

Transgender is of course an absurd notion. Claiming to be a woman when you have male parts is an attack on reality, common sense and seventh grade biology. That is not to say that homosexual attraction is non-existent. It is simply to say that a male is a male and a female is a female – not at all profound. If you are a man who is sexually attracted to another man, you are still a man, and you will never be anything else regardless of the number of sessions you spend with a sympathetic psychiatrist or how many surgeries you may have. Your DNA still identifies you as a man. As Paul noted in Romans 1:22 of these people, they leave all logic and common sense behind, *"Professing themselves to be wise, they became fools."* (And we are the ones who are constantly being accused of being unscientific.)

In this passage God says that there is a corresponding penalty for this particular type of sin. He declares that homosexual activity brings with it *"that recompence of their error which was meet."* Or another way of saying that is that there will be particular natural consequences, or as He puts it, repayment (recompence) for this type of sin. Probably no social group has paid a higher price for its defiance of God than homosexuals.

Homosexual acts, which generally include anal intercourse, are of all human interaction the most high-risk and unsanitary. The actions themselves invite all manner of disease, and we have likely not seen an end to particular homosexual STDs. AIDS was a disease which attacked almost exclusively homosexuals. I seriously doubt that AIDS will be the last of homosexual STDs.

However, beyond disease, homosexuals suffer particular psychological issues relating to their lifestyle. Male homosexuals have a life expectancy in the mid-50s. Multiple studies of homosexual male suicide rates reveal that homosexuals are at least three times as likely to commit suicide as non-homosexuals, and most experts agree that homosexual males commit suicide at least at a rate of five to one over non-homosexuals. Some studies even suggest a higher rate than that, but few would argue for a rate lower than 3 to 1.

The American Association of Suicidology reports on its website the most recent statistics for despair among young homosexuals.

> *In 2015 the Youth Risk Behavior Surveillance System of the Centers for Disease Control and Prevention conducted a study on the behavior of youth in the US in the past year. They observed the following:*
>
> - *In the past 12 months, 60.4% of LGB youth felt hopeless or sad every day for 2+ weeks, compared to 26.4% of heterosexual youth.*
> - *In the past 12 months, 42.8% of LGB youth seriously considered suicide, compared to 14.8% of heterosexual youth.*
> - *In the past 12 months, 38.2% of LGB youth made a suicide plan, compared to 11.9% of Heterosexual youth.*
> - *In the past 12 months, 29.4% of LGB youth attempted suicide, compared to 6.4% of heterosexual youth.*
> - *In the past 12 months, 9.4% of LGB youth made a suicide attempt that required the attention of a medical professional, compared to 2% of heterosexual youth.* [This represents a rate of 4.7 to 1]

As we mentioned earlier in this chapter, God has placed within each person a natural knowledge of right and wrong. The homosexual lifestyle in particular puts one at odds with God's created intent for sex. No matter how affirming society may be toward homosexuality, that inner voice is a very depressing, frustrating thing to have to live with constantly. For many homosexuals it is too much.

Nothing could be more clear from the Bible than that homosexuality is an abominable sin, condemned for its particular affront to a Holy God and an attack on His created order and natural law. In spite of the clear teaching of Scripture, today homosexuality has almost totally permeated the American mind as a normal part of society. Even though a tiny, but growing, minority of Americans practice this lifestyle, and many still think of homosexual acts as repugnant and disgusting, it has unfortunately become acceptable by most.

With regard to this whole issue, the only thing that is NOT acceptable is criticism of homosexuals, transgenders, and deviant sexual practice. This is particularly true of Millennials who have been brought up on homosexual propaganda through their schools, the theater and their TV sets. This is one last stage of a society's abandonment from God before complete and total chaos sets in.

God, speaking through the prophet Isaiah issued a warning that parallels this whole section of Romans Chapter One. *"Woe unto them that call evil good, and good evil; that put darkness for light, and light for darkness; that put bitter for sweet, and sweet for bitter!"* (Isaiah 5:20) America has much to answer for.

Step #5 of National Decline – Complete Chaos and Violence – Romans 1:28-32

> *And even as they did not like to retain God in their knowledge, God gave them over to a reprobate mind, to do those things which are not convenient; Being filled with all unrighteousness, fornication, wickedness, covetousness, maliciousness; full of envy, murder, debate, deceit, malignity; whisperers, Backbiters, haters of God, despiteful, proud, boasters, inventors of evil things, disobedient to parents, Without understanding, covenant-breakers, without natural affection, implacable, unmerciful: Who knowing the judgment of God, that they which commit such things are worthy of death, not only do the same, but have pleasure in them that do them.*

We are just beginning to see the first disturbing scenes of the final step in God's abandonment of America. It is now dangerous for a conservative to speak on most college campuses. Demonstrations for Biblical principles are now often met with violent counter-protests from such groups as Antifa which promote violent overthrow of America and of our free enterprise economy.

Many young people, particularly young men, are increasingly isolated. They lose themselves in social media and violent video games. In a recent CharismaNews.com article, violent video games are connected to fourteen different mass shooters, including the shooters at Columbine, Aurora theater, Tucson (shooter of Rep. Gabbrielle Giffords), Sandy Hook Elementary, Charleston church, and the killer of 68 young people at a youth camp in Norway. There are likely more mass killers that started out with violent video games that we do not know about – it seems to represent a trend.

Our cities are fast becoming unprecedented harbors for the homeless, many of which are simply living in despair for a great number of reasons. Some of it is drug related. Some of it is mental health, and much of the mental health is the loss of hope and any spiritual anchor. The streets of many major cities are now infested with needles and human excrement. Many simply prefer not to engage at any level of personal responsibility. In the best of economic times where holding a job would be relatively easy, many are simply not interested. It will only get much worse.

This passage of scripture describes a future time of chaos and treachery, accompanied by murder, maliciousness, betrayal, and all forms of violence and sexual deviancy. This is what awaits America as it enters that downstream rapids out of which it is impossible to navigate.

During the years 1789-99 France went through a period of terror and violence known as the French Revolution. France had long been known as a permissive society, and although formally a Catholic nation, the French Revolution was characterized by hatred of the Catholic Church, its corruptions, and its land holdings. It was the secular counterpart to the Bible-based theistic American Revolution, and the contrasts couldn't be sharper.

Known as the *Reign of Terror*, this period was characterized by violent demonstrations, mass executions, and regicide. Whichever party was in power took deadly aim at opponents and subjected hundreds to the guillotine. During one stretch under the reign of Maximilien Robespierre, an average of 29 people per day were put to the guillotine in Paris. To be accused was to be executed. There was no due process.

So how did France extricate itself from this *Reign of Terror*? To restore some semblance of tranquility, they turned to a dictator, Napoleon Bonaparte. This is the logical conclusion of a society after a long term of violence and upheaval. This violence and precursor to dictatorship and a police state is the destiny of America, described in the last five verses of Romans 1.

America is nearing the end of its journey down that ever accelerating river, and the waterfall looming at the end of that rapids will produce a terrifying crash. That crash could be financial, or it could be military in nature. However it comes about, the America that we have known and love will be no more, as the reproach of sin takes its final toll. But it may not have to end this way.

Chapter 15

Can the Blessing Be Restored?

Therefore also now, saith the LORD, turn ye even to me with all your heart, and with fasting, and with weeping, and with mourning: And rend your heart, and not your garments, and turn unto the LORD your God: for he is gracious and merciful, slow to anger, and of great kindness, and repenteth him of the evil. Who knoweth if he will return and repent, and leave a blessing behind him; even a meat offering and a drink offering unto the LORD your God? Joel 2:12-14

We do not know for sure the date that the above words were written. Most scholars believe that the Prophet Joel wrote these words around 800 BC or shortly thereafter. The date is not so important as the message. The message contains an answer to the question, "Can the Blessing Be Restored?" Joel's answer is simply "Who knows?" We have no certainty as to whether a restoration is possible. What we do know from Scripture is that it is possible for a person, or for a nation, to reach a point of rebellion so onerous to God that His Spirit no longer draws that person or nation to a place of repentance and revival.

Has America reached that point? Some pastors contend that God has given up on America. But they do not know that. They contend that America's sins have taken us past the possibility of return. Romans 1 tends to suggest that once a nation advances down that path of rebellion, God gives them up to the consequences of their own sins. Once on that path, I believe it is very difficult to turn a culture of licentiousness back to morality.

But is it too late? I must conclude with Joel that I do not know the answer to that question, "Can the Blessing Be Restored?" Or asked another way, "*Behold, I am the LORD, the God of all flesh: is there any thing too hard for me?*" (Jer. 32:27) I do know that if nothing changes, judgment and severe persecution will shortly follow. We need a general revival of God's people, and then a general awakening in our culture, and that is our only hope for restoration. God can do that.

The above context from Joel precedes a call to repentance – a call for a solemn assembly to gather together and plead with God for forgiveness.

> *Blow the trumpet in Zion, sanctify a fast, call a solemn assembly: Gather the people, sanctify the congregation, assemble the elders, gather the children, and those that suck the breasts: let the bridegroom go forth of his chamber, and the bride out of her closet. Let the priests, the ministers of the LORD, weep between the porch and the altar, and let them say, Spare thy people, O LORD, and give not thine heritage to reproach, that the heathen should rule over them: wherefore should they say among the people, Where is their God?* Joel 2:15-17

Joel calls for a national assembly. The urgency of this call cannot be overstated. Everything else in life must yield to this singular priority. No one is given a pass, not even nursing infants. Not even those on their honeymoons. Restoration of God's blessing will never come until it is the most important thing in the world to God's people, yes, *all* of God's people. It might take a monumental calamity to drive us to our knees.

The solution is simple, really. However, simple is not the same thing as easy. I almost hesitate to quote the familiar passage from II Chronicles because we have become so familiar with it without actually acting on it, that it has lost its persuasive power and urgency. Most of us can quote it. "*If my people, which are called by my name, shall humble themselves, and pray, and seek my face, and turn from their wicked ways; then will I hear from heaven, and will forgive their sin, and will heal their land.*" II Chron. 7:14

This familiar passage has become to us the solution that the other guy needs to heed. What do we think of when we hear it? Usually we think of our national sins, abortion, homosexuality, immorality. These are usually someone else's sins. In hearing this verse we rarely think of our own sins. Some Christians view it even as a call for the ungodly to get their act together. However, this passage is not written to society in general, it is written specifically to God's people. Some, no doubt, have taken it to heart and have applied it as best they know how. But this is not simply a once-every-Sunday type of effort.

I can say from personal experience that while all the aspects of this solution are simple, they are not easy. What does total commitment cost? All the sins of pride and the encroaching immorality of our media-enabled culture are difficult to expunge. The solution lies in not just a few pastors engaging but rather, for _me_ to engage. It calls for personal cost-counting. What must I do to truly fulfill my part of this promise? It calls for a sacrifice of time, resources and self-esteem. It costs us control of our lives. Do we really want revival? Are we afraid of what it might mean? What it might cost?

Vice President Mike Pence has quoted this passage in a general call to come back to our founding principles, but he left out the most important factor. His quote went like this, *"If my people, which are called by my name, shall humble themselves, and pray, and seek my face, then will I hear from heaven, and will forgive their sin, and will heal their land."* Perhaps in an effort to avoid controversy or criticism, he left out the one phrase that gives this promise its efficacy, *"and turn from their wicked ways."* We cannot continue with the sexual revolution, and with the homosexual revolution, and with the abortion, and with the rebellious pride that characterizes our Christian culture, and expect the blessing of God, no matter how much time we spend on our knees.

Years ago, I heard a sad report, one that surprised me but one that explains a lot. There was in one of America's large cities, at a large hotel resort, a conference for pastors, Bible-believing pastors. The conference was such that it occupied most of the hotel rooms. The hotel's television choices included a pornographic channel. The hotel reported that there was little difference in the usage of the pornographic channel when the pastors occupied the rooms as compared to a normal occupancy. Turning from our wicked ways involves all of us.

Within the State of Michigan the past few years there has been an effort among pastors in several places around the State to gather regularly for prayer, pleading with God for a revival among His people. Many pastors have become engaged, but many pastors have declined to meet with their brethren, generally for two reasons.

First, there is a pernicious doctrine held by many pastors that goes something like this, "I want revival, and I believe if God wants us to have revival, He will send it in His own time. If He doesn't want us to have revival, He won't send it. It's in His hands, not mine." I suspect that this is more often an excuse than a real doctrine. It allows a pastor to remain in his own comfort zone for spiritual sounding reasons.

Even the most ardent Calvinist/Dispensationalist needs to recognize that the powerful experience of Pentecost came after a ten-day prayer meeting (*These all continued with one accord in prayer and supplication.* Acts 1:14), a time of consecration and preparation; that in the parable of the persistent friend, Jesus said that God *wants* to give His Spirit to His beloved children, but to get it we must persistently ask, seek, and knock. All three of those words are Greek present tense, meaning ask continuously, seek continuously, knock continuously. And what is the object of this asking, seeking, and knocking?

> *I say unto you, Though he will not rise and give him because he is his friend, yet because of his importunity he will rise and give him as many as he needeth. And I say unto you, Ask, and it shall be given you; seek, and ye shall find; knock, and it shall be opened unto you. For every one that asketh receiveth; and he that seeketh findeth; and to him that knocketh it shall be opened. If a son shall ask bread of any of you that is a father, will he give him a stone? or if he ask a fish, will he for a fish give him a serpent? Or if he shall ask an egg, will he offer him a scorpion? If ye then, being evil, know how to give good gifts unto your children: <u>how much more shall your heavenly Father give the Holy Spirit to them that ask him?</u>* Luke 11:8-13

What we are to ask for continuously is the power of God's Spirit in our lives. If Luke's account leaves you dispensationally lacking, then perhaps God's command through the apostle Paul will be more appealing to you:

> *And be not drunk with wine, wherein is excess; but be filled with the Spirit; Speaking to yourselves in psalms and hymns and spiritual songs, singing and making melody in your heart to the Lord; Giving thanks always for all things unto God and*

the Father in the name of our Lord Jesus Christ; Submitting yourselves one to another in the fear of God. Eph. 5:18-21

Here being filled with the Spirit is a process, just as getting drunk with wine is a process. We don't sit around hoping that we don't get drunk. We know that to get drunk we have to actually do something to get drunk. In contrast, if we want the filling of God's Spirit we have to do something to get the Spirit's filling. In Luke that process is a continual asking. In this passage, Paul adds preparing your heart with hymns and thankfulness, and outward actions of love and self-denial toward other Christians. The work of God's Spirit is not something that ambushes the unprepared.

That last clause, *"Submitting yourselves one to another in the fear of God,"* takes me to that second reason many pastors refuse to join other pastors in prayer. That second reason is that they are afraid they might have to pray with a man who views a few things differently, or a pastor who uses a different version of the Bible than he uses. The "I will submit to no such compromiser" attitude will get us nowhere. The contempt some pastors hold in their hearts toward other brothers is a sin, pure and simple. *"We know that we have passed from death unto life, because we love the brethren. He that loveth not his brother abideth in death."* I John 3:14 Wow! Strong words.

I do believe that if restoration ever comes, it will come as the result of another Great Awakening, a spiritual revival on a national scale, the likes of which we have not seen in America since the mid-1700s. During the Great Awakening, led mostly by an Anglican minister and a Congregationalist minister, all denominations came together in a national revival. Many of these denominations held distinctives which normally were not compromised. Some even just a few decades before had literally executed those who did not share their distinctives.

There were many nay-sayers. George Whitefield was criticized by his Anglican brethren for being willing to take communion with Baptists. After all, Baptists, with their idea of *soul liberty*, were considered ill-educated, reckless and without any strong doctrine. Virtually every denomination was split during that time between those seeking God's Spirit (the "new lights") and those content to live without it (the "old lights").

However, that love of the brethren and mutual submission ultimately spilled over old denominational walls, and it had a tremendous impact on the colonies and eventually on the righteousness of a new nation. God's Spirit was able to do a mighty work among them, all because they were willing to submit themselves one to another in the fear of God.

The ONLY solution to America's problem is a revival among God's people, and a general moral awakening among the nation as a whole. There is no plan B. There are no solutions to America's problem in Washington, or in any of the State capitols. The solution, like the great spiritual awakenings of the past, must first start in our pulpits, spread to the pews, and at last reach the streets. For now, it's up to you, pastors and lay leaders.

We will need to come together in humility and submission with all of God's people who want a real Holy Spirit revival, not just the few in our own little circles that we are comfortable with. It cannot be just a Baptist revival, or a King James Version revival. Those may be important distinctives, but this problem is far bigger than our comfort zones, some of which are tiny circles. This must be a national turning to God and must encompass far more than our own tiny circles.

It will involve standing shoulder to shoulder with men that think differently from you, but who love God's Word, trust in Jesus, and love America. *"Who art thou that judgest another man's servant? to his own master he standeth or falleth.... But why dost thou judge thy brother? or why dost thou set at nought thy brother? for we shall all stand before the judgment seat of Christ... So then every one of us shall give account of himself to God."* Both you and your brother, both servants of God, will stand individually before your own master. Let's be willing to leave some of those things to God.

If our distinctives keep us from loving the brethren or from warring together with other good men who don't view everything just like we do, that is a prideful sin. We can agree to disagree on some fine points, and still humbly approach the throne of Grace together for the sake of our country, our churches, our families, and most importantly for the sake of God's Kingdom. It doesn't mean we have to compromise or change our beliefs, but we must have a change of heart, one which allows for *"Submitting yourselves one to another in the fear of God."*

Many pastors will say, "America is too far gone. It is hopeless. We are destined for God's judgment." Few who say that really believe it. Persecution is not a pleasant experience. Being jailed and tortured is a fearsome thing, and if a pastor really believed he was about to face that, he would be down on his knees continually seeking God's deliverance. No, once again, this excuse allows a pastor to remain comfortable and uncommitted for spiritual sounding reasons.

The bottom line is this. This exceptionally blessed nation that once was America is now on the brink. America will be lost irretrievably without a revival of God's Spirit. That revival will not come without action on the part of all of God's people, but especially the Bible believing pastors. We cannot just sit around and wait for it to happen. We cannot look at some brothers with disdain and contempt if we truly seek the power of God's Spirit. We will need to come together as God's people and pray for it, preparing our hearts, confessing our sins, and submitting to one another.

What do we have to lose? What if we go through all the motions of fasting, praying, submitting ourselves, and loving a brother who sees some minor point differently, and revival never comes? Will the prayer, the fasting, the brotherly love have been a loss after all? No, it will have been well worth it, time well spent, and it will have better prepared us for what comes next. This is probably our last call. Will we respond?

On March 2, 1863, Senator James Harlan of Iowa introduced a resolution in the U.S. Senate asking President Lincoln to proclaim a national day of prayer and fasting. The following proclamation was signed by President Lincoln on March 30, 1863, for a day of national prayer and fasting to be observed the following April 30, 1863.

Lincoln's proclamation is the best summary I could possibly use for this book. It confirms the history I have been describing, and it confirms the solution I am advocating.

**Washington, D.C.
March 30, 1863**

By the President of the United States of America.

A Proclamation.

Whereas, the Senate of the United States, devoutly recognizing the Supreme Authority and just Government of Almighty God, in all the affairs of men and of nations, has, by a resolution, requested the

President to designate and set apart a day for National prayer and humiliation.

And whereas it is the duty of nations as well as of men, to own their dependence upon the overruling power of God, to confess their sins and transgressions, in humble sorrow, yet with assured hope that genuine repentance will lead to mercy and pardon; and to recognize the sublime truth, announced in the Holy Scriptures and proven by all history, that those nations only are blessed whose God is the Lord.

And, insomuch as we know that, by His divine law, nations like individuals are subjected to punishments and chastisements in this world, may we not justly fear that the awful calamity of civil war, which now desolates the land, may be but a punishment, inflicted upon us, for our presumptuous sins, to the needful end of our national reformation as a whole People? We have been the recipients of the choicest bounties of Heaven. We have been preserved, these many years, in peace and prosperity. We have grown in numbers, wealth and power, as no other nation has ever grown. But we have forgotten God. We have forgotten the gracious hand which preserved us in peace, and multiplied and enriched and strengthened us; and we have vainly imagined, in the deceitfulness of our hearts, that all these blessings were produced by some superior wisdom and virtue of our own. Intoxicated with unbroken success, we have become too self-sufficient to feel the necessity of redeeming and preserving grace, too proud to pray to the God that made us!

It behooves us then, to humble ourselves before the offended Power, to confess our national sins, and to pray for clemency and forgiveness.

Now, therefore, in compliance with the request, and fully concurring in the views of the Senate, I do, by this my proclamation, designate and set apart Thursday, the

30th. day of April, 1863, as a day of national humiliation, fasting and prayer. And I do hereby request all the People to abstain, on that day, from their ordinary secular pursuits, and to unite, at their several places of public worship and their respective homes, in keeping the day holy to the Lord, and devoted to the humble discharge of the religious duties proper to that solemn occasion.

All this being done, in sincerity and truth, let us then rest humbly in the hope authorized by the Divine teachings, that the united cry of the Nation will be heard on high, and answered with blessings, no less than the pardon of our national sins, and the restoration of our now divided and suffering Country, to its former happy condition of unity and peace.

In witness whereof, I have hereunto set my hand and caused the seal of the United States to be affixed.

Done at the City of Washington, this thirtieth day of March, in the year of our Lord one thousand eight hundred and sixty-three, and of the Independence of the United States the eighty seventh.

By the President: Abraham Lincoln
William H. Seward, Secretary of State.

One Final Thought

The following verses contain the faith of most of our founding fathers and the philosophers that they admired. The Bible tells us:

> *For God so loved the world, that He gave His only begotten Son, that whosoever believeth in Him should not perish, but have everlasting life.*
>
> *For God sent not His Son into the world to condemn the world; but that the world through Him might be saved.*
>
> *He that believeth on Him is not condemned: but he that believeth not is condemned already, because he hath not believed in the name of the only begotten Son of God.* (John 3:16-18)
>
> *Jesus saith unto him, "I am the way, the truth, and the life: no man cometh unto the Father, but by me."* (John 14:6)

In the language of Jesus' time, the words faith, believe and trust all come from the same root word. To believe in Jesus Christ is to rest your entire faith on Him for your eternal destiny. The opposite of resting your faith on Jesus is resting your faith on your own good works, which God calls *"filthy rags."* (Isaiah 64:6) God created each human as an eternal being. Each one of us will spend forever somewhere, either in Heaven or in Hell.

The Bible says *"All have sinned . . . "* (Romans 3:23) The Bible says *"The wages* [the just penalty] *of sin is death, but the gift of God is eternal life through Jesus Christ our Lord."* (Romans 6:23) You must believe that Jesus is God's only way to Heaven and that He died on the cross to pay the penalty for your sin. You must confess your sin to God, you must repent of your sins, and you must trust Jesus as your only hope of salvation. Then you may rest in God's promise, *"that whosoever believeth in Him should not perish, but have everlasting life."*

Other Books by Kenneth L. Bradstreet:

The King James Version in History (2004)
The Michigan Bradstreets, an American Family (Coming in 2020)

Appendix A
Early Education Laws of New England

Original Massachusetts Bay School Law (1642)

Forasmuch as the good education of children is of singular behoof and benefit to any Commonwealth; and whereas many parents & masters are too indulgent and negligent of their duty in that kind. It is therefore ordered that the Select men of every town, in the several precincts and quarters where they dwell, shall have a vigilant eye over their brethren & neighbors, to see, first that none of them shall suffer so much barbarism in any of their families as not to endeavor to teach by themselves or others, their children & apprentices so much learning as may enable them perfectly to read the English tongue, & knowledge of the Capital Laws: upon penalty of twenty shillings for each neglect therein. Also that all masters of families do once a week (at the least) catechize their children and servants in the grounds & principles of Religion, & if any be unable to doe so much: that then at the least they procure such children or apprentices to learn some short orthodox catechism without book, that they may be able to answer unto the questions that shall be propounded to them out of such catechism by their parents or masters or any of the Select men when they shall call them to a trial of what they have learned of this kind. And further that all parents and masters do breed & bring up their children & apprentices in some honest lawful calling, labor or employment, either in husbandry, or some other trade profitable for themselves, and the Commonwealth if they will not or cannot train them up in learning to fit them for higher employments. And if any of the Select men after admonition by them given to such masters of families shall find them still negligent of their duty in the particulars aforementioned, whereby children and servants become rude, stubborn & unruly; the said selectmen with the help of two magistrates, or the next county court for that shire, shall take such children or apprentices from them & place them with some masters for years (boys till they come to twenty one, and girls eighteen years of age complete) which will more strictly look unto, and force them to submit unto government according to the rules of this order, if by fair means and former instructions they will not be drawn into it. [Spelling updated]

The Old Deluder, Satan Act (1647)

It being one chief project of that old deluder, Satan, to keep men from the knowledge of the Scriptures, as in former times by keeping them in an unknown tongue, so in these latter times by persuading from the use of tongues, that so that at least the true sense and meaning of the original might be clouded and corrupted with false glosses of saint-seeming deceivers; and to the end that learning may not be buried in the grave of our forefathers, in church and commonwealth, the Lord assisting our endeavors.

It is therefore ordered that every township in this jurisdiction, after the Lord hath increased them to fifty households shall forthwith appoint one within their town to teach all such children as shall resort to him to write and read, whose wages shall be paid either by the parents or masters of such children, or by the inhabitants in general, by way of supply, as the major part of those that order the prudentials of the town shall appoint; provided those that send their children be not oppressed by paying much more than they can have them taught for in other towns.

And it is further ordered, that when any town shall increase to the number of one hundred families or householders, they shall set up a grammar school, the master thereof being able to instruct youth so far as they may be fitted for the university, provided that if any town neglect the performance hereof above one year that every such town shall pay 5 pounds to the next school till they shall perform this order. [Spelling updated]

Appendix B
Blue-Backed-Speller, Moral Catechism

Excerpts from Webster's Moral Catechism, found in Websters "Blue-Backed Speller" beginning in 1794.

A MORAL CATECHISM: OR, LESSONS FOR SATURDAY.

Question. WHAT is moral virtue?
Answer. It is an honest upright conduct in all our dealings with men.

Q. Can we always determine what is honest and just?
A. Perhaps not in every instance, but in general it is not difficult.

Q. What rule have we to direct us?
A. God's word contained in the Bible has furnished all necessary rules to direct our conduct.

Q. In what part of the Bible are these rules to be found?
A. In almost every part; but the most important duties between men are summed up in the beginning of Matthew, in Christ's sermon on the mount.

OF HUMILITY.

Q. What is humility?
A. A lowly temper of mind.

Q. *What are the advantages of humility?*
A. The advantages of humility in this life are very numerous and great. The humble man has few or no enemies. Every one loves him and is ready to do him good. If he is rich and prosperous people do not envy him; if he is poor and unfortunate, every one pities him, and is disposed to alleviate his distress.

Q. *What is pride?*
A. A lofty high-minded disposition.

Q. *Is pride commendable?*
A. By no means. A modest self-approving opinion of our own good deeds is very right. It is natural; it is agreeable; and a spur to good actions. But we should not suffer our hearts to be blown up with pride, whatever great and good deeds we have done; for pride brings upon us the ill will of mankind and displeasure of our Maker.

Q. *What has Christ said respecting the virtue of humility?*
A. He has said, "Blessed are the poor in spirit, for their's [sic] is the kingdom of heaven." Poorness of spirit is humility; and this humble temper prepares a man for heaven, where all is peace and love.

OF MERCY.

Q. *What is mercy?*
A. It is a tenderness of heart.

Q. *What are the advantages of this virtue?*
A. The exercise of it tends to happify every one about us. Rulers of a merciful temper will make their *good* subjects happy; and will not torment the *bad* with needless severity. Parents and masters will not abuse their children and servants with harsh treatment. More love, more confidence, more happiness, will subsist among men, and of course society will be happier.

Q. *What does Christ say of the merciful man?*
A. He says he is "blessed for he shall obtain mercy." He who shows mercy and tenderness to others, will be treated with tenderness and compassion himself.

OF PEACE MAKERS.

Q. *Who are peace makers?*
A. All who endeavour to prevent quarrels and disgrace among men; or to reconcile those who are separated by strife.

Q. *Is it unlawful to contend with others on any occasion?*
A. It is impossible to avoid some differences with men; but disputes should be always conducted with temper and moderation. The man who keeps his temper will not be rash, and do or say things he will afterwards repent of. And though men should sometimes differ, still they should be friends. They should be ready to do kind offices for each other.

Q. *What is the reward of the peace maker?*
A. He shall be "blessed, and called the child of God." The mild, peaceable and friendly man resembles God. What an amiable character is this! To be like our heavenly Father, that lovely, perfect, and glorious being, who is the source of all good, is to be the best and happiest of men.

OF PURITY OF HEART.

Q. *What is a pure heart?*
A. A heart free from all bad desires and inclined to conform to the divine will in all things.

Q. *Should a man's intentions as well as his actions be good?*
A. Most certainly. Actions cannot be called *good*, unless they proceed from good motives. We should wish to see and make all men better and happier--we should rejoice at their prosperity. This is benevolence.

Q. What reward is promised to the pure in heart?
A. Christ has declared "they shall see God." A pure heart is like God, and those who possess it shall dwell in his presence, and enjoy his favour forever.

OF REVENGE.

Q. What is revenge?
A. It is to injure a man because he has injured us.

Q. Is this justifiable?
A. Never, in any possible case. Revenge is perhaps the meanest as well as wickedest vice in society. Nothing but murder can equal it.

Q. But suppose a man insults us in such a manner that the law cannot give redress?
A. Then forgive him. "If a man strikes you on one cheek, turn the other to him," and let him repeat the abuse, rather than strike him.

Q. But if we are in danger from the blows of another, may we not defend ourselves?
A. Most certainly. We have always a right to defend our persons, property and families. But we have no right to fight and abuse people merely for revenge. It is nobler to forgive. "Love your enemies--bless them that curse you--do good to them that hate you--pray for those that use you ill"—these are the commands of the blessed Saviour of men. The man who does this is great and good; he is as much above the little mean revengeful man, as virtue is above vice, or as heaven is higher than hell.

OF GENEROSITY.

Q. What is generosity?
A. It is some act of kindness performed for anther, which strict justice does not demand.

Q. *Is this a virtue?*
A. It is indeed a noble virtue. To do justice, is well; but to do more than justice, is still better, and may proceed from nobler motives.

Q. *What has Christ said respecting generosity?*
A. He has commanded us to be generous in this passage, "Whoever shall compel (or urge) you to go a mile, go with him two."

OF TRUTH.

Q. *What is truth?*
A. It is speaking and acting agreeably to fact.

Q. *Is a duty to speak truth at all times?*
A. If we speak at all, we should tell the truth. It is not always necessary to tell what we know. There are many things which concern ourselves & others, which we had better not publish to the world.

Q. *What are the ill effects of lying and deceiving?*
A. The man who lies, deceives or cheats, loses his reputation. No person will believe him even when he speaks truth; he is shunned as a pest to society. Falsehood and cheating destroy all confidence between man and man; they raise jealousies and suspicions among men; they thus weaken the bands of society and destroy happiness. Besides, cheating often robs people of their property, and makes them poor and wretched.

OF CHARITY AND GIVING ALMS.

Q. *What is charity?*
A. It signifies giving to the poor, or it is a favourable opinion of men and their actions.

Q. *When and how far is it our duty to give to the poor?*
A. When others really want what we can spare without material injury to ourselves, it is our duty to give them something to relieve their wants.

Q. *When persons are reduced to want by there [sic] own laziness and vices, by drunkenness, gambling and the like, is it a duty to relieve them?*
A. In general it is not. The man who gives money and provisions to a lazy vicious man, becomes a partaker of his guilt. Perhaps it may be right, to give such a man a meal of victuals to keep him from starving, and it is certainly right to feed his wife and family and make them comfortable.

Q. *Who are the proper objects of charity?*
A. Persons who are reduced to want by sickness, unavoidable losses by fire, storms at sea or land, drouth or accidents of other kinds. To such persons we are commanded to give; and it is our own interest to be charitable; for we are all liable to misfortunes, and may want charity ourselves.

Q. *In what manner should we bestow favours?*
A. We should do it with gentleness and affection; putting on no airs of pride and arrogance. We should also take no pains to publish our charities; but rather to conceal them; for if we boast of our generosity we discover that we give for mean selfish motives. Christ commands us, in giving alms, not to let our left hand know what our right hand doeth.

Q. *How can charity be exercised in our opinions of others?*
A. By thinking favorable of them and their actions. Every man has his faults; but charity will not put a harsh construction on another's conduct. It will not charge his conduct to bad views and motives, unless this appears very clear indeed.

OF AVARICE.

Q. *What is avarice?*
A. An excessive desire of gaining wealth.

Q. *Is this commendable?*
A. It is not; but one of the meanest of vices.

Q. *Can an avaricious man be an honest man.*
A. It is hardly possible; for the lust of gain is almost always accompanied with a disposition to take mean and undue advantages of others.

OF INDUSTRY.

Q. *What is industry?*
A. It is a diligent attention to business in our several occupations.

Q. *Is labour a curse or a blessing?*
A. Hard labour or drudgery is often a curse by making life toilsome and painful. But constant moderate labor is the greatest blessing.

Q. *Why then do people complain of it?*
A. Because they do not know the evils of not labouring. Labor keeps the body in health, and makes men relish all their enjoyments. "The sleep of the labouring man is sweet," so is his food. He walks cheerfully and whistling about his fields or shop, and scarcely knows pain. The rich and indolent first lose their health for want of action-- They turn pale, their bodies are enfeebled, they lose their appetite for food and sleep, they yawn out a tasteless stupid life without pleasure, and often useless to the world.

Q. *What are the other good effects of industry?*
A. One effect is to procure an estate. Our Creator has kindly united our duty, our interest and happiness: for the same labour which makes us healthy and cheerful, gives us wealth. Another good effect

of industry is, it keeps men from vice. Not all the moral discourses ever delivered to mankind, have so much influence in checking the bad passions of men, in keeping order and peace, and maintaining moral virtue, in society as *industry*. Business is a source of health; of prosperity, or virtue, and obedience to law. To make good subjects and good citizens, the first requisite is to educate every young person, in some kind of business. The possession of millions should not excuse a young man from application to business, and that parent or guardian who suffers his child or his ward to be bred in indolence, becomes accessary to the vices and disorders of society, he is guilty of "not providing for his household, and is worse than an infidel."

OF CHEERFULNESS.

Q. *Is cheerfulness a virtue?*
A. It doubtless is, and a moral duty to practise it.

Q. *Can we be cheerful when we please?*
A. In general it depends much on ourselves. We can often mould our temper into a cheerful frame--We can frequent company and other objects calculated to inspire us with cheerfulness. To indulge a habitual gloominess of mind is weakness and sin.

Q. *What shall one do when overwhelmed with grief?*
A. The best method of expelling grief from the mind, or of quieting its pains, is to change the objects that are about us; to ride from place to place and frequent cheerful company. It is our duty so to do, especially when grief sits heavy on the heart.

Q. *Has not religion a tendency to fill the mind with gloom?*
A. True religion never has this effect. Superstition and false notions of God often make men gloomy; but true rational piety and religion have the contrary effect. They fill the man with joy and cheerfulness; and the countenance of a truly pious man should always wear a secure simile. [Note how within this principle and

the following principle, the concepts of religion and Christianity are used interchangeably.]

Q. *What has Christ said concerning gloomy Christians?*
A. He has pronounced them hypocrites; and commanded his followers not to copy their sad countenances and disfigured faces; but even in their acts of humiliation to "anoint their hands and wash their feet." Christ intended by this, that religion does not consist in, nor require a monkish sadness and gravity; on the other hand he intimates that such appearance of sanctity are generally the marks of hypocrisy. He expressly enjoins upon his followers, marks of cheerfulness. Indeed the only true ground of perpetual cheerfulness, is a consciousness of ever having done well, and an assurance of divine favour.

Appendix C
McGuffey's Third Reader Excerpts

The following are from the Eclectic Third Reader, lessons 13 & 14, published by William H. McGuffey in 1837. Bear in mind as you read this that you are reading from a public school reading book designed for those about 9 or 10 years of age. The McGuffey readers were the most widely circulated public school reading textbooks in the history of America.

Following are excerpts from two lessons in the third reader, each originally with 14 numbered paragraphs concerning the Bible, in all 28 paragraphs. It deals with the proofs of authenticity of both the Old and New Testaments, issues of translation into the English language – just about everything a Bible college student would learn in a college level Bibliology class. Both sections end with a series of questions for the teacher to ask the students. As you can see from the following text, if a ten year old can handle such a selection, that ten year old is going to be a very good reader indeed, and not too bad a Bible student.

Lesson XVIII. [Excerpts]
The Bible. – S. H. Tyng

>   RULE. – *Read for improvement, and not for show. The great object of reading is to improve your minds in useful knowledge, to establish your hearts in virtue, and to prepare you for a right performance of the duties of life.*

1. The word Bible means book, and the sacred volume is so called because it is the book of books – the best book.

The word Scriptures signifies writings. The Bible was not written at one time, or by one person, but consists of various parts, written at different times by different men. It is divided into two Testaments, called the Old and the New, chiefly with reference to the time when they were published. The Old was published before the coming of Christ, and the New after His death.

2. *The excellency of the Bible might be proved sufficiently from its sanctifying and transforming influence upon the minds of all who read it with a proper spirit. This is manifest more especially from the fact of its having God for its author. That God is its author is evident from its being the only book which teaches everything that our Creator requires of us, either to know, or believe, or do, that we may escape his deserved displeasure, obtain his sovereign favor, and dwell forever in the bliss of his immediate presence.*

3. *It opens to us the mystery of the creation the nature of God, of angels, and of men, the immortality of the soul, the end for which man was created. It teaches the origin of evil, and the inseparable connection between sin and misery, the vanity of the present world, and the glory reserved in a future state for the pious servants of God....*

9. *The writings of all uninspired men are modern, compared with the Holy Scriptures. The earliest profane history which is known is that of Herodotus, in Greek which was written no earlier than the time of Malachi, the last of the Old Testament writers...*

10. *The books of these ancient, uninspired writers are of quite a different character from the Holy Scriptures. They are filled with silly and absurd fables and contain many impurities. They make no discovery of the just character of the only living and true God, though they contain much concerning religion....*

11. *The inspiration of the Holy Scriptures is evident from their divine sentiments in religion. The glorious character under which they represent Almighty God, the purity and*

reasonableness of their morality, the majestic simplicity of their style, their wonderful efficacy on the minds of believers, the faithfulness and disinterestedness of the writers, the miracles by which they confirmed their doctrines, the astonishing preservation of the several books to our times, and the fulfillment of their numerous and various prophecies all prove their having come by inspiration....

13. *To be inspired of God signifies to be supernaturally influenced by his Holy Spirit. Thus the ancient prophets are said to have spoken by divine inspiration...*

Lesson XIX. More about the Bible...[Excerpts]

1. *The design of the Bible is evidently to give us correct information concerning the creation of all things by the omnipotent word of God, to make known to us the state of holiness and happiness of our first parents in paradise, and their dreadful fall from that condition by transgression against God, which is the original cause of all our sin and misery.*

2. *It is also designed to show us the duty we owe to Him, who is our almighty Creator, our bountiful Benefactor, and our righteous Judge; the method by which we can secure His eternal friendship, and are prepared for the possession of everlasting mansions in His glorious kingdom.*

3. *The scriptures are especially designed to make us wise unto salvation through faith in Christ Jesus, to reveal to us the mercy of the Lord in Him, to form our minds after the likeness of God our Savior, to build up our souls in wisdom and faith, in love and holiness, to make us thoroughly furnished unto good works, enabling us to glorify God on earth, and to lead us to an imperishable inheritance among the spirits of just men made perfect, and finally to be glorified with Christ in heaven.*

4. *If such be the design of the Bible, how necessary must it be for everyone to pay a serious and proper attention to what it reveals. The word of God invites our attentive and prayerful*

regards in terms the most engaging and persuasive, It closes its gracious appeals by proclaiming, "Whosoever will, let him take the water of life freely." The infinite tenderness of the divine compassion to sinners flows in the language of the inspired writers, with which they address the children of men, and the most gracious promises of the Lord of glory accompany the divine invitation....

11. As to the preservation of the sacred books down to our times, it is certain that although the original copies may have been lost, the books of the New Testament have been preserved without any material alterations, much less corruption. They are, in all essential matters, the same as when they came from the hands of their authors. In taking copies of these books by writing from time to time, as the art of printing was then unknown, some letters have been omitted, altered, or even changed in some manuscripts, but no important doctrine, precept or passage of history, has been designedly or fraudulently corrupted...

13. The manuscripts of the sacred books are found in every ancient library in all parts of the Christian world, and amount in number to several thousands. About five hundred have been actually examined and compared by learned men with extraordinary care. Many of them were evidently transcribed as early as the eighth, seventh, sixth, and even the fourth centuries.

14. Thus we are carried up to very near the times of the apostles, and the first promulgation of the inspired writings. The prodigious number of these manuscripts, the remote countries where they have been collected, and the identity of their contents with the quotations which the fathers of different ages have made, demonstrate the authenticity of the New Testament. It has been, indeed, asserted by learned men, that if the New Testament were lost, its contents might be wholly supplied by the quotations from it which are found in the writings of the fathers of the first four centuries of the Christian church.

Appendix D

Essex Convention

Following is an article from the Salem Gazette, published December 26, 1814, about a convention held in Essex County, Massachusetts, at the behest of the state legislature, for the purpose of enacting ordinances designed to curtail violations of the Sabbath. It is a simple illustration of how the States guarded their sovereignty over religious issues, and their understanding of the First Amendment.

ESSEX CONVENTION. A Convention, composed of forty three members, from thirteen different towns, was holden 21st Dec., 1814, at Topsfield Hotel, County of Essex, Mass., for the purpose of devising and adopting measures for the observation of the Lord's Day. Hon. John Heard, Esq. was chosen Moderator; and Mr. John Adams, Clerk.

After the Convention was organized, the Throne of Grace was addressed on the occasion, by the Rev. Mr. Allen, of Bradford. Rev. Mr. Abbott of Beverly, Rev. Mr. Edwards of Andover, and Hon. Mr. Cleaveland of Topsfield, were chosen a Committee of Arrangements.

The Committee, after having attended to the duties of their appointment, reported for the consideration of the Convention the following Resolutions:

1. Resolved, that this Convention regard the Report of the Legislature of this Commonwealth in their session of June last, on the subject of the due observation of the Sabbath, with grateful respect; and devoutly wish there may be a concert of prudent and firm measures in all the towns

of the County, to carry the recommendations of our civil fathers into full effect.

2. Resolved, that the early and discreet measures pursued by the public officers of several towns in this County, to restrain the violators of the Sabbath, meet with their warmest approbation and that they respectfully recommend to them to persevere in the same, till the important object be fully attained.

3. Resolved, that this Convention warmly recommend to the Tythingmen and officers in other towns of the County, to engage in the prudent and faithful discharge of their duties with respect to the Lord's Day; and to give the more effect to their operations, to commence them on the first day of the New Year.

4. Resolved, that it be recommended to the friends of the Lord's Day in every town, to hold frequent meetings, for the purpose of extending support and countenance to public officers in the faithful discharge of their duties. And as very much will depend on the wisdom, firmness and perseverance of the civil officers, whose duty it is to preserve the Sabbath from violation.

5. Resolved, that it be recommended to the friends of 'the Sabbath in every town. to make all honorable and prudent exertions to secure, in the coming Spring, the election of the best men to the office of Tythingmen: and to such men when elected, it is recommended, that no motives of personal convenience should induce them to shrink from the faithful discharge of their important duties.

6. Resolved, as the opinion of this convention, that a mild but faithful and persevering execution of the measures now recommended, Will, with the divine blessing, soon prevent those flagrant violations of the Sabbath, which in late years, especially Since the commencement of the present unhappy war, have given it the appearance of a day devoted to business and pleasure; will secure undisturbed peace to worshiping assemblies; will have an important influence in producing a stricter

regard for this Divine institution among the rising generation and the unreflecting; and contribute, we devoutly hope, to the return to the divine favor to our guilty and suffering country.

The foregoing resolutions were unanimously adopted.

The Rev. Dr. Worcester, of Salem, Capt. John Pearson, of Newburyport, Rev. Mr. Allen, of Bradford, Hon. Mr. Cleaveland, of Topsfield, Dea. Rantoul, of Beverly, Rev. Mr. Edwards, of Andover, were chosen a standing committee.

Rev. Mr. Edwards was chosen a delegate to attend the next meeting of the Middlesex Convention to be holden in Concord on the last Wednesday in January, 1815.

Voted, that the papers containing the doings of this Convention be committed to the Clerk, and that he be requested to procure their publishment in the public papers of Boston, Salem, Newburyport, and Haverhill.

Voted, that this convention be adjourned, to meet again at this place, on the last Wednesday of April next, at 10 o'clock, A. M.

John Heard, Moderator.
John Adams, Clerk.
Salem Gazette, Dec. '26, 1814

Index

A

Abington School District v. Schempp 181
abortion xxi, 155, 164, 182, 197, 262, 263
Adams, President John 78, 98, 99, 100, 119, 153, 155, 158, 159, 189
Adams, President John Quincy 119, 189
adultery 125, 231, 232, 249
After the Revolution
    book by Joseph Ellis xvii, 35, 40
A Great and Godly Adventure
    book by Godfrey Hodgson 206
Alaska 73, 129
Alexis de Toqueville xiii, 224
Alien Contract Labor Law 16, 17, 169, 171
American Creation
    book by Joseph Ellis xvi
American Exceptionalism
    book by Charles A Murray 206, 207, 211, 212, 214, 215, 229
American Historical Association xix
American Sphinx
    book by Joseph Ellis xvi
A Nation Abandoned by God
    sermon by Rev John MacArthur 247
Andover Theological Seminary 49

Anglican 16, 30, 56, 57, 60, 113, 144, 145, 265
Aquinas, Thomas 82
Aristotle 80
Articles of Confederation 11, 77, 120, 130, 147
Astor, John Jacob 1

B

Bacon, Sir Francis 51, 66, 99, 100, 102, 105, 106, 115, 120
Baptist xv, 25, 57, 59, 60, 172, 179, 265, 266
Barton, David 59, 60, 119
Berkely University xix
Bill of Rights 11, 46, 74, 75, 76, 107, 130, 131, 137, 139, 147, 148, 156, 178, 179, 180, 181, 185
Binney, Horace 5, 8
Black, Justice Hugo 173, 179, 180
Blackstone, Sir William 10, 66, 82, 88, 89, 90, 94, 118, 119, 120, 122, 123, 124, 125, 218, 231, 248
Blaine, Speaker James
    US House of Representatives 173, 174, 175, 178, 181
Blue Backed Speller xvii, 34, 35, 36, 40, 42, 43
Bob Jones University 58
Boston xix, 2, 32, 49, 52, 55, 293

Bowers v. Hardwick 254
Bradford, William 29, 208
Bradstreet, Nehemiah Cleveland 189, 201
Brandeis, Justice Louis 165, 183, 187
Brewer, Justice David J 17
Brown University 57
Burke, Edmund 198
Bush, President George W 207, 215, 233

C

Canada 231
Chacon, Richard J. 213
Channing, William Ellery 49
Charles II, King of England 107
Charles I, King of England 30
Chatfield, Pastor Rusty v, 244
Chatfield, Rep Lee 244
Church of the Holy Trinity v. United States 2, 15, 16, 17, 131, 171, 218
Cicero 81
Clapper, James xiv
Clinton, President William Jefferson xxi, 254
Coke, Edward 86, 87
Coleman, Rev Benjamin 55
College of William & Mary 56
Columbia University 57
Commentaries on the Laws of England
    books by Sir William Blackstone 10, 82, 89, 119, 122, 123
Communists xi
Confession of Faith
    tract written by Sir Francis Bacon 100
Congregationalists 30, 57
Corlet, Elijah 53
Cotton, Rev John 32, 50, 51
Cromwell, Oliver 30
Crown College 58

D

Dartmouth College 56, 57
Darwinism 15
Defense of Marriage Act 254
deism 3, 8, 61, 105, 109, 119, 132, 221, 222
Delaware 22, 132, 134
Denham, Sir John 70
Dilworth, Rev Thomas 33, 34, 37
Dudley, Thomas 28, 30, 51
Dunster, Henry 53

E

Eliot, Charles William 49, 50
Elizabeth I, Queen of England 18
Ellis, Joseph xvi, xvii, xviii, xix, xx, 35, 36, 37, 40, 42
Endecott, John 28, 30
Engel v. Vitale 181
Essex County 146, 231, 291
Everson v. Board of Education 179, 180, 181, 184
evolution 45, 220, 249, 250

F

Faith & Freedom
    book by Benjamin Hart xxv
Feinstein, Senator Dianne 163
Fifteenth Amendment 166
First Amendment xv, 11, 13, 14, 22, 148, 174, 176, 179, 180, 181, 291
Florida 192
Fortune Magazine 1
Founding Brothers
    book by Joseph Ellis xvi, xviii, xix
Fourteenth Amendment 165, 166, 167, 169, 170, 172, 173, 175, 176, 177, 178, 179, 180, 181, 185, 187

Franklin, Benjamin xxii, xxv, 67, 78, 97, 132, 210, 221, 222, 223, 224
French Revolution 68, 259

G

Gates, Bill 1
George Washington's Sacred Fire
    book by Jerry Newcombe and Peter Lillback xxi
Ginsberg, Justice Ruth Bader 162
Girard, Stephen 1, 2, 3, 4, 5, 6, 7, 14, 15, 17, 27, 218, 223
Gorsuch, Justice Neal 162, 163

H

Hamilton, Alexander 99, 100, 136, 142, 157, 160, 194, 196, 214
Hart, Benjamin xxv
Harvard, Rev John 50, 51
Harvard Seal 55, 56
Harvard University 15, 48, 49, 50, 51, 52, 53, 54, 55, 56, 58, 244
Hawaii 73, 129, 254
Henry, Patrick 119, 138
Hibbens, Rev William 52
Hilton, Ronald xix
His Excellency
    book by Joseph Ellis xvi
History of Harvard University
    book by Josiah Quincy 51
Hodgson, Godfrey 206, 207, 208, 209, 210, 211, 215, 219, 232, 233
Holmes, Justice Oliver Wendell 165, 183, 187
homosexuality 125, 164, 182, 185, 231, 232, 249, 252, 254, 255, 256, 257, 258, 262, 263
homosexual revolution 252
Hooke, Robert 97
Hooker, Rev Richard 70, 108, 109

Hume, David 118, 119, 120
Hummel, Charles E 102

I

Illinois 11, 21, 132
incorporation doctrine 172, 175, 178, 179, 181, 184, 186
Indiana 11, 21, 132
Information to Those Who Would Remove to America
    pamphlet by Benjamin Franklin xxv

J

Jackson, Justice Robert 86
James I, King of England 18, 86, 87
Jay, John 136
Jefferson, President Thomas xvi, xix, xxii, 58, 59, 60, 67, 78, 85, 93, 94, 98, 99, 100, 102, 105, 109, 112, 113, 115, 117, 119, 120, 149, 158, 159, 179, 180, 189, 210, 212, 222, 223, 224, 225, 227
Johnson, House Speaker Rick 236, 237
Johnson, Samuel 69, 70
Jones, Anita xix

K

Kavanaugh, Justice Brett xiv
Kent, Justice James 23, 24
King James Version 3, 266
King, Martin Luther 87, 94, 206

L

Latin American Indigenous Warfare and Ritual Violence
    book by Chacon and Mendoza 213
Lawrence v. Texas 182, 184, 254
Leahy, Senator Patrick 162

Letter From Birmingham Jail
   letter written by Martin Luther
   King 88
Leverett, John 55
Lex Rex
   book by Samuel Rutherford 82,
   106, 107
Liberty University 58
Lillback, Peter xxi
Limbaugh, Rush 198, 217
Lincoln, President Abraham 72, 73, 85,
   92, 94, 123, 128, 129, 164, 167,
   168, 169, 189, 237, 245, 267, 269
Locke, John 66, 70, 82, 89, 94, 99, 100,
   103, 105, 106, 107, 108, 109, 112,
   113, 115, 117, 118, 120, 123, 218
Losing Ground
   book by Charles A Murray 206

M

MacArthur, Rev John 247
MacCallum, Martha 190
Madison, President James 119, 136, 138,
   142, 143, 146, 147, 156, 159, 177,
   179, 210, 215
Manning, Rev James 57
Marbury v. Madison 158, 159, 160, 161
Marsden, George M 61
Maryland xxv, 132, 135, 136, 159, 176
Mason, George 138
Massachusetts 28, 29, 30, 31, 50, 51,
   131, 132, 134, 135, 136, 139, 145,
   146, 149, 153, 231, 273, 291
Massachusetts Bay Colony 28, 29, 30,
   31, 50, 146, 273
Masters College 58
Mayflower Compact 19, 131
McGuffey Readers 27, 43, 44, 287
McGuffey, William H 27, 43, 44,
   45, 287
Meadows, Rep Mark 199

Mendoza, Ruben G. 213
Methodist 60
Michigan 1, 11, 13, 60, 155, 190, 196,
   236, 244, 263
Minnesota 11
Mississippi 21, 132
Missouri 165
Monroe, President James 138
Montesquieu, Charles 66, 118, 120, 121,
   122, 123, 218
More Equal than Others
   book by Godfrey Hodgson 206
Morse, Rev Henry 49
Morse, Samuel 49
Mount Holyoke College xviii, xix
Murray, Charles A 206, 207, 211, 212,
   213, 214, 215, 219, 229, 232

N

National Archives 74, 76, 160
natural law 67, 79, 80, 81, 82, 85, 86, 87,
   88, 89, 90, 91, 92, 94, 95, 106,
   108, 109, 114, 125, 229, 257
Nevada 73, 129
Newcombe, Jerry xxi
New England Primer xvii, 32, 33, 34,
   36, 43
New Hampshire 134, 136, 137, 143, 145
New Jersey 30, 56, 134
Newton, Sir Isaac 66, 83, 84, 97, 99,
   100, 102, 103, 104, 105, 106,
   115, 120
New York xiii, xix, 1, 2, 3, 15, 16, 23, 30,
   48, 57, 134, 137, 138, 139, 140,
   141, 144, 171, 185, 186, 189, 236
New York Times xix
North American Indigenous Warfare
   and Ritual Violence
   book by Chacon and Mendoza 213
North Carolina 140, 141, 144, 145

Northwest Ordinance 11, 13, 14, 46, 68, 69, 218, 248
Nuremberg Trial 85, 86, 87

O

Obama, President Barack 26, 161, 190, 205, 207, 208
Obergefell v. Hodges 182, 183, 184, 185, 254
Ohio 176
Ohio River 11

P

Paine, Thomas xv, xxii, 80, 210, 224
Pearl, Nancy xviii
Pence, Vice President Mike 198, 263
Pennsylvania xxv, 5, 6, 7, 8, 10, 14, 57, 61, 132, 134, 145, 223
Pensacola Christian College 58
People v. Ruggles 23
Pepperdine Law Review 14
Pershing, General John 245, 246
Peter, Rev Hugh 52
Philadelphia xxii, 1, 2, 3, 4, 5, 6, 7, 8, 10, 14, 98, 120
Philadelphia Bible Riots 3, 14
Philosophiæ Naturalis Principia Mathematica. See ; See *Principia*
Pilgrims xv, 27, 206, 217
Plato 80
Plymouth Colony 29, 208
Presbyterian 43, 45, 56, 59, 60
Presser v. Illinois 175
Princeton University 56, 58, 59
Principia
book by Sir Isaac Newton 83, 84, 103
Puritan 27, 29, 30, 51, 146, 228, 230

Q

Quakers 31
Quincy, Josiah 51

R

Reagan, President Ronald 88, 94, 215
Reasonableness of Christianity
book by John Locke 105, 106, 113
Rehnquist, Chief Justice William 180, 181
Rhode Island 57, 130, 140, 141, 144
Rice, Rev John Holt 59
Rockefeller, John D 1
Roe v. Wade 155, 182, 184, 254
Roosevelt, President Franklin D 91, 246
Rush, Benjamin 98, 99, 119
Rutgers University 57
Rutherford, Rev Samuel 66, 82, 106, 107

S

Scalia, Justice Antonin 129, 162, 163
Scopes, John 45
Scopes Monkey Trial 45, 249
Second Inaugural Address
by Abraham Lincoln 92, 225, 227
Sekulow, Jay 14
sexual revolution 1960s 251
Slaughter-House Cases 175
South Carolina 136, 145
Stanford University xix
Story, Justice Joseph 6, 8, 10, 14, 24, 61

T

Tappin, David 49
Tedesco, Jeremy 14
Tenth Amendment 76, 131, 135, 148, 151, 156, 165, 170, 172, 173, 175, 178, 181, 185, 186
Thatcher, Margaret 92

The Bell Curve
   book by Charles A Murray 206
The Jefferson Lies
   book by David Barton 59, 119
The Life of Sir Isaac Newton
   book by Sir David Brewster 103
The Myth of American Exceptionalism
   book by Godfrey Hodgson 206, 207, 208, 209, 210
The Observations on the Prophesies of Daniel and the Apocalypse of St. John
   book by Sir Isaac Newton 103
The Old Deluder Satan Law 31, 274
The Spirit of the Laws
   book by Charles Montesquieu 120
Thirteenth Amendment 166
Thomas, Justice Clarence 162, 183
Trumbull, John 100
Trump, President Donald xxiii
Two Treatises of Government
   book by John Locke 82, 106, 107, 108, 113, 114

U

United States v. Cruikshank 175, 176, 177, 178, 181
University of Michigan 60
University of Pennsylvania 57
University of Virginia 6, 58, 59, 149

V

Vanderbilt, Cornelius 1
Vermont 134
Vidal v. Girard's Executors 1, 4, 14, 15, 17, 27, 28, 61, 218
Virginia 18, 19, 30, 56, 60, 131, 137, 138, 139, 140, 141, 143, 144, 145, 149, 158, 223

W

Wallace v. Jaffree 180, 181
Ware, Henry 49
Warren Court 184
Warren, Rev Walpole 16, 17
Washington, President George xi, xii, xiii, xvi, xx, xxi, xxii, 11, 30, 68, 99, 212, 219, 220, 221, 222, 223, 224, 232
Webber, Samuel 49
Webster, Daniel 5, 7
Webster Dictionary 42
Webster, Noah xvii, xxi, 34, 35, 36, 37, 40, 42, 43, 209, 277
Weld, Rev Thomas 52
Whitefield, Rev George 265
Willard, Joseph 47, 48, 49, 50
Will, George 199
Williams, Rev Roger 50
Wilson, President Woodrow 245, 246
Winthrop, John 28, 30, 50, 51
Wisconsin 11
world view xi, xiii, xxi, 14, 26, 66, 67, 68, 78, 80, 95, 100, 103, 117, 118, 119, 120, 125, 132, 150, 153, 184, 187
World War I Bibles 245
World War II Bibles 246

Y

Yale University 56, 207